"Rob is one of the most gifted storytellers of our time. In *100 Bible Verses That Made America*, he uses his knack for story to trace the staples of Scripture in structuring and sturdying our nation, past and present—how the Bible is the foundation of America's plight to provide liberty and justice for all. Bravo, Rob!"

—ANDREW GREER, SINGER-SONGWRITER AND COHOST OF *DINNER CONVERSATIONS WITH MARK LOWRY AND ANDREW GREER*

"What an incredible book. Rob Morgan masterfully demonstrates how the God of history is the same today and tomorrow. He skillfully integrates the truth about American history through story, scripture, theology, and an extraordinarily well-written narrative. His exceptional skill to 'tell the story' transforms this book into a compelling, enriching, encouraging, and insightful historical document that is both devotional and inspirational. This is a *must-read* for any person interested in a serious, honest study of the relationship between the Bible, Judeo-Christian principles, and American history."

—DR. VERNON M. WHALEY, DEAN, SCHOOL OF MUSIC, LIBERTY UNIVERSITY

"The US has been built on the Bible since the pilgrims crossed the Atlantic. Throughout history the scriptures have inspired us to ingenuity, comforted us in trials, and given us a template to care well for one another. In *100 Bible Verses That Made America*, you'll be encouraged to learn afresh how the foundation of our country—and of your life—is grounded on the solid rock of Scripture."

—GREGG MATTE, PASTOR, FIRST BAPTIST CHURCH, HOUSTON, TEXAS

"America needs this book to point us to the Book! I've always loved biographies and history. Throw in the Gospels, and I'm caught hook, line, and sinker. Americans have long been told the United States and its educational system were founded on Judeo-Christian principles. Robert J. Morgan shares proof of this in a compelling, documented manner. Oh, how we need to return to our biblical foundations. I love this book!"

—DR. LYN COOK, CO-OWNER, COOKS PEST CONTROL, AND AUTHOR, *EMPLOYEE NUMBER 2*

T0034278

Praise for *100 Bible Verses That Made America*

"Robert J. Morgan has authored an exceptional book that covers the fine points of the making of America, coupled with one hundred Bible verses. His reach to pre-American influences is masterful, as is his intertwining of significant events (the death of Alexander Hamilton, prayers by George Washington, FDR, and Eisenhower, for example) that unfolded to arguably make America what it is today—though a keen thinker might proffer that America is decisively, if not hopelessly, divided today. If there is hope for unity in the current day of political reality in America, perhaps this careful pathway offered by Morgan is a helpful assist to the national conversation."

—DR. MICHAEL D. CHARLES, CHAPLAIN (COL) USA, RET., VETERAN OF SEVEN DEPLOYMENTS TO AFGHANISTAN AND IRAQ

"The spiritual history of America lives in the latest book by my friend Robert J. Morgan: *100 Bible Verses That Made America*. I am so grateful for this inspiring and exciting description of great Americans and their faith and the principles that make our nation great."

—DR. JACK GRAHAM, PASTOR, PRESTONWOOD BAPTIST CHURCH, DALLAS, TEXAS

"Robert J. Morgan sets out with undeniable clarity the reliance on Scripture by many of our most important government leaders throughout history. It is irrefutable that the structural foundation and underpinnings of our great country are in large part rooted in the Word of God. I encourage you to be involved in the political process and to study this book."

—WILLIAM L. WALLER JR., CHIEF JUSTICE OF MISSISSIPPI, BG (R) MSARNG

"Rob Morgan is a student of the Bible. He is also a student of American history. *100 Bible Verses That Made America* explores the crossroads of faith and our nation's freedoms, of Scripture and one nation's statehood."

—MARK LOWRY, GRAMMY-WINNING SINGER-SONGWRITER

"Rob Morgan is a pastor with a heart for people to know God. *100 Bible Verses That Made America* is a great reminder of our heritage of faith. If we forget our history, we are adrift. We are all indebted to Rob for directing us toward God's involvement with our national destiny. I highly recommend this book for all who wonder if God is still at work in the earth."

—ALLEN JACKSON, PASTOR, WORLD OUTREACH CHURCH, MURFREESBORO, TENNESSEE

"I love the simple but powerful way Robert J. Morgan connects us to our nation's past. His simple layout allows me to memorize these verses and appreciate their significance. These one hundred Bible promises are God-breathed. The one hundred stories are God-blessed."

—GREG VAUGHN, GRACE MINISTRIES FOUNDER AND PRESIDENT

"For years debate has raged over a simple question: Was America founded as a Christian nation? That discussion brings emotions to the surface from all sides of the political spectrum. The very fact that good and evil coexist in our Western culture makes it impossible to provide a clear and crisp answer. But one thing is for sure: Christianity and the ideas of the Enlightenment merged on the shores of a young America. The wisdom of the Bible leaked into the culture of the New World and created a conscience, individually and collectively, that is evident to this day. Rob Morgan persuasively captures this theme most effectively in *100 Bible Verses That Made America*. Reflect on it. Share it with your children and your children's children."

—EDWARD M. SMITH, PHD, PRESIDENT, WILLIAMSON COLLEGE

"Within the pages of this book, Rob Morgan shows you how—from George Washington's inauguration to the National Prayer Breakfast—the Scriptures have played a major role in the life of America and its leaders. The stories recounted here will reveal the foundation of America's beginnings, stir a deeper love for the Bible, and increase your faith. May this book be a catalyst to once again bring an awakening to the hearts of our nation."

—DANIEL FLOYD, FOUNDING AND SENIOR PASTOR, LIFEPOINT CHURCH, FREDERICKSBURG, VIRGINIA

"I must confess, I cried off and on all the way through the reading of this book. The stories of sacrifice and faithfulness of regular human beings who used the Word of God as their compass brought me to my knees. No doubt, if we today would use the same guiding tool, God might 'forgive our sins and heal our land.'

"Robert J. Morgan, a master storyteller, has done the hard work of finding true stories and breathing life into them so we may be challenged to walk boldly in the twenty-first century. I accept the challenge and will be using this book as a daily devotional. This book bolsters my courage to stand strong for the cause of Christ."

—KAY DeKALB SMITH, SINGER, SPEAKER, HUMORIST

100
BIBLE
VERSES
That
MADE
AMERICA

For podcasts,

study guides,

small group and video curriculum,

and other resources related to

100 Bible Verses That Made America, visit

www.robertjmorgan.com/100verses

100
BIBLE
VERSES
That
MADE
AMERICA

Defining Moments That Shaped
Our Enduring Foundation of Faith

ROBERT J. MORGAN

W PUBLISHING GROUP

AN IMPRINT OF THOMAS NELSON

Published in Nashville, Tennessee, by W Publishing Group, an imprint of Thomas Nelson.

Published in association with Yates & Yates, www.yates2.com.

Thomas Nelson titles may be purchased in bulk for educational, business, fund-raising, or sales promotional use. For information, please e-mail SpecialMarkets@ThomasNelson.com.

ISBN 978-0-7852-2211-8 (TP)
ISBN 978-0-7852-2212-5 (eBook)

Library of Congress Cataloging-in-Publication Data

Names: Morgan, Robert J., 1952- author.
Title: 100 Bible verses that made America : defining moments that shaped our enduring foundation of faith / Robert J. Morgan.
Other titles: One hundred Bible verses that made America
Description: Nashville, Tennessee : W. Publishing Group, [2019] | Includes bibliographical references. | Summary: "Robert Morgan explores 100 Bible verses that shaped America, unpacking stories from our nation's past and reminding us of the importance of Scripture to our nation still today"— Provided by publisher.
Identifiers: LCCN 2019033229 (print) | LCCN 2019033230 (ebook) | ISBN 9780718079628 (hardcover) | ISBN 9780785222125 (ebook)
Subjects: LCSH: Bible—Criticism, interpretation, etc. | United States—Church history. | Christianity—Influence. | Bible—Influence. | United States—History—Religious aspects—Christianity. | Bible and politics—United States—History.
Classification: LCC BR515 .M5955 2019 (print) | LCC BR515 (ebook) | DDC 277.3—dc23
LC record available at https://lccn.loc.gov/2019033229
LC ebook record available at https://lccn.loc.gov/2019033230

Printed in the United States of America

23 24 25 26 27 LBC 10 9 8 7 6

To
Hope

I now make it my earnest prayer that God . . . would most graciously be pleased to dispose us all to do justice, to love mercy, and to demean ourselves with that charity, humility and pacific temper of mind which were the characteristics of the Divine Author of our blessed Religion (Jesus Christ), and without a humble imitation of whose example in these things, we can never hope to be a happy nation.

—GEORGE WASHINGTON, IN HIS LETTER
TO THE GOVERNORS OF THE THIRTEEN
NEW UNITED STATES, JUNE 8, 1783

Contents

Prologue   April 30, 1789   *The Invisible Hand*   xix

1. December 21, 1511   Antonio de Montesinos and His Blowtorch   1
                        Matthew 3:3

2. April 20, 1534   Jacques Cartier and the Northwest Passage   4
                        John 1:1

3. September 10, 1608   Jamestown   7
                        2 Thessalonians 3:10

4. July 20, 1620   The Pilgrims   10
                        Ezra 8:21

5. September 22, 1620   The Mayflower Compact   13
                        Psalm 107:30

6. April 8, 1630   The City on a Hill   16
                        Matthew 5:14

7. September 8, 1636   The Founding of Harvard   19
                        John 8:32

8. May 31, 1638   Thomas Hooker, the Father of Democracy   22
                        Deuteronomy 1:13

9. December 29, 1649   "God Stept In and Helped"   25
                        2 Timothy 2:3

10. November 22, 1739   William Tennent's Log Cabin Seminary   28
                        Acts 17:6

11. May 5, 1740   Citizens of Heaven   31
                        2 Corinthians 12:4

12. October 23, 1740   The News from Heaven   34
                        John 3:7

CONTENTS

13. July 8, 1741	America's Most Famous Sermon Deuteronomy 32:35	37
14. October 16, 1746	The Prayer That Sunk a Navy Romans 8:31	40
15. October 9, 1747	"I Dared to Rejoice in God" Isaiah 40:1	43
16. January 30, 1750	The Catechism of the Revolution Romans 13:1	47
17. June 7, 1753	The Liberty Bell Cracks the Case Leviticus 25:10	50
18. August 17, 1755	Divine Body Armor 2 Samuel 10:12	53
19. December 7, 1771	Sermon at an Execution Romans 6:23	56
20. March 5, 1774	Parson Parsons Galatians 5:1	59
21. September 7, 1774	The First Prayer of the Continental Congress Psalm 35:1	62
22. March 23, 1775	America's Orator Gives the Speech of His Life Jeremiah 8:11	65
23. April 19, 1775	The Shot Heard Round the World Joel 3:19	68
24. April 23, 1775	The Origin of America's Military Chaplains Nehemiah 4:14	71
25. June 17, 1775	The Boy Who Saw the Battle of Bunker Hill Psalm 62:8	74
26. January 21, 1776	The Fighting Parson of the Revolution Ecclesiastes 3:8	77
27. March 5, 1776	Dorchester Heights Exodus 14:25	80
28. May 17, 1776	When Politics Got into the Pulpit Psalm 76:10	83
29. August 29, 1776	The Fog of War James 5:16	86

CONTENTS

30. May 28, 1777	The Prayers That Turned the Tide Ezekiel 45:9	90
31. September 30, 1777	A Speech to Bewildered Men Proverbs 18:10	93
32. October 26, 1777	Watchman, What of the Night? Isaiah 21:11–12	96
33. December 31, 1777	How Prayer Funded the Army at Valley Forge Exodus 35:21	99
34. September 26, 1780	The Sword of the Lord and of Gideon Judges 7:20	102
35. October 19, 1781	The Victory Sermon at Yorktown 1 Samuel 7:12	106
36. December 11, 1783	God's Instructions to a New Nation Micah 6:8	110
37. June 28, 1787	The Prayer That Saved the Constitution Psalm 127:1	113
38. October 26, 1788	Kindling the Second Great Awakening 1 Kings 10:7	116
39. September 26, 1789	The Founder Who Walked with God Genesis 5:24	120
40. November 26, 1789	An American Holiday Is Born Psalm 97:1	124
41. December 10, 1795	Invaluable Treasure 1 Peter 3:15	127
42. April 25, 1799	The Father of American Geography Psalm 11:3	130
43. June 6, 1799	Patrick Henry's Sealed Envelope Proverbs 14:34	133
44. June 4, 1800	Noah Webster and His Dictionary Acts 26:24–25	136
45. August 6, 1801	America's Pentecost Mark 16:15	139
46. July 11, 1804	The Death of Alexander Hamilton Acts 4:12	142

CONTENTS

47. June 27, 1810	The Haystack Prayer Meeting Revelation 14:13	145
48. April 19, 1813	The Father of American Medicine Matthew 25:23	149
49. August 24, 1814	The Tornado That Saved Washington James 1:17	152
50. March 31, 1816	Circuit Riders Who Tamed the Frontier 1 John 3:8	156
51. May 11, 1816	"Give Me That Book!" Psalm 68:11	159
52. December 30, 1823	Preaching in Sodom Genesis 19:14	162
53. July 4, 1826	Benjamin Rush's Amazing Dream Matthew 5:9	165
54. April 23, 1833	The Nation's Schoolmaster Matthew 7:12	168
55. December 4, 1833	The Tappan Brothers 1 Corinthians 3:11	171
56. June 21, 1834	Better Make It a Hundred Romans 8:37	174
57. November 7, 1837	Freedom of the Press Jude 1:3	177
58. March 1, 1841	The Friend of Both Washington and Lincoln Psalm 65:11	180
59. May 24, 1844	The Artist Who Struck Lightning Numbers 23:23	184
60. June 8, 1845	Old Hickory's Firm Foundation 2 Peter 1:4	187
61. February 23, 1848	Death in the House John 11:25	190
62. September 17, 1849	Go Down, Moses Exodus 7:16	193
63. June 5, 1851	Book of the Century John 15:15	196

CONTENTS

64. July 5, 1852   Frederick Douglass and the Fourth of July   199
    Isaiah 1:15

65. September 23, 1857   Revival Sweeps the Country   203
    Hebrews 4:16

66. January 1, 1863   The Day the Nation Felt Clean   206
    Revelation 19:6

67. July 5, 1863   Wrestling in Prayer for Gettysburg   209
    Colossians 4:12

68. September 6, 1863   Revival in the Ranks   213
    John 3:15

69. August 16, 1864   Providence Spring   216
    Numbers 20:11

70. April 14, 1865   Lincoln's Last Words   219
    Mark 11:22

71. November 20, 1866   The Christian General   222
    1 John 1:7

72. March 4, 1881   The Prayer That Saved a President   225
    Psalm 86:16

73. December 6, 1884   A Virtual Bible Engraved in Stone   228
    Psalm 68:35

74. December 24, 1898   Christmas Eve in the War Zone   232
    Joshua 1:5

75. November 21, 1899   A President Like That   235
    Matthew 13:45–46

76. September 14, 1901   The Assassination of William McKinley   239
    Luke 22:42

77. March 26, 1905   The Queen of American Hymn Writers   242
    Deuteronomy 8:2

78. December 3, 1911   The Biblical Secret of America's Retailer   246
    Matthew 6:33

79. July 16, 1914   The Concoction   249
    1 Thessalonians 1:5

80. July 12, 1917   The Book in the Trenches   252
    Philippians 2:16

CONTENTS

81. March 4, 1933   May He Guide Me   255
Proverbs 29:18

82. October 8, 1934   A Letter to Almighty God   258
Romans 5:8

83. January 17, 1941   The Verse That Made Churchill Weep   261
Ruth 1:16

84. December 7, 1941   From Pearl Harbor to Calvary   264
Luke 23:34

85. February 3, 1942   The Four Chaplains   267
John 15:13

86. June 6, 1944   FDR's Prayer on D-Day   270
Matthew 6:10

87. December 14, 1944   Patton's Prayer for Clear Skies   273
Judges 6:12

88. April 12, 1945   You Are the One in Trouble Now   276
1 Kings 3:9

89. May 14, 1948   The Rebirth of the State of Israel   279
Deuteronomy 1:8

90. January 20, 1953   Eisenhower and His Preacher   283
2 Chronicles 7:14

91. August 28, 1963   Let Freedom Ring!   287
Amos 5:24

92. March 15, 1965   Bloody Sunday   290
Matthew 16:26

93. December 24, 1968   For All the People Back on Earth   293
Genesis 1:1

94. January 22, 1973   The Conscience of an Honest Woman   296
John 4:15

95. January 19, 1979   The Holy Spirit Was Present   299
Romans 3:23

96. September 19, 1979   The National Day of Prayer   302
Zechariah 4:6

97. August 7, 1982   Ronald Reagan's Remarkable Letter   305
John 3:16

CONTENTS

98. February 22, 1990 Why Did God Spare Me?   309
           Isaiah 40:8

99. September 11, 2001 The Day We'll Never Forget   312
           Psalm 23:4

100. February 7, 2019 The National Prayer Breakfast   315
           2 Timothy 1:7

Conclusion   *The Miracle of America*   319
Acknowledgments   323
Notes   325
About the Author   359

Prologue

April 30, 1789: The Invisible Hand

1:00 p.m.

The Virginian, tall and stately and ramrod straight, stepped onto the crowded second-floor balcony of the old Federal Building in lower Manhattan and took his place beside a large decorative Bible. A thunderous roar erupted from the sea of people on Wall Street, followed by tense silence as everyone strained to hear the man's voice. He would not say much—only two words—but both syllables would shape the ages to come. This man was about to change history. He was about to take the oath of office as the first president of the United States of America.

General Washington was dressed in a modest, double-breasted brown suit with buttons embossed with eagles. A sword dangled at his side. His face was careworn. The Bible before him, bound in rich brown leather, had been hastily borrowed from the altar of the nearby St. John's Lodge. It rested on a red cushion held by Samuel Otis, secretary of the Senate, and it was opened to Genesis 49, the passage containing the blessings of Jacob to his twelve sons who were destined to become a great nation.

After placing his hand on the Bible, the general listened to the oath of office, which was quoted by Robert Livingstone, chancellor of New York. After hearing the final words—"preserve, protect, and defend the Constitution of the United States"—Washington said, "I do," and then he did something extraordinary. To the thrill of the crowd and in full view of posterity, he removed his hand from Genesis 49 then reverently bent down and kissed the Bible.[1]

"It is done!" Livingston cried to the crowd. "Long live George Washington, president of the United States!" The multitude burst into cheers—shouting, yelling, weeping, and rejoicing as the father of their nation quietly turned and disappeared into the building to give his inaugural address to members of Congress.

In that speech, Washington said:

> No people can be bound to acknowledge and adore the Invisible Hand which conducts the affairs of men more than the people of the United States. Every step by which they have advanced to the character of an independent nation, seems to have been distinguished by some token of providential agency. . . . The propitious smiles of Heaven can never be expected on a nation that disregards the eternal rules of order and right, which Heaven itself has ordained.[2]

On that spring day in 1789, hundreds of eyewitnesses saw Washington lay his hands on God's Word and kiss its pages. And those who heard his remarks took notice of his reverence toward the God of heaven who has revealed His "eternal rules of order and right," an unmistakable reference to Scripture.

The founders of the United States of America revered the Bible because it reflected their awareness of God's authority over the nations. Washington did not place his hand on the Declaration of Independence or the Constitution of the United States, as hallowed as those documents are. Nor did he kiss the pages of any other religious or secular tome. It was the Bible that sanctified the moment. The Bible, he knew, had ushered American history to this point.

It is the Bible that made America.

Not every Founding Father was a Christian, a Bible-believer, or a paragon of virtue. Not every president has honored the Bible. Not every leader has appreciated its influence. Some of the Founding Fathers—Thomas Jefferson, Ethan Allen, Thomas Paine—were disciples of Enlightenment rationalism. But even they were intimately acquainted with the contents of the Bible. They vigorously studied Scripture and respected its ethical teachings.

I am not commending all those whose stories I tell in these pages, but I *am* commending the book they held in their hands. Trying to explain American history without its Bible is like trying to understand the human body without its bloodstream. Had there been no Bible, there would be no America as we know it. The nation would not have been born as it was.

Perhaps it would not have been born at all.

John Adams wrote, "The Bible contains the most profound philosophy, the most perfect morality, and the most refined policy that was ever conceived on earth. . . . I believe [it] to be the only system that ever did or ever will preserve a republic in the world."[3]

John Jay, the first chief justice of the US Supreme Court, said, "The Bible is the best of all books, for it is the Word of God and teaches us the way to be happy in this world and the next. Continue therefore to read it and to regulate your life by its precepts."[4]

"In regard to this Great Book," wrote Abraham Lincoln in a letter dated September 7, 1864, "I have but to say it is the best gift God has given to man. All the good the Savior gave to the world was communicated through this Book."[5]

"Hold fast to the Bible," wrote Ulysses S. Grant on June 6, 1872, "as the sheet-anchor of your liberties; write its precepts in your hearts, and practice them in your lives."[6]

Calvin Coolidge said, "The foundation of our society and our government rest so much on the teachings of the Bible that it would be difficult to support them if faith in these teachings would cease to be practically universal in our country."[7]

Vice President Theodore Roosevelt, addressing the Long Island Bible

Society just weeks before being thrust into the presidency by the assassination of William McKinley, said, "A very large number of people tend to forget that the teachings of the Bible are so interwoven and entwined with our whole civic and social life that it would be literally—I do not mean figuratively, I mean literally—impossible for us to figure to ourselves what that life would be if these teachings were removed."[8]

President Franklin Roosevelt said, "We cannot read the history of our rise and development as a Nation without reckoning with the place the Bible has occupied in shaping the advances of the Republic."[9]

The Bible is a lamp to our feet and a light to our path; when it burns low, our culture grows dark. The best way to keep America strong is to know her history, to honor her roots, to preserve her legacy, and to cherish the eternal God who, in His providence, placed this continent between two shimmering seas, and who, in His goodness, provided a Book that became her moral and intellectual foundation: the Holy Bible.

———

Washington's Inaugural Bible has been carefully preserved as one of the nation's prized possessions. Other presidents have borrowed it from time to time, placing their hands on it as they repeated the oath of office: Warren Harding, Dwight Eisenhower, Jimmy Carter, and George H. W. Bush. George W. Bush wanted to use Washington's Bible, but his inauguration was threatened by rain, and no one wanted to risk damaging its hallowed pages.

Only once has Washington's Bible faced the prospect of destruction: on September 11, 2001. It was on loan to the historic Fraunces Tavern Museum in lower Manhattan when terrorists destroyed the nearby Twin Towers of the World Trade Center. For two days, no one knew if Washington's Bible had escaped ruin. The area was sealed off as rescue workers searched for survivors. Finally, on September 13, police officers in an unmarked cruiser entered the area, accompanying the custodians of the Bible. The air was still thick with dust and smoke, and the tavern was strewn with rubble, but the building itself seemed unharmed. Inside, untouched and unscathed, was Washington's Inaugural Bible.[10]

The Bible, in its essential nature, is an indestructible book. For millennia its critics have tried to ban it, burn it, and bar it from those who want or need it. Still, the Bible endures as the central Book of human literature, as the centerpiece of spiritual life, and as the compelling document that shaped the United States of America.

Patrick Henry reportedly said, "The Bible . . . is a book worth more than all the other books that were ever printed."

That's my opinion too. I'm writing from a conviction that the Bible is unique in human literature: a Book breathed out by God, recorded by those who were borne along by the Holy Spirit, and remains unerring in its teachings. Its message can change your life—your emotions, your situation, your mind, your heart, your family, and your future. The Scriptures can make us wise for salvation through faith in Jesus Christ.

"My words are few and plain," George Washington once wrote. "Listen well to what I tell you and let it sink deep into your hearts. . . . You do well to wish to learn our arts and ways of life and above all—the religion of Jesus Christ. This will make you a greater and happier people than you are."[11]

The following pages are a scriptural tour of American history—one hundred moments when the Bible has made the difference in the chronicles of our nation and in the lives of our leaders. May these snapshots sink deeply into our hearts to help revive our devotion to God and to His powerful Word. And may God send a fresh Great Awakening for our times, sparked by His Word and fanned by His Spirit, who alone—through Jesus Christ—can make us "a greater and happier people" than we are.

December 21, 1511

Antonio de Montesinos and His Blowtorch

> *For this is he who was spoken of by the prophet Isaiah,*
> *saying:*
>> *"The voice of one crying in the wilderness:*
>> *'Prepare the way of the LORD;*
>> *Make His paths straight.'"*
>
> —MATTHEW 3:3

The horde of Spanish conquistadors and soldiers who followed Christopher Columbus to the New World wreaked devastation. Many of these Spaniards claimed to be religious, but their actions proved they were not true followers of Christ. Many of them massacred, enslaved, and brutalized the American indigenous peoples. The conquistadors were motivated by greed, lust, and power, and they dreamed of glory and conquest. They were cruel.

One Spaniard was different. His name was Antonio de Montesinos, and he was part of a team of Dominican missionaries who landed on the island of Hispaniola (modern Haiti / Dominican Republic). Friar Antonio was appalled at the carnage inflicted on the local tribes by Spanish authorities. Thankfully, he was no coward, and he became "the first man to raise his voice publicly in America against slavery and all forms of oppression."[1]

On December 21, 1511, Antonio climbed into the pulpit of a straw-thatched church, faced the Spanish authorities who had gathered, and preached one of history's most blistering Christmas sermons:

> In order to make your sins against the Indians known to you I have come up on this pulpit, I who am the voice of Christ crying in the wilderness of this island, and therefore it behooves you to listen, not with careless attention, but with all your heart and senses, so that you may hear it: for this is going to be the strangest voice that ever you heard, the harshest and hardest and most awful and most dangerous that ever you expected to hear. . . . This voice says that you are in mortal sin, that you live and die in it, for the cruelty and tyranny you use in dealing with these innocent people. Tell me, by what right or justice do you keep these Indians in such a cruel and horrible servitude? On what authority have you waged a detestable war against these people, who dwelt quietly and peacefully on their own land? . . . Are these not men? Have they not rational souls? Are you not bound to love them as you love yourselves?[2]

The sermon hit the Spanish community like a blowtorch, and the friar found himself being shipped back to Spain like an outlaw. But when Antonio faced King Ferdinand II, the priest persuaded the king of the horror unfolding in the Americas. As a result, the king convened a commission that established the Laws of Burgos, the first ordinance in the Americas aimed at protecting indigenous peoples.

There's also an important postscript to the story. One of the slave owners who heard Antonio's sermon, Bartolome de Las Casas, was incensed at first. But later he became so convicted that he divested himself of all his slaves, became an outspoken defender of Christian charity toward indigenous Americans, and made sure Antonio's sermon was preserved for posterity.[3]

Antonio de Montesinos is known as the first defender of human rights in the Americas.[4] Modern visitors to the Dominican Republic are reminded of him, as his memory is enshrined in a fifty-foot-tall statue, established in 1982 and erected near the site of his fearless sermon.

I find great comfort in this story of courage. Not everything done in the name of religion is Christian. Yet, rather than defending the indefensible or being put on the defensive, we should be the voices crying in the wilderness, calling our culture to repentance and obedience to the grace of Jesus Christ.

April 20, 1534

Jacques Cartier and the Northwest Passage

> *In the beginning was the Word, and the Word was with God, and the Word was God.*
>
> —JOHN 1:1

On behalf of King Francis I, Jacques Cartier sailed from France on April 20, 1534, with two ships and sixty-one sailors. They had all confessed their sins before sailing, and they prayed for the safety and success of their voyage. Their goal: to determine if a northwest passage existed that would link the Atlantic Ocean to the Pacific. European explorers were fascinated with the possibility of reaching Asia by sailing westward around the continent through a northern waterway that would connect the two great oceans.

Encountering good weather, Cartier crossed the Atlantic in less than three weeks. On May 10, he spotted what today is called Newfoundland. As he explored the coastline, he and his men paused on June 10 to worship God—the first recorded instance of public worship in Canada.[1]

At first, Cartier and his men were discouraged by the desolate nature of the coastline, and the explorer commented that it reminded him of the land God gave Cain.[2] But after the sailors began encountering tribes of Native Americans, their attitude changed. Eager to share the gospel, Cartier erected large crosses and sought to explain their meaning to local tribal leaders. On the shore of Gaspe Bay, Cartier wrote, "We kneeled down together before them, with our hands toward heaven yielding God thanks; and we made signs unto them, showing them the heavens and that all our salvation depended only on Him which in them dwelleth; whereat they showed a great admiration, looking first at one another and then at the cross."[3]

The next year, Cartier returned on a second voyage, this time with three ships; on October 3, 1535, he entered a Native American village named Hochelaga, the site of present-day Montréal. Cartier was deeply moved when local tribesmen gathered around him bringing their sick and afflicted. The villagers thought the French explorers might be celestial beings.

> To a man of Cartier's habit of mind, the scene must have been an affecting one, suggesting as it did the many similar occurrences in the Savior's life upon earth; and in recalling the words of power from the Divine lips—*I will, be thou clean—Receive thy sight—Take up thy bed*—he must have longed for the gift of healing, if only for a few moments. . . . As his heart went out in sympathy for this poor people whose bodily ailments were but a faint type of their spiritual condition . . . he . . . sought to direct them as best he could to the Great Healer of men—to one who could do for them that which he was powerless to effect.[4]

Cartier couldn't heal the villagers of their sickness, but he knew how to give them the gospel. Lifting his voice, the explorer began reciting the first chapter of John, starting with verse 1: "In the beginning was the Word, and the Word was with God, and the Word was God." The gospel of John, Cartier knew, presents Jesus Christ as God Himself, who, in love, came down from heaven as the Great Communication—the Word—the message of eternal life. Cartier spoke of the passion, death, and resurrection of Christ, then he earnestly prayed for the physical and spiritual needs of those gathered around him. The villagers were "marvelously attentive, looking up to heaven and imitating us in gestures."[5]

Jacques Cartier didn't find the elusive Northwest Passage, but his three voyages to North America brought the symbol of the cross and the message of the gospel to the vast areas of the St. Lawrence River, the waterway that slices through eastern Canada and links the Atlantic not with the Pacific but with the Great Lakes. In the process, he also gave Canada its name, from the Iroquois word *Kanata*, meaning "village."

September 10, 1608

Jamestown

If anyone will not work, neither shall he eat.

—2 Thessalonians 3:10

French explorers notwithstanding, the Spanish Empire dominated the Americas for a hundred years, shipping back enough gold to make Spain the richest nation on earth. But England had no intention of being left out. Sir Walter Raleigh journeyed to the New World and staked out a portion of land he named Virginia for England's virgin Queen Elizabeth. His efforts faltered, but after Elizabeth's death her nephew, James I, granted a charter for an attempt led by Captain Christopher Newport.

On April 26, 1607, three ships arrived in the Chesapeake Bay, and within a few weeks the settlers established the colony of Jamestown up the James River from the current site of Newport News. About the same time, King James also authorized a new version of the Bible, lending his name to two legacies—Jamestown and the King James Bible.

The Jamestown venture wasn't a spiritual enterprise but a commercial endeavor. Unlike the Pilgrims and Puritans, who would cross the Atlantic a few years later to settle areas farther north, there was little Christian spirit at Jamestown. Consequently, things didn't go well. The community was splintered by conflict, greed, drought, and disease. No strong leader emerged, and the settlers bickered like children. The water from the James River made them sick, and they were tormented by mosquitoes and malaria. They suffered attacks from local indigenous tribes.

All told, half the settlers perished during the summer and fall of 1607.

A single pastor was present—Reverend Robert Hunt. On June 21, 1607, he presided over the first communion service in British America. It was held under a sail suspended between trees, and the pulpit was a board nailed between trees. Hunt appealed for a spirit of unity and pointed out that the very sacrament of communion represented the urgency of living in harmony. Hunt's voice of reason didn't last long. He died about the time a primitive chapel was constructed and was buried under its floor.[1]

After Hunt's death, Jamestown again deteriorated into chaos, splintered by weak leadership and laziness. Many settlers refused manual labor. They had come to dig for gold, but they had no intention of digging for crops. To make matters worse, a fire broke out and destroyed many of their huts and houses. Once again, it looked as if the colony would perish.

On September 10, 1608, Captain John Smith became leader of the Jamestown community. Appalled by the idleness of some of the settlers, Captain Smith made an important ruling based on 2 Thessalonians 3:10: "If anyone will not work, neither shall he eat." He told them

> that their late experience and misery were sufficient to persuade everyone to mend his ways; that they must not think that either his pains or the purses of the adventurers at home would forever maintain them in sloth and idleness; that he knew that many deserved more honor and a better reward than was yet to be had, but that far the greatest part of them must be more industrious or starve; that it was not

reasonable that the labors of thirty or forty honest and industrious men should be consumed to maintain one hundred and fifty loiterers; that, therefore, every one that would not work should not eat.[2]

People grudgingly went to work, the death rate dropped, supply ships arrived, a well was dug, crops were grown, and the colony began to slowly establish a foothold. Although Jamestown still faced many difficult days, an important precedent had been set in the early history of America—the biblical principle of hard work.

When Paul wrote to the Thessalonians in the first century, he knew some of them were wasting their time and simply waiting around for Christ to return to earth. In 1 Thessalonians 3, he addressed the issue of idleness, reminding them that when he visited the city, he didn't sponge off the Christians there but "worked with labor and toil night and day, that we might not be a burden to any of you" (1 Thessalonians 3:8). Then he proceeded to lay down the principle that became so important to the mind-set of America—"If anyone will not work, neither shall he eat."

Jamestown became the first permanent English settlement in North America. Smith's knowledge of a single principled verse of Scripture—2 Thessalonians 3:10—ushered in a work ethic that has, over the centuries, created the most industrious and productive nation in history.

4

July 20, 1620

The Pilgrims

Then I proclaimed a fast there at the river of Ahava, that we might humble ourselves before our God, to seek from Him the right way for us and our little ones and all our possessions.

—EZRA 8:21

After King Henry VIII severed ties with Rome and appointed himself head of the Church of England in 1553, three groups of Protestants emerged: (1) Anglicans who continued the traditions of their church; (2) Puritans who wanted to work within Anglicanism to reform and purify it; and (3) Puritans who were Separatists and dissenters determined to establish their own independent congregations. Over the next hundred years, the Puritans and Separatists faced extreme pressure from the English Crown, compelling many of them to flee their country.

The great Puritan migration, led by John Winthrop, occurred between 1620 and 1640, resulting in the establishment of the Massachusetts Bay

Colony and the founding of Boston. But before these Puritans were the Separatists—those who came to Plymouth Rock on Cape Cod aboard the *Mayflower* in 1620.

The Pilgrims, as we call them, were dissenters who had been "harried out of the land" by various British monarchs. Many of them had fled to Holland, where one Leyden congregation, led by Rev. John Robinson, flourished and tripled in size.[1] But these dissenters grew concerned at how easily their children were being assimilated into the Dutch culture. They were strangers in the land. Somehow an idea arose in their hearts to immigrate to the New World, where they could establish a colony to freely pursue their English customs while retaining religious liberty.

It was a breathtaking idea. With the exception of Jamestown, no English colony had survived in the New World. And Jamestown was hardly an exception—it was a disaster. Of the thirty-six hundred settlers sent to Jamestown between 1619 and 1622, three thousand perished.[2] Going to the New World must have seemed to these dissenters like colonizing the moon. Yet they felt compelled to go.

"It is not with us as with other men," they said, "whom small things can discourage, or small discontentments cause to wish themselves home again." As one of them, William Bradford, would later write: "They knew they were pilgrims."[3]

Their beloved pastor, John Robinson, was heartbroken when he realized he couldn't leave the bulk of his congregation to travel with the Pilgrims. He hoped to join them later, though death kept him from fulfilling his dream. Unable to go himself, Robinson led his church in an emotional send-off. About 125 church members had signed up for the first voyage, with the rest planning to come later.

Robinson proclaimed "a day of solemn humiliation" on which he delivered a passionate sermon based on Ezra 8:21, which is about Ezra leading the remnant of Jews from exile to the promised land. Robinson's text apparently encompassed the following verses of that chapter:

Then I proclaimed a fast there at the river of Ahava, that we might humble ourselves before our God, to seek from Him the right way for us and our little ones and all our possessions. For I was ashamed to request of the king an escort of soldiers and horsemen to help us against the enemy on the road, because we had spoken to the king, saying, "The hand of our God is upon all those for good who seek Him, but His power and His wrath are against all those who forsake Him." So we fasted and entreated our God for this, and He answered our prayer. (vv. 21–23)

Robinson didn't choose this passage at random. The eighth chapter of Ezra tells the story of Ezra's leading a remnant of Jewish pilgrims back to the promised land of Israel from their exile in Babylon. It would be a hard and dangerous trip, but Ezra wanted to direct the hearts and minds of his people to the protective hand of the God who was leading them. Robinson must have felt like a modern-day Ezra, and, indeed, in many ways he was.

After his sermon, Robinson led the congregation in "powering out prayers to the Lord." He then traveled with the Pilgrims to the Dutch port of Delfshaven, where "their Reverend Pastor fell down on his knees and they all with him with watery cheeks commended them with the most fervent prayers to the Lord."[4]

From Delfshaven the Pilgrims sailed to Southampton, where they boarded a creaky little ship called the *Mayflower*.

September 22, 1620

The Mayflower Compact

So He guides them to their desired haven.

—Psalm 107:30

The *Mayflower* sailed from Plymouth Harbor on Wednesday, September 6, 1620, and the voyage to America felt like a nightmare. The ship was about the length of a tennis court, and it hadn't been designed for passengers, only for cargo. As a result, all 102 passengers and the 25 or so crew members were crammed into tight spaces. The passengers spent most of their time in the darkness of the gun deck, which measured twenty-five by fifteen feet at its broadest point and was barely over five feet high. The children could stand up, but everyone else was forced to crawl on hands and knees.

The ship rolled and pitched and made slow progress—the voyage lasted sixty-six days. Seasickness was rampant, and there was little means of sanitation. A large contingent of stowaway cockroaches and rats accompanied the Pilgrims, and the heavy seas hit the walls of the

Mayflower like sledgehammers, sending rivulets of cold water into the hold, drenching the Pilgrims and turning everything into a sodden mess.

The Pilgrims, however, never lost sight of God. Midway through the voyage on September 22, they read the scripture for the day and felt it was placed in the Bible just for them. It was Psalm 107, a glorious psalm of thanksgiving, which expresses the gratitude of various groups of people who experienced God's watchful care over their lives. One portion of the psalm was spoken by those on dangerous voyages who rejoice because their God controls the elements and knows how to guide them to safe harbors and to their desired haven. Verses 23–31 say:

> Those who go down to the sea in ships,
> Who do business on great waters,
> They see the works of the LORD,
> And His wonders in the deep.
> For He commands and raises the stormy wind,
> Which lifts up the waves of the sea.
> They mount up to the heavens,
> They go down again to the depths;
> Their soul melts because of trouble.
> They reel to and fro, and stagger like a drunken man,
> And are at their wits' end.
> Then they cry out to the LORD in their trouble,
> And He brings them out of their distresses.
> He calms the storm,
> So that its waves are still.
> Then they are glad because they are quiet;
> So He guides them to their desired haven.
> Oh, that men would give thanks to the LORD for His goodness,
> And for His wonderful works to the children of men!

When the *Mayflower* finally sailed into its "desired haven" of Cape Cod, the Pilgrims hammered out a formal and binding agreement, which is known as the Mayflower Compact and was signed aboard ship on November 11, 1620:

> In the Name of God, Amen. We, whose names are underwritten . . . having undertaken for the Glory of God, and the Advancement of the Christian Faith, and the Honor of King and Country, a Voyage to plant the first Colony in the northern parts of Virginia, do by these Presents, solemnly and mutually, in the Presence of God and of one another, covenant and combine ourselves together into a civil Body Politick.[1]

In their book *The Light and the Glory*, Peter Marshall and David Manuel wrote:

> The Mayflower Compact would become the cornerstone of American representative government. Although the Pilgrims had no idea of the significance for America of what they had done, it marked the first time in history since the children of Israel in the Sinai wilderness (with the exception of John Calvin's Geneva) that free and equal men had voluntarily covenanted together to create their own new civil government based on Biblical principles.[2]

April 8, 1630

The City on a Hill

"You are the light of the world. A city that is set on a hill cannot be hidden."

—Matthew 5:14

On April 8, 1630, a fleet of four ships left the Isle of Wight, carrying seven hundred Puritan immigrants to the New World. Among them was John Winthrop, a noted English lawyer who was distressed by the persecution directed toward his fellow Puritans from King Charles I. Joining Winthrop aboard the flagship, *Arabella,* were two young sons; his wife, Margaret, wasn't able to join him until the next year. John and Margaret, in an unusual act of devotion, forged a plan for keeping their love alive during their separation. They covenanted to think about each other for an hour every Monday and Friday afternoon.[1]

At some point before, during, or just after the voyage, Winthrop prepared and preached one of the most influential sermons in American history, "A Model of Christian Charity," also known as the "City Upon a

Hill" sermon. In his sermon, Winthrop painted a compelling vision for the future of American society. Borrowing the words of Jesus from Matthew 5:14, he offered an image that has been repeated for nearly four hundred years by presidents and patriots—America is a shining city on a hill.

Winthrop preached to his fellow Puritans, saying,

The only way to . . . provide for our posterity is to follow the counsel of Micah, to do justly, to love mercy, and to walk humbly with our God. For this end we must be knit together in this work as one man; we must entertain each other in brotherly affection. We must be willing to abridge ourselves of superfluities for the supply of other's necessities. We must uphold a familiar commerce together in all meekness, gentleness, patience, and liberality. We must delight in each other; make others' conditions our own; rejoice together, mourn together, labor and suffer together, always having before our eyes our commission and community in this work, as members of the same body.

So shall we keep the unity of the Spirit in the bond of peace. The Lord will be our God and delight to dwell among us as His own people and will command a blessing upon us in all our ways. So that we shall see much more of His wisdom, power, goodness, and truth than formerly we have been acquainted with.

We shall find that the God of Israel is among us, when ten of us shall be able to resist a thousand of our enemies; when He shall make us a praise and glory that men shall say of succeeding [settlements], "The Lord make it like that of New England." For we must consider that we shall be a City upon a Hill. The eyes of all people are upon us . . . .

Beloved, there is now set before us life and good, death and evil, in that we are commanded this day to love the Lord our God, and to love one another, to walk in His ways and to keep His commandments and His ordinance and His laws . . . that we may live and be multiplied, and that the Lord our God may bless us in the land wither we go to possess it.[2]

Winthrop's vision of America was compelling, but it bears remembering that Jesus Christ coined this phrase in His Sermon on the Mount to refer not to America herself but to His followers, His church on earth. He told us:

"You are the light of the world. A city that is set on a hill cannot be hidden. Nor do they light a lamp and put it under a basket, but on a lampstand, and it gives light to all who are in the house. Let your light so shine before men, that they may see your good works and glorify your Father in heaven." (Matthew 5:14–16)

7

September 8, 1636

The Founding of Harvard

And you shall know the truth, and the truth shall make you free.

—JOHN 8:32

The Puritans arrived in Massachusetts Bay by boatloads during the Great Migration of the 1630s, and many of them were well-educated graduates of England's leading universities, especially Emmanuel College, Cambridge. Many were theologians, pastors, and Bible scholars. One thing was paramount on their minds as they settled into the New World: to establish a school in the colonies, especially for the training of ministerial students. As explained in the 1643 booklet *New England's First Fruits*:

> After God had carried us safe to New England and we had built our houses, provided necessaries for our livelihood, reared convenient places for God's worship, and settled the civil government: One of the next things we longed for and looked after was to advance learning and

perpetuate it to posterity; dreading to leave an illiterate ministry to the churches, when our present ministers shall lie in the dust.[1]

On September 8, 1636, the legislature of the Colony of Massachusetts Bay voted to create the first college in America.[2] The records say: "The Court agree to give Four Hundred Pounds towards a School or College, whereof Two Hundred Pounds shall be paid the next year, and Two Hundred Pounds when the work is finished."[3] In 1637, the General Court appointed twelve eminent men as trustees of the college.

That same year, a young clergyman from England arrived on American shores—John Harvard, who was described as a godly man and a lover of learning. Harvard, born in 1607, was the son of a butcher and tavern owner in a village near London. In 1625, the bubonic plague wiped out most of Harvard's family. His mother, however, survived and was able to send him to Emmanuel College, Cambridge. John was ordained a dissenting minister, which meant he joined the Puritans who resisted the oversight of the Anglican Church. He married Ann Sadler in 1637, and the next year they emigrated to New England, where John became an assistant preacher in Boston.

John was battling tuberculosis, and he died the next year at age thirty. He bequeathed half of his property and all of his library of approximately three hundred volumes to the new college.[4] (Unfortunately a fire in 1764 consumed Harvard's original library, with the exception of one book, which was in the hands of a student at the time and thus escaped the flames. The book's title was *The Christian Warfare Against the Devil, World, and Flesh . . . And Means to Obtain Victory.*[5])

In appreciation for his generosity the new school was named for him— Harvard. The doors opened, and a student handbook was published, *Laws and Statutes for Students of Harvard College*, which said,

Let every Student be plainly instructed, and earnestly pressed to consider well, the main end of his life and studies is *to know God and Jesus*

Christ, which is eternal life. Joh. 17:3. . . . And seeing the Lord only giveth wisdom, let every one seriously set himself by prayer in secret to seek it of him. Prov. 2:3.

Every one shall so exercise himself in reading the Scriptures twice a day, that he shall be ready to give such an account of his proficiency therein, both in *Theoretical* observations of the Language and *Logic*, and in *Practical* and spiritual truths, as his Tutor shall require, according to his several ability—seeing *the entrance of the word giveth light, it giveth understanding to the simple.* Psalm 119:130.[6]

Sometime later, Harvard adopted the motto "Veritas Christo et Ecclesiae," Latin for "Truth for Christ and the Church." The motto was followed by an explanatory reference to John 8:32, which provides the only sure foundation for a sound education: "And you shall know the truth, and the truth shall set you free."[7]

It bears remembering that the first educators in America and the founders of our great institutions of learning were anchored to their conviction of objective, absolute truth, based on the reality of God and the trustworthiness of Scripture. This was the firm foundation of American education.

May 31, 1638

Thomas Hooker, the Father of Democracy

Choose wise, understanding, and knowledgeable men from
among your tribes, and I will make them heads over you.

—Deuteronomy 1:13

Thomas Hooker was born in Leicestershire, England, in 1586. He studied theology at Cambridge and became one of the most powerful and popular preachers in England. But he encountered pressure from the government due to his Puritan views and fled, first to Holland and then, by disguising himself for protection, to America as part of the great Puritan migration.

In 1633, he became the pastor of a small church near the present site of Cambridge, Massachusetts. His pulpit skills were extraordinary, and he has been called "perhaps the greatest of the seventeenth-century American preachers."[1]

Hooker believed in extending the right to vote to more people, and that put him at odds with some of his fellow Puritan leaders. In 1636,

Hooker, his wife, his congregation of about a hundred, plus 160 cattle, left Cambridge and Boston, migrating south to establish the city of Hartford.

Here on May 31, 1638, Hooker preached a midweek sermon from Deuteronomy 1:13, which has been called "among the most important sermons in colonial New England."[2] Hooker was drawn to this verse because it's where Moses recounted how he developed a political structure that effectively oversaw the new nation of Israel. As Moses led the Israelites out of Egypt and into the wilderness, he was overwhelmed with his responsibility. But he told the Israelites to choose wise, understanding leaders for themselves from among their tribes, and the people did so. The resulting organization provided relief to Moses and accountable leaders for the people. To Hooker, it was a pattern for how nations should be governed.

A manuscript of Hooker's sermon doesn't exist, but one listener, Henry Wolcott Jr., took notes in shorthand, recording thirteen short paragraphs giving Hooker's key points, one of which is:

The choice of public magistrates belongs unto the people by God's own allowance. . . . The privilege of election, which belongs to the people, therefore must not be exercised according to their humours, but according to the blessed will and law of God. . . . They who have power to appoint officers and magistrates, it is in their power, also, to set the bounds and limitations. . . . The foundation of authority is laid, firstly, in the free consent of the people.[3]

Hooker's concept of democracy was considered radical in a world dominated by monarchs and emperors. Many historians believe the ideas he expressed set the stage for Connecticut to adopt a new constitution the following January, which is known as the Fundamental Orders of Connecticut. This is considered the first written constitution to embody a democratic tone, and it became the model for constitutions in other colonies. Ultimately, it paved the way for the Constitution of the United States. That's why Connecticut is known to this day as the Constitution State.

The Fundamental Orders of Connecticut, inspired by the ideas of Deuteronomy 1:13 as preached by Thomas Hooker, said in its opening preamble,

> Forasmuch as it hath pleased the Almighty God by the wise disposition of His Divine Providence so to order and dispose of things that we, the inhabitants and residents of Windsor, Hartford and Wethersfield, are now cohabiting and dwelling in and upon the river of Connecticut and the lands thereunto adjoining, and well knowing where a people are gathered together the Word of God requires that to maintain the peace and union of such a people there should be an orderly and decent government established according to God, to order and dispose of the affrays of the people at all seasons as occasion shall require; do therefore associate and connive ourselves to be as one public state or commonwealth, and do, for ourselves and our successors . . . enter into combination and confederation together, to maintain and preserve the liberty and purity of the gospel of our Lord Jesus which we now profess.[4]

The Fundamental Orders of Connecticut represent the beginnings of democracy in America. Some have called Hooker the Father of Democracy, and his ideas were firmly rooted in the priesthood of the believers based on the gospel of Christ.[5]

9

December 29, 1649

"God Stept In and Helped"

You therefore must endure hardship as a good soldier of Jesus Christ.

—2 TIMOTHY 2:3

J ohn Eliot was born in England, attended Cambridge, came to Christ under the ministry of Thomas Hooker, and emigrated to Boston, where the church of Roxbury hired him as pastor in 1632. He kept the job fifty-seven years. In 1646, when he was forty-two years old, Eliot grew burdened for nearby Native Americans and began studying one of the Algonquin languages (Wôpanâak). It was a daunting task, especially because of the length of the words. For example, the phrase "our lusts" was expressed:

NUMMATCHEKODTANTAMOONGANUNNONASH[1]

Eliot persevered until he could speak the language well enough to preach with the help of an interpreter.[2] Speaking of himself in the third person, Eliot later wrote of his first attempt:

He then preached Jesus Christ unto them, as the only means of recovery from sin and wrath and eternal death; he explained to them who Christ was, and whither he was gone, and how he will one day come again to judge the world. He spake to them of the blessed state of all those who believe in Christ and know Him feelingly.[3]

In a short time, a number of Native Americans confessed Christ as Savior. The converts established their own village and named it *Noonanetum*, or Rejoicing. As time went by, other villages arose, and Eliot traveled up and down the coast, all the time maintaining his primary ministry as a pastor in Roxbury. In a letter dated December 29, 1649, he wrote:

I was not dry night nor day from the third day of the week unto the sixth, but so travelled, and at night pull off my boots, wring my stockings, and on with them again, and so continued . . . yet God stept in and helped: I considered . . . 2 Tim. 2:3, "Endure hardness as a good soldier of Christ."[4]

We all should consider that verse. There's nothing easy about life or about serving God in a hostile age or resistant environment. Paul was facing execution for his faith in Christ when he wrote those words to Timothy, and he wanted to impart tenacity and toughness into his young disciple.

Men and women who, like John Eliot, helped establish the gospel in America faced miserable conditions and great hardships. But they considered 2 Timothy 2:3 and persevered. Under Eliot's ministry, Native American churches were planted in Natick, Plymouth, Cape Cod, Nantucket, and Martha's Vineyard. Eliot lived to see his ministry found fourteen praying villages, each with between twenty-five hundred and four thousand people, and twenty-four Native American preachers—all while serving his church in Roxbury.[5] The school he founded, Roxbury Latin School, is today the oldest school in continuous existence in North America.[6]

Eliot's most prodigious feat was the production of the first Bible published in America, which was also the first Bible translation into a Native American language. The New Testament came out in 1661, and the Old Testament three years later.[7] It's hard to imagine how Eliot accomplished such a thing—reducing a near-impossible language to writing, training Native Americans to read, then translating the entire Bible for them. That in itself is "a work which excited the wonder and admiration of both hemispheres, and has rendered his name ever memorable in the annals of literature and piety."[8]

In his eighties Eliot grew too weak to preach at his church in Roxbury, and he asked the church to seek another pastor. "I wonder for what the Lord Jesus Christ lets me live," he said. "He knows that now I can do nothing for him!"[9] As he sought some final work to do for Christ, he heard of a youth who had fallen into a fire and been blinded. Eliot invited the child to live with him, devoting many hours to helping him memorize chapters of Scripture and learning to pray. Eliot was a man of prayer. When confronted with distressing news, he would say, "Brethren, let us turn all this into prayer."[10]

John Eliot passed away on May 21, 1690, in his eighty-sixth year. His last words were: "Welcome joy! Pray, pray, pray!"[11]

November 22, 1739

William Tennent's Log Cabin Seminary

> *Those who have turned the world upside down have come here too.*
>
> —ACTS 17:6

Rev. William Tennent Sr. came to America from Ireland in 1716, and five years later he settled in Bucks County, Pennsylvania, just north of Philadelphia. He was at midlife, but his true life's work was just beginning. He purchased a hundred acres of land and built a log school for the training of pastors. The students, which included his sons, studied there by day and took up lodging in the neighborhood at night.[1] Tennent's wife, Catherine, cared for the boys like sons. This rough building became the first Presbyterian seminary in America, and the log cabin became a bonfire for the Great Awakening.[2]

On November 22, 1739, celebrated evangelist George Whitefield (pronounced Wit-field) visited the school and found about three thousand people gathered outside. They had come to hear Whitefield, but William

Tennent, not knowing when the famous evangelist would arrive, had started the sermon and was preaching away with great power. Seeing Whitefield ride up, Tennent brought his sermon to a rapid close, led the group in singing a psalm, and turned the crowd over to Whitefield.

"At first, the people seemed unaffected," Whitefield later wrote, "but in the midst of my discourse, the power of the Lord Jesus came upon me, and I felt such a struggling within myself for the people, as I scarce ever felt before. The hearers began to be melted down immediately."[3]

Whitefield provided us with an important description of Tennent's Log College:

> The place wherein the young men study now is . . . a log house, about twenty feet long, and near as many broad and to me it seemed to resemble the schools of the old prophets; for that their habitation were [primitive] . . . From this despised place, seven or eight worthy ministers of Jesus have lately been sent forth; more are almost ready to be sent, and a foundation is now laying for the instruction of many others. The devil will certainly rage against them, but the work, I am persuaded, is of God, and therefore will not come to naught. Carnal ministers oppose them strongly . . . as persons that turn the world upside down.[4]

Turning the world upside down is what the followers of Christ have been doing for two thousand years. When the apostle Paul and his companions ventured into the ancient city of Thessalonica and began preaching the gospel, they won many to Christ. But in the process, they encountered tremendous anger and opposition. The critics railed against them, saying, "These who have turned the world upside down have come here too."

I like that phrase! Though it was uttered in disdain, it aptly describes those who hold up the cross of Jesus Christ. We are turning the world upside down.

Tennent's handful of graduates turned the Colonies upside down as evangelists of the Great Awakening, the massive spiritual revival that swept over the Colonies, bringing multitudes to faith in Christ and changing the fabric of early American culture.

Thomas Murphey wrote:

> It is doubtful whether ever before or since then lads were collected in the same school who were afterward to accomplish so much good in their own day, and to send down such streams of blessings to unborn generations. . . . It is absolutely startling to glance at the list of the eminent ministers—great preachers, the greatest in the early annals of our church—who obtained their training for the ministry . . . in this humble institution. . . . They went forth preaching the Gospel in every quarter, bringing thousands of souls to Christ, building up the churches in many regions, establishing schools and academies . . . and starting streams of godly influences that flowed over the whole land, the currents of which have not subsided even to this present day.[5]

Tennent died on May 6, 1746, at age seventy-three, but his graduates and supporters joined together to establish a more permanent training school for Presbyterian ministers in the Colonies: the College of New Jersey, today known as Princeton University. Rev. Douglas K. Turner wrote, "The germ of this distinguished seat of learning [Princeton] . . . is to be found in Mr. Tennent's seminary."[6]

May 5, 1740

Citizens of Heaven

*He was caught up into Paradise and heard inexpressible
words, which it is not lawful for a man to utter.*

—2 CORINTHIANS 12:4

S everal months after George Whitefield preached at William Tennent's
log cabin, he did the same for Tennent's son, William Tennent Jr.,
who was pastoring in Freehold, New Jersey. Whitefield, then twenty-five,
spent the night with the younger Tennent and wrote on May 5, 1740: "Oh
how sweetly did the time glide on and our hearts burn within us, when
we opened the Scriptures and communicated our experiences to each
other! Our Lord was with us, as with the two disciples going to Emmaus."[1]

William Tennent Jr. had become the pastor of the Old Scots
Presbyterian Church in Freehold following the death of his brother,
who had been the previous pastor. The church's location was strategic—
situated in the heart of the Middle Colonies—and Tennent served the
church for forty-three years. He was a fiery champion of the mighty

revival known as the Great Awakening and the ensuing drive for religious liberty and American independence.

Tennent's powerful ministry was fueled, in part, by something he experienced in college. He had worn himself out with his studies, and his friends grew alarmed at his weight loss. He became little more than a living skeleton. His best friend, a doctor, was especially concerned.

One day as Tennent was talking to a friend, he collapsed and, from all appearances, died. In those days it was difficult to gauge the moment of death. But Tennent seemed to be gone, so his body was prepared for burial, and his funeral was announced for the next day.[2]

When his physician friend returned from a trip and heard the news, he went straight to Tennent's body and examined it carefully for any possible sign of life. Convinced the young scholar wasn't dead, the doctor moved the body to a warm bed, and the funeral was postponed.

Tennent's brother, certain his sibling was gone, grew angry. For three days and nights the two men engaged in an ongoing debate about when the funeral should occur. The doctor sat by the bedside unwilling to declare the man dead. Events finally came to a climax when the brother came to take Tennent's body for the funeral. As they quarreled, suddenly the "corpse" opened his eyes and uttered a loud and dreadful groan.[3]

Plans for the funeral were hastily scrapped and the mourners sent home. Tennent recovered and later gave this testimony:

As to dying—I found my fever increase, and I became weaker and weaker, until all at once I found myself in heaven, as I thought. I saw no shape as to the Deity, but *glory all unutterable!* . . . I can say, as St. Paul did, I heard and I saw things all unutterable; I saw a great multitude before this glory, apparently in the height of bliss, singing most melodiously. I was . . . about to join that great and happy multitude, when one came to me, looked me full in the face, laid his hand on my shoulder and said, "You must go back." . . . Nothing could have shocked me more; I cried out, Lord, must I go back? With this shock I opened my eyes in this world.[4]

Tennent compared his experience to a similar episode in the life of Saint Paul in 2 Corinthians 12, when the apostle was caught up to Paradise "whether in the body or out of the body I do not know, God knows" (v. 3). Paul heard great and inexpressible words, which encouraged him for the rest of his earthly life and enabled him to press onward with the gospel, despite suffering and difficulties.

The same was true for William Tennent Jr. and his fellow evangelicals. They turned the world upside down because they focused on eternal realities. The Bible plainly states, "our citizenship is in heaven" (Philippians 3:20). We don't think of ourselves as citizens of earth going to heaven but as citizens of heaven passing through earth. The history of America—and the testimony of our own lives—reveals an incredible secret. Those who most anticipate a future in glory are the most likely to change the world here and now.

12

October 23, 1740

The News from Heaven

You must be born again.

—John 3:7

He set the Colonies on fire—George Whitefield, one of the most electrifying preachers in Christian history. A British Anglican, he made seven trips to the Colonies and preached so extensively that 80 percent of the population heard him, usually in the open air. His crowds numbered thousands, and his voice was commanding though he had only the air for amplification. He was America's first celebrity, the most famous person in the Colonies before George Washington, and he has been called America's Spiritual Founding Father.[1] His key verse—the text for many of his sermons and the theme of his lifelong ministry—was John 3:7: "You *must* be born again" (emphasis mine). It was such a constant chorus that a woman reportedly asked Whitefield why he so often insisted on preaching on the words "You must be born again." He replied, "Because, Madam, you must."[2]

Whitefield's 1739-1740 tour of the Colonies began in Philadelphia and coincided with the high tide of the Great Awakening. He generated audiences like none had ever seen before—often exceeding the population of the cities he visited. A spirit of revival radiated from his ministry for miles in all directions.

Nathan Cole, a farmer in Connecticut, described Whitefield's visit to his area on October 23, 1740.[3] Like virtually everyone in the Colonies, Cole had heard reports of the remarkable meetings Whitefield was conducting and longed to hear the preacher for himself. His interest wasn't just curiosity; he had a spiritual hunger and wondered if he might find God through the young evangelist's words.

One morning about eight or nine o'clock, a rider passed the Cole farmstead shouting that Mr. Whitefield was to preach at Middletown at ten o'clock. Cole threw down his tool and ran with all his might to the house, hollering for his wife to get ready to go to the event, which was about twelve miles away. Running to his barn, he threw the saddle on his horse, galloped back, and hoisted his wife behind him. Together they traveled as fast as the horse could run. When the horse showed signs of giving out, Cole dismounted and ran alongside until the animal had regained strength, then jumped back on; in this manner they made their way to Middletown, fearing they would be too late. Cole later said they traveled as if fleeing for their lives.

By and by they saw a strange cloud forming, like a yellow fog rising from the earth. They heard a noise like thunder shaking the ground. Coming closer, they saw the cloud and noise represented thousands of people, rushing as they were, hoping to arrive on time. Every horse was galloping with all its might, as thousands of people clogged the roads and pathways leading to Middletown.

Cole's wife exclaimed, "Law, our clothes will be all spoiled; see how they look." Everything within sight was covered by the dust—the trees, ground, horses, people, and even the sky were tinted an orange-brown color.

Over on the river, ferry boats were disgorging passengers in great numbers as a multitude of thousands assembled in a field outside town. Cole later wrote:

> When I saw Mr. Whitefield come upon the [platform], he looked almost angelical—a young, slim, slender youth before some thousands of people and with a bold, undaunted countenance, and my hearing how God was with him everywhere as he came along, it solemnized my mind and put me into a trembling fear before he began to preach; for he looked as if he was clothed with authority from the great God.[4]

The sermon resulted in Nathan Cole's conversion, and in the conversions of many others. George Whitefield's repeated visits to America, between 1738 and 1770, led thousands to be born again. The Great Awakening united the Colonies in a way that transcended regional differences, infused the land with spiritual liberty, populated their pulpits with clergymen proclaiming freedom, and laid a moral foundation for the American Revolution.

13

July 8, 1741

America's Most Famous Sermon

Their foot shall slip in due time.

—DEUTERONOMY 32:35

There were limited forms of entertainment in colonial times, and little reason for people to gather in assemblies except in times of crisis. That's why churches were so important and sermons so influential. People gathered weekly to fellowship, pray, worship, and learn from Scripture. Many of the events that shaped the mind-set of colonial America occurred because of biblical sermons preached by gifted pastors.

No one embodies that more than Jonathan Edwards.

Jonathan was the fifth child (and the only son of eleven children) of Rev. Timothy Edwards and Esther Stoddard Edwards. He was born on October 5, 1703, in West Windsor, Connecticut. Jonathan was a brilliant child, mastering Latin, Greek, and Hebrew by age twelve. He entered Connecticut Collegiate School (today Yale University), and graduated valedictorian of his class.

At age seventeen, while working on his master's degree, he began meditating on 1 Timothy 1:17: "Now to the King eternal, immortal, invisible, to God who alone is wise, be honor and glory forever and ever. Amen." That verse sparked a spiritual experience that made Edwards feel "swallowed up" in God. Scholars describe this as his conversion experience. Edwards wrote: "From about that time, I began to have a new kind of apprehensions and ideas of Christ, and the work of redemption, and the glorious way of salvation by Him."[1]

At age eighteen, Edwards took his first pastorate in a Presbyterian church in New York City, and he became a professor at Yale from 1724 to 1726.

In November 1726, his grandfather, Solomon Stoddard, asked Edwards to join him in the pastorate at Northampton Church, and when his grandfather passed away, Edwards became the sole pastor of the church. In the mid-1730s, a revival broke out in Northampton, and in 1740, the great evangelist George Whitefield came to preach. His visit further enflamed Edwards to give himself to the cause of revival.

The next year Edwards prepared a sermon titled "Sinners in the Hands of an Angry God," based on Deuteronomy 32:35. This passage is part of the song of Moses, composed near the end of Moses's life, in which he predicted blessings for Israel and judgment on those who rejected God. Using poetic language, Moses warned the Israelites against drifting from the ways of the Lord, for such backsliders will discover their foot will slip in due time, and the day of calamity will come swiftly.

Many of Edwards' sermons were uplifting, positive, and full of the grace and love of God. But on this occasion, his sermon was a warning against taking God for granted or rejecting His entreaties. In a calm tone he warned his listeners:

> Unconverted men walk over the pit of hell on a rotten covering, and
> there are innumerable places in this covering so weak that they will not
> bear their weight, and these places are not seen. The arrows of death
> fly unseen at noon-day; the sharpest sight cannot discern them . . . .

This that you have heard is the case of every one of you that are out of Christ—that world of misery, that lake of burning brimstone, is extended abroad under you. There is a dreadful pit of the glowing flames of the wrath of God; there is hell's wide gaping mouth open; and you have nothing to stand upon, nor any thing to take hold of; there is nothing between you and hell but the air. . . .

Your wickedness makes you as it were heavy as lead, and to tend downwards with great weight and pressure towards hell; and if God should let you go, you would immediately sink and swiftly descend and plunge into the bottomless gulf, and your healthy constitution, and your own care and prudence, and best contrivance, and all your righteousness, would have no more influence to uphold you and keep you out of hell than a spider's web would have to stop a falling rock. . . .

And now you have an extraordinary opportunity, a day wherein Christ has thrown the door of mercy wide open, and stands in calling and crying with a loud voice to poor sinners.[2]

In the pews, Edwards's words stuck with supernatural force. People began to moan, to weep audibly, and even to scream. The ensuing revival became part of the Great Awakening—a movement of the Holy Spirit over New England and the Colonies.

The Great Awakening in the American Colonies was part of a much broader revival that swept over the Western church in those days. In England the revival is commonly known as the Wesley Revival; in Germany it became known as Pietism. These three great revival movements changed history, awakening the church in Germany, saving England from going down the path of the French Revolution, and giving America the moral and spiritual impetus to become a free and independent nation.

How we need another Great Awakening today!

October 16, 1746

The Prayer That Sunk a Navy

If God is for us, who can be against us?

—ROMANS 8:31

In the 1740s, the American Colonies became a rope in the tug-of-war between Britain and France. One of the harshest periods of conflict, King George's War, raged from 1744 to 1748, some thirty years before the Declaration of Independence.

In the midst of the conflict, in October 1746, Bostonians heard with alarm that the French admiral duc d'Anville was preparing to sail his fleet from Nova Scotia to Boston Harbor to attack the city and ravage New England. It was the largest naval armada to have threatened the American coastline.[1]

The governor of the Massachusetts colony had no adequate way to protect Boston, the jewel of American cities, or its fifteen thousand inhabitants. The French were coming to burn the city to the ground. Sunday, October 16, 1746, was appointed a citywide day of prayer and fasting. Panicked citizens gathered into the city's churches, with hundreds of them crowding into the historic Old South Meeting House. The only thing pleasant that day was the weather, which was peaceful and calm. Not a breeze ruffled the waters in the bay, and no threatening clouds drifted through the skies.

The pastor of Old South Church was Rev. Thomas Prince, a powerful force in the Great Awakening, a friend of George Whitefield, and a man of prayer. Climbing into the high pulpit, Rev. Prince earnestly interceded on behalf of the Colonies. "Deliver us from our enemy," he reportedly prayed. "Send Thy tempest, Lord, upon the waters to the eastward! Raise Thy right hand. Scatter the ships of our tormentors and drive them thence."[2]

Suddenly a powerful gust of wind struck the church so hard the shutters banged, startling the congregation.[3] Rev. Prince paused and looked up in surprise. Sunlight no longer streamed through the windows, and the room reflected the ominous darkness of the sky. Gathering his thoughts, Rev. Prince continued with greater earnestness, saying, "Sink their proud frigates beneath the power of Thy winds." Gusts of wind caused the church bell to chime "a wild and uneven sound . . . though no man was in the steeple."[4]

Raising his hands toward heaven, Rev. Prince bellowed, "We hear Thy voice, O Lord! We hear it! Thy breath is upon the waters to the eastward, even upon the deep. Thy bell toils for the death of our enemies!" Overcome by emotion, he paused as tears ran down his cheeks, then he ended his prayer saying, "Thine be the glory, Lord. Amen and amen!"[5]

That day a storm of hurricane force struck the French ships. The greater part of the fleet was wrecked, and the duc d'Anville either took his own life or died from a stroke. Only a few sailors survived. In his book *Anatomy of a Naval Disaster: The 1746 French Expedition to North America*, Professor James Pritchard wrote, "Not a single French military objective had been achieved. Thousands of soldiers and sailors were dead. . . . No one knows how many men died during the expedition; some estimates range as high as 8,000. So great was the calamity that naval authorities hastened to wind up its affairs and bury quickly and effectively the memory of its existence."[6]

Back in Boston, the governor set aside a day of thanksgiving, and according to historian Catherine Drinker Bowen, "There was no end to the joyful quotation: *If God be for us, who can be against us?*"[7] Somehow that verse came to people's minds, reminding them that when God is our advocate, no enemy—not even an entire navy—can overcome us. This verse comes from the majestic song of Paul at the end of Romans 8, in which he exalts in the grace of the God whose love for us is unending.

"What then shall we say to these things?" asked Paul. "If God is for us, who can be against us? He who did not spare His own Son, but delivered Him up for us all, how shall He not with Him also freely give us all things?" (Romans 8:31–32).

In nearby Braintree on that never-to-be-forgotten day, a child named John Adams knelt with his family as his father thanked God "for this most timely evidence of His favor."[8]

A century later Henry Wadsworth Longfellow immortalized the event in his poem "A Ballad of the French Fleet," written in the voice of Rev. Prince, who said, in part:

> There were rumors in the street,
> In the houses there was fear
> Of the coming of the fleet,
> And the danger hovering near,
> And while from mouth to mouth
> Spread the tidings of dismay,
> I stood in the Old South,
> Saying humbly, "Let us pray!"[9]

October 9, 1747

"I Dared to Rejoice in God"

"Comfort, yes, comfort My people!" says your God.

—Isaiah 40:1

When David Brainerd, twenty-nine, died on October 9, 1747, he could not have imagined how his influence, amplified by the Great Awakening, would reverberate through the centuries to fuel the age of Christian missions. Brainerd, who was born in 1718, experienced a profound conversion to Christ in 1739 and enrolled at Yale. When his spiritual enthusiasm resulted in his expulsion, Brainerd embarked on the task of evangelizing Native Americans—preaching throughout the Northeast, battling the elements, fighting off depression, and suffering from tuberculosis.

Brainerd's story is gripping because he suffered mental depression and physical weakness while battling intense loneliness in an undying quest to find and finish the work God had assigned him. Jonathan Edwards said of Brainerd, "He exceeded all melancholy persons that ever I was acquainted with."[1]

43

Because of these factors, Brainerd was cast on the mercy of God more than most of us, and all of us can relate to parts of his struggle. He learned to draw from the Lord's comfort, practice the Lord's companionship, and employ the Lord's strength. When he had nowhere else to turn, Brainerd inevitably turned to the comfort of Scripture.

Brainerd kept a diary and wrote with tremendous honesty. In his entry for May 18, 1743, he wrote:

My circumstances are such that I have no comfort, of any kind, but what I have in God. I live in the most lonesome wilderness; have but one single person to converse with, that can speak English. Most of the talk I hear, is either Highland-Scotch or Indian. I have no fellow-Christian to whom I might [unburden] myself, and lay open my spiritual sorrows, and with whom I might take sweet counsel in conversation about heavenly things, and join in social prayer. I live poorly with regard to the comforts of life: most of my diet consists of boiled corn, hasty pudding, and etc. I lodge on a bundle of straw, my labor is hard and extremely difficult, and I have little appearance of success, to comfort me.

Two days later he added:

Was much perplexed some part of the day; but towards night, had some comfortable meditations on Isaiah 40:1 ["Comfort ye, comfort ye my people, saith your God" (KJV)] and enjoyed some sweetness in prayer. Afterward my soul rose so far above the deep waters, that I dared to rejoice in God: I saw, there was sufficient matter of consolation in the blessed God.[2]

I love that phrase: "I dared to rejoice in God." Sometimes we feel guilty if we rejoice in our hearts, for we're so aware of our problems and pressures. The weakness and weariness of life makes us consider worry the most appropriate emotional response to it all. But when we find the comfort of God within the pages of His Word, and when we experience the sweetness of prayer, we can dare to rejoice in Him.

Brainerd did see some outward success during his brief ministry. On August 8, 1745, he wrote, "In the afternoon I preached to the Indians, their number was now about sixty-five persons, men, women, and children. . . . The power of God seemed to descend upon the assembly 'like a mighty rushing wind,' and with an astonishing energy bore down all before it. I stood amazed at the influence which seized the audience almost universally, and could compare it to nothing more aptly, than the irresistible force of a mighty torrent."[3]

In July 1747, Brainerd rode to Jonathan Edwards's house, almost too weak to sit in the saddle. Edwards's family cared for him in his final days, and Brainerd maintained his journal nearly to the end. His last entry from October 2 reads, "My soul was this day, at turns, sweetly set on God: I longed to be *with him*, that I might *behold his glory*. . . . Oh, come, Lord Jesus, come quickly! Amen."[4]

Brainerd died on October 9, 1747, and two years later Edwards published *The Life of David Brainerd*, composed mainly of Brainerd's journal entries. It electrified the nation, inspired America's first generation of missionaries, and has never gone out of print.[5] Brainerd could only experience his life in the moment, but we can evaluate it from the perspective of history. He battled depression and illness, sought comfort from God, drew from the words of scriptures such as Isaiah 40, and pursued his work for God until he literally gave out. And he died young with little outward success to encourage him.

And yet how great his impact!

William Carey, known as the Father of Modern Missions, referred to Brainerd's diary as "almost a second Bible."[6] Missionary pioneer Henry Martyn wrote: "I long to be like him!"[7] Almost every pioneer missionary kept a copy of Brainerd's life near at hand. John Piper called *The Life of David Brainard* "a biography that has inspired more missionary service, perhaps, than any other book outside the Bible. . . . His story has become a spiritual classic."[8]

How amazing to think that our greatest ministry often comes after we're gone!

16

January 30, 1750

The Catechism of the Revolution

Let every soul be subject to the governing authorities. For there is no authority except from God, and the authorities that exist are appointed by God.

—ROMANS 13:1

Without America's pre-Revolutionary preachers, it's hard to conceive of the Fourth of July. In his book *A City Upon a Hill: How Sermons Changed the Course of American History*, Larry Witham wrote, "During the decade-long [Puritan] Great Migration . . . ninety Puritan ministers . . . made the Atlantic crossing. They all preached in the same plain meetinghouses, of which 220 were built in the 1600s. In the next century, nearly ten times that many went up. By the American Revolution, New England had more clergy per population than anywhere else, and these five generations of clergy delivered at least five million sermons. A churchgoer listened to seven thousand sermons in a lifetime."[1]

These sermons often touched on themes of liberty, freedom, and obedience to God alone. Among the most influential pulpiteers was Congregational pastor Jonathan Mayhew, whose best-known sermon helped shape the American experience.

On January 30, 1750, Mayhew stood in the pulpit of Boston's Old West Church and preached on the occasion of the 101st anniversary of the execution of King Charles I. His message from Romans 13, titled "A Discourse Concerning Unlimited Submission and Non-Resistance to the High Powers," became "the most famous sermon preached in pre-Revolutionary America."[2]

When published, Mayhew's sermon spread like electricity through the Colonies. John Adams, fourteen at the time, read it over and over "till the Substance of it, was incorporated into my Nature and indelibly engraved on my Memory."[3] Adams later called Mayhew's sermon "the catechism" for the American Revolution.[4] Others have called it "the first volley of the American Revolution, setting forth the intellectual and scriptural justification for rebellion against the crown."[5]

In his sermon Mayhew avowed that Paul's command to be subject to governing authorities did not imply blanket submission to tyrants. Based on his understanding of Romans 13, we are to be under the authority of the government, but the government itself is to respect the higher authority of God. When a government exercises power apart from God's oversight, we have an obligation to resist. Mayhew put it like this:

[Romans 13] urges the duty of obedience from this topic of argument, that civil rulers, as they are supposed to fulfill the pleasure of God, are the ordinance of God. But how is this an argument for obedience to such rulers as do not perform the pleasure of God, by doing good; but the pleasure of the devil, by doing evil; and such as are not, therefore, *God's ministers*, but the devil's! . . .

Common tyrants, and public oppressors, are not entitled to obedience from their subjects, by virtue of any thing here laid down by the inspired apostle. . . .

When once magistrates act contrary to their office . . . when they rob and ruin the public, instead of being guardians of its peace and welfare; they immediately cease to be the *ordinance* and *ministers of God*; and no more deserve that glorious character, than common *pirates* and *highwaymen*.[6]

Fifteen years later Mayhew, forty-five, preached another seditious sermon on a blistering August afternoon in 1765. Sitting in Mayhew's Boston congregation were clandestine members of the Sons of Liberty. The day after his sermon a mob attacked the mansion of Thomas Hutchison, the British governor of Massachusetts Bay Province. Hutchison and his family escaped harm, and Mayhew condemned the violence.

Mayhew died the next year of an illness. He was only forty-six, but his published sermons were papers that kindled the fires of the American Revolution, which erupted ten years to the week after his death.

June 7, 1753

The Liberty Bell Cracks the Case

Proclaim liberty throughout all the land to all its inhabitants.

—LEVITICUS 25:10

When William Penn founded Pennsylvania, he hung a bell from a tree in Philadelphia and rang it to gather citizens for announcements and proclamations. The town grew over time, and a louder bell was needed. In 1751, Isaac Norris, speaker of the Pennsylvania legislature, built a tower on the south side of the State House (Independence Hall) and placed an order for "a good bell of about two thousand pounds weight." Norris, a devoted Bible student, chose the inscription from Leviticus 25:10: "Proclaim Liberty thro' all the Land to all the Inhabitants Thereof."[1]

Whitechapel Bell Foundry in London forged the Pennsylvania State House Bell and shipped it to America. When it arrived in Philadelphia in August 1752, the city buzzed with excitement and everyone gathered to see the bell and hear its glorious tone. Workers erected a makeshift stand,

and the bell was rung with such force that, to the horror of all present, it cracked with the first strike of the clapper![2]

Norris wrote a furious letter to the Whitechapel Foundry, which claimed the bell must have been damaged in transit. The cracked bell was taken down and entrusted to John Pass and John Stow, Philadelphia metalworkers. They created a new mold before taking sledgehammers and shattering the bell into small pieces, which were then melted down and remolded in the cast. When the second bell was unveiled, the population of Philadelphia came out again. The city council provided a feast of meats, cheeses, potatoes, bread, and beer.[3] The moment came, and a worker again struck the clapper to the side of the bell. This time it didn't crack—but neither did it ring. It clunked.

The bell was again smashed to pieces, melted down, and recast. On June 7, 1753, workers hoisted the third version of the one-ton bell into the steeple of the State House. Many people still didn't like its tone, but it started doing its official work, summoning the Pennsylvania colonial legislators to session. It was also used to announce the news of the day— the accession of George III to the British throne, the end of the French and Indian War, and, increasingly, the politics of the Revolution. As a British ship sailed up the Delaware River to deliver the dreaded Stamp Act to America, the State House bell rang to warn the city. For the next decade, the Old State House bell rang at every major step along the road to the Revolutionary War. Its most famous moment came at 11:00 a.m. on July 8, 1776, when it summoned people to Independence Hall to hear the reading of the Declaration of Independence. Afterward all the bells of all the churches in Philadelphia pealed until the evening.

When British troops invaded Philadelphia, the State House bell was moved to Allentown and hidden beneath the floor of a church. When Philadelphians returned to their city, the bell came back, but the State House steeple had deteriorated, and the bell was stowed until 1785. In time, it was rehung and started ringing again, announcing the news of the day until sometime in the 1830s or 1840s when it developed its now-famous crack. No one is exactly sure how or why the bell cracked.

But truly, the old State House bell chimed louder after its clapper was silenced. Abolitionists campaigning for the emancipation of slaves noticed its words: "Proclaim liberty throughout the land *for all its inhabitants*." They began using the symbol of the old State House bell in their pamphlets and posters, and they are the ones who gave it a new name—the Liberty Bell.

Years later, as the body of Abraham Lincoln was taken by train to Illinois for burial, his family stopped in Philadelphia. The slain president's open casket was positioned in front of the Liberty Bell, his head resting against the backdrop of its iconic and biblical words: "Proclaim liberty throughout the land for all its inhabitants."[4]

August 17, 1755

Divine Body Armor

Be of good courage, and let us be strong for our people
and for the cities of our God.

—2 SAMUEL 10:12

I n the mid-1700s, both France and England had colonies in America. The strife between them led to the French and Indian War, which preceded the American Revolution by just over a decade. The French colonies, having a smaller population, allied themselves with various Native American tribes to fight the English. The British administrator of Virginia, Robert Dinwiddie, selected a twenty-one-year-old soldier named George Washington to travel from Williamsburg to northwest Pennsylvania on a diplomatic mission to avoid war.[1] The negotiations failed, but the attempt was well publicized and made young Washington a household name.

Later, during the ill-fated Battle of the Monongahela (near present-day Pittsburgh), Washington, who was recovering from illness, exhibited remarkable courage and leadership when British forces marched into an ambush and suffered a disastrous defeat. Washington's survival was miraculous. After the battle, he wrote his mother, saying, "I luckily escaped without a wound, though I had four bullets through my coat and two horses shot under me. . . . I was not half recovered from a violent illness that had confined me to my bed and a wagon for above ten days."[2]

Washington believed God had providentially protected him, and it infused him with confidence in God's guarding, guiding hand. Writing to his brother, John, he said, "By the all-powerful dispensation of Providence I have been protected beyond all human probability or expectation; for I had four bullets through my coat and two horses shot under me yet escaped unhurt, although death was leveling my companions on every side."[3]

The Native Americans were equally perplexed at Washington's survival. One of the chiefs had repeatedly fired at him and ordered his young warriors to do the same, all of them being true marksmen. But their bullets were "turned aside by some invisible and inscrutable interposition."[4] Chief Red Hawk claimed to have personally shot at Washington eleven times. Another chief, perplexed at Washington's survival, is said to have predicted, "He will become the chief of nations, and a people yet unborn will hail him as the father of a mighty empire."[5]

Washington's incredible survival created a sensation in the Colonies, and many felt God's hand was on him for a special purpose. That opinion was expressed in a famous sermon preached in Hanover County, Virginia, on August 17, 1755, by Samuel Davies.

Davies, a Presbyterian evangelist whose wife had died from a miscarriage shortly before their first anniversary, was battling tuberculosis. He wanted to use every moment for the Lord. He wrote hymns, advanced the Great Awakening, served as president of Princeton University, and preached sermons that left a lasting impression on the Colonies.

In his August 17 sermon, "Religion and Patriotism," Davies preached to Captain Overton's Independent Company of Volunteers and encouraged the troops to bravery as he quoted his text, 2 Samuel 10:12: "Be of good courage, and let us be strong for our people and for the cities of our

God." He spoke of the defeat at Monongahela but reminded the soldiers that "God governs the world."[6]

"As a remarkable instance of this," he said, "I may point out to the public that heroic youth, Colonel Washington, whom I cannot but hope Providence has hitherto preserved in so signal a manner for some important service to his country."[7]

Davies didn't live long enough to see how prophetic his words were. He died in 1761, at age thirty-seven. His text, however, lives on. It's remarkable how often the Bible commands us to be strong and to stay encouraged. The eye of providence that preserved young Washington hasn't lost its keenness. The hand that steers the stars and turns the pages of history is the same that arranges our days and bestows the grace needed for each one.

December 7, 1771

Sermon at an Execution

For the wages of sin is death, but the gift of God is eternal life in Christ Jesus our Lord.

—Romans 6:23

In 1723, a Native American boy was born in a wigwam in the village of Mohegan in Connecticut. He was named Occom. He later wrote, "My parents lived a wandering life, as did all the Indians at Mohegan. They chiefly depended upon hunting, fishing, and fowling for their living."[1]

Occom was a teenager at the time of the Great Awakening, and his heart was opened to the gospel. He committed his life to Christ and sought to learn to read the Bible. Hearing about a school (later named Dartmouth) started by Rev. Eleazer Wheelock, a Congregational pastor, Occom enrolled. Wheelock taught the boy to read, mentored him, and prepared him to serve Christ.

On August 29, 1759, Samson Occom was ordained into the Presbyterian ministry.[2] He labored among Native Americans, and in 1765, at the suggestion of George Whitefield, sailed to England to raise money for a charity school (John Hancock helped pay his fare). Occom took England by storm, with large crowds gathering for his sermons—everyone, including the king, wanted to meet him. Occom returned to America a celebrity.

His best-known moment came when a fellow Mohegan, Moses Paul, asked Occom to preach his execution sermon. Paul had been convicted of murder, and in those days it was customary to have a sermon before the hanging. On September 2, 1771, a crowd gathered at the First Church of New Haven as Moses Paul was escorted by guards and Occom stood in the pulpit.

It is an unwelcome task for me to speak upon such an occasion, but since it is the desire of the poor man himself, who is to die a shameful death this day, in conscience I cannot deny him. . . .

The sacred words I have chosen to speak from, upon this undesirable occasion, are found in the Epistle of St. Paul to the Romans, 6:23: "For the wages of sin is death, but the gift of God is eternal life through Jesus Christ our Lord." Death is called the king of terrors, and it ought to be the subject of every man and woman's thoughts daily. . . . We must all come to it, how soon we cannot tell. . . .

Sin has made man proud, tho' he has nothing to be proud of . . . Sin is the cause of all the miseries that attend poor sinful man, which will finally bring him to death, death temporal and eternal. . . .

But heaven and happiness is a free gift; it comes by favor . . . this life is given in and through our Lord Jesus Christ. It could not be given in any other way, but in and through our Lord Jesus Christ; Christ Himself is the gift. . . .

O poor Moses, see what you have done! And now repent, repent. . . . O fly, fly, to the blood of the Lamb of God for the pardon of all your aggravated sins. . . . O Moses! This is good news for you on this last day of your life; here is a crucified Savior at hand for your sins. . . . O, poor Moses, now believe on the Lord Jesus Christ with all your heart, and thou shall be saved eternally.[3]

The demand for copies of Samson Occom's sermon resulted in it being printed, the first publication of a North American Indian in English. It spread over the Colonies, appearing in multiple editions, and became the unexpected means of bringing many to faith in Christ.

To this day, debates rage about whether Moses Paul received a fair trial, but no one doubts the eloquence of Samson Occom. He went on to publish many more sermons and hymns—the country's first Native American writer, preacher, and hymnist. His text that day—Romans 6:23—was the core message of his life because it's at the heart of the gospel message: "The wages of sin is death, but the gift of God is eternal life through Jesus Christ our Lord."

March 5, 1774

Parson Parsons

> *Stand fast therefore in the liberty by which Christ has*
> *made us free, and do not be entangled again with a yoke*
> *of bondage.*
>
> —GALATIANS 5:1

Though Jonathan Parsons enrolled at Yale to prepare for the ministry, he had never been truly born again through the power of Christ. He entered the pastorate at age twenty-five, got married, and went about his work, reportedly more concerned about his clothing than about his calling. This changed during the Great Awakening, when Parsons was gripped by the gospel and soundly converted. He became parson of a Presbyterian church in Newburyport, Massachusetts—a seaport town north of Boston—and continued there until his death thirty years later.[1]

When evangelist George Whitefield came through the area, he found a true friend in Parsons, who always asked him to preach. But by 1770, Whitefield seemed far older than his fifty-five years. His great exertions—crossing the Atlantic over and over, trudging through all kinds of weather on horseback, and preaching to thousands without amplification—had worn him out. On Saturday, September 29, 1770, Whitefield rode wearily into Exeter, where Parsons met him to escort him on to Newburyport. The crowds in Exeter asked Whitefield for a sermon, and though he could barely stand, he attempted to preach and, as he pressed into his sermon, found strength to proclaim the gospel.

Afterward, Parsons accompanied Whitefield to Newburyport and welcomed him into his home for the night. The exhausted evangelist wanted to go upstairs to bed, but a crowd had gathered in the street. Whitefield agreed to speak to them, and the doors were opened, filling the room with people. Standing on the landing of the staircase, a candle in his hand, Whitefield preached Christ. When the candle burned down and flickered out, Whitefield continued up the stairs, got into bed with his Bible and a copy of Isaac Watts's hymnbook nearby, and died. He was buried in the vault beneath the floor of Parson's church, where he remains to this day.[2]

Jonathan Parsons became known as Whitefield's deathbed friend, further spurring on his ministry through sermons, spoken and printed. Meanwhile, the forces of Revolution were igniting, and Parsons used his powerful preaching to proclaim liberty throughout the land. On March 5, 1774, he preached a rousing sermon from Galatians 5:1, which became a motto of Revolutionary sentiment: "Stand fast therefore in the liberty by which Christ has made us free."[3]

The text rang out from many pulpits in the days before the American Revolution. There is a thin line between spiritual liberty and political liberty. When people find freedom from sin, they want the freedom to proclaim it to others.

In his sermon at Newburyport, marking the fourth anniversary of the Boston Massacre, Parsons said that liberty is "a legacy left us by Christ, the purchase of His blood."[4]

And will any tamely submit to be entangled with the yoke of bondage, now that Christ has made us free! We desire liberty with peace, and would gladly live as friends, but if the blessing of liberty cannot be had with peace, it is lawful and right to enter into a contrary state. If former friends now resolved to entangle us with a yoke of bondage, God forbid that we should suffer them to cut off our limbs and mangle our whole body to gratify their injurious demands. . . . If it should be so that our natural and constitutional liberties cannot be recovered and maintained without repelling force by force, who could hesitate for a moment about the propriety of taking up arms?[5]

Later, when news came of the Battles of Lexington and Concord,

Jonathan Parsons stood up in his pulpit to preach to the people of liberty and their rights. He was an old man then, just closing his three-score and ten years, but his eyes were not dimmed nor his form bent with age. As he closed his final appeal, his people hung breathless upon his words, and each seemed more anxious than the other to catch his every utterance. "Men of America, citizens of this great country hanging upon the precipice of war, loyalty to England lies behind you . . . duty to freedom, duty to your country, duty to God, is before you."[6]

On July 19, 1776, Parsons died and was buried beside Whitefield beneath the floor of his church. As his biographer said, "He had lived to hear Independence declared, to see Washington in command of the army, and his son the colonel of the 6th Connecticut Regiment."[7]

21

September 7, 1774

The First Prayer of the
Continental Congress

Plead my cause, O LORD, with those who strive with me.

—PSALM 35:1

mid fear and rising tensions, delegates from across the Colonies arrived in Philadelphia on September 4, 1774, to convene the First Continental Congress. Before tackling the weighty issues of the day, they acted on a motion by Thomas Cushing from Massachusetts to begin their business with prayer. Some opposed the motion because of the diversity of denominations represented by the delegates. But Samuel Adams, the firebrand of the Revolution and a devout member of the Congregational Church, rose and "asserted that he was no bigot, and could hear a prayer from any gentleman of piety and virtue, who was at the same time a friend to his country."[1]

Adams nominated a local Anglican pastor, Jacob Duché, to lead in prayer, and the delegates agreed. About the same time, a rumor swept through Philadelphia, which later proved untrue, that Boston was being shelled by British cannons. So the next morning when the delegates assembled in Carpenter's Hall for the agreed-upon prayer, they were tense and confused. In that room were such icons as George Washington, John Adams, Samuel Adams, John Hancock, and Patrick Henry.

Duché opened his Anglican prayer book to the prescribed reading for the day, and the delegates instantly sensed the selection of scripture was providential—Psalm 35: "Plead my cause, O LORD, with those who strive with me; fight against those who fight against me. . . . Let those be put to shame and brought to dishonor who seek after my life; let those be turned back and brought to confusion who plot my hurt" (vv. 1, 4).

Duché then led in a powerful prayer, lasting about ten minutes, which has been called "the most famous prayer of the American Revolution."[2] He said, in part:

O Lord our Heavenly Father, high and mighty King of kings and Lord of lords, who dost from Thy throne behold all the dwellers on earth and reignest with power supreme and uncontrolled over all the Kingdoms, Empires, and Governments; look down in mercy, we beseech Thee, on these our American States, who have fled to Thee from the rod of the oppressor and thrown themselves on Thy gracious protection, desiring to be henceforth dependent only on Thee . . . .

Be Thou present, O God of wisdom, and direct the councils of this honorable assembly; enable them to settle things on the best and surest foundation that the scene of blood may be speedily closed; that order, harmony and peace may be effectually restored; and truth and justice, religion and piety prevail and flourish amongst the people. Preserve the health of their bodies and the vigor of their minds; shower down on them and the millions they represent, such temporal blessings as Thou seest expedient for them in this world and crown them with everlasting glory in the world to come. All this we ask in the name and through the merits of Jesus Christ, Thy Son and our Savior.[3]

Afterward, John Adams described the event in a letter to his wife, Abigail:

Mr. Duché appeared . . . and read several prayers in the stablished form, and then read the Collect for the seventh day of September, which was the Thirty-fifth Psalm. You must remember this was the next morning after we heard the horrible rumor of the cannonade of Boston. I never saw a greater effect upon an audience. It seemed as if Heaven had ordained that Psalm to be read on that morning. After this Mr. Duché, unexpectedly to everybody, struck out into an extemporary prayer, which filled the bosom of every man present. I must confess I never heard a better prayer or one so well pronounced . . . such fervor, such ardor, such earnestness and pathos, and in language so elegant and sublime, for America, for the Congress, for the Province of Massachusetts Bay, and especially for the town of Boston. It has had an excellent effect upon everybody here.[4]

According to other accounts, many of the delegates were in tears, and some were on their knees.[5] It was as though the Lord Himself had come down into the room to receive the prayers of the frightened but determined revolutionaries. Duché's prayer so braced the Continental Congress that he henceforth started each day's session in prayer, becoming, in effect, America's first Congressional chaplain.

March 23, 1775

America's Orator Gives the
Speech of His Life

Saying, "Peace, peace!" when there is no peace.

—JEREMIAH 8:11

P atrick Henry was a natural orator. "There was lightning in his eyes which seemed to drive the spectator.... In the tones of his voice, but more especially in his emphasis, there was a peculiar charm, a magic, of which . . . no one can give any adequate description. They can only say that it struck upon the ear and upon the heart in a manner which language cannot tell."[1]

One of Henry's speeches was described as "more than that of mortal men.... His talents seemed to swell and expand themselves, to fill the vaster theater.... There was no rant . . . no straining of the voice . . . no confusion of the utterance. His countenance was erect; his eye, steady; his action, noble; his enunciation, clear and firm. [He was the greatest] orator of America."[2]

Henry was a diligent student of Scripture and a follower of Christ.[3] His speeches were filled with biblical allusions and delivered with the power and cadence of an Old Testament prophet.

On March 20, 1775, the Second Virginia Convention gathered at St. John's Church in Richmond to debate the rising tensions with England. Henry advocated raising a militia and preparing a military defense, but other delegates cautioned patience, hoping for a peaceful solution. On March 23, Henry gave perhaps the most eloquent speech in American history. It was filled with scriptural phrases, especially as he neared its climax and began quoting the words of Jeremiah. Addressing the president of the convention, he said,

> Let us not, I beseech you, sir, deceive ourselves longer. Sir, we have done everything that could be done to avert the storm which is now coming on. We have petitioned—we have remonstrated—we have supplicated—we have prostrated ourselves before the throne. . . . Our petitions have been slighted; our remonstrances have produced additional violence and insult; our supplications have been disregarded; and we have been spurned with contempt from the foot of the throne . . . .
>
> Sir, we are not weak, if we make a proper use of those means which the God of nature hath placed in our power. Three millions of people, armed in the holy cause of liberty and in such a country as that which we possess, are invincible by any force which the enemy can send against us. Besides, sir, we shall not fight our battles alone. There is a just God who presides over the destinies of nations . . .
>
> Gentlemen may cry, peace, peace, but there is no peace. The war is actually begun . . . !
>
> Is life so dear, or peace so sweet, as to be purchased at the price of chains and slavery? Forbid it, Almighty God. I know not what course others may take; but as for me, give me liberty or give me death![4]

Patrick Henry quoted Jeremiah because there were loud voices in ancient Judah predicting that God would spare the nation from the coming Babylonian invasion. No repentance was needed, nor was any preparation necessary. Jeremiah accused them of crying, "Peace, peace," when there was no peace. What was truly needed was spiritual repentance and military readiness—the same thing Patrick Henry advocated.

In my own mind I often ponder whether we're living in the days of Isaiah or Jeremiah. The prophet Isaiah lived at a time when revivals still occurred, and spiritual awakenings periodically restored a degree of biblical morality to the culture. But by the time of Jeremiah, the revivals came no longer and the nation crumbled around him. Jeremiah knew there was no hope of peace, for he lived in a nation that had thoroughly rejected God.

I believe we're still in the days of Isaiah. I sense another revival is coming!

April 19, 1775

The Shot Heard Round the World

For they have shed innocent blood....

—JOEL 3:19

T he opening shots of the American Revolution were aimed at a preacher and his congregation, who, bolstered by Scripture, were ready for the moment.

Jonas Clark preached in the village of Lexington, Massachusetts, "with uncommon energy and zeal." His voice "extended far beyond the bounds of his meeting house and could be heard distinctly by those who were anywhere in the immediate neighborhood."[1] Many of his sermons lasted an hour, and one of his public prayers extended beyond two hours.[2] But he preached Scripture, and he preached freedom.

As tensions rose with Britain, Pastor Clark taught his church about "personal, civil, and religious liberty."[3] One historian said, "Long before it was certain that the quarrel must come to blows, he had so thoroughly indoctrinated his people with these great truths that no better spot on the continent could have been found" for the Revolution to begin.[4]

His preaching . . . had been . . . preparation for the noble stand taken by his people on the morning of the 19th of April. The militia on the Common, that morning, were the same who filled the pews of the meeting house on the night before. . . . [Because of Clark's sermons] no population within the compass of the Colonies were better prepared for the events of the 19th of April than the people of Lexington; no people to whom the events of that day could more safely have been entrusted. . . . No single individual probably did so much to educate the people up to that point . . . as their honored and beloved pastor.[5]

As the British occupied Boston, General Horatio Gates took out after Samuel Adams and John Hancock, who were sequestered in Pastor Clark's farmhouse. Late on April 18, Paul Revere galloped in with news the British were coming. Adams and Hancock turned to Clark and asked if the people of Lexington would stand up to the invaders. The pastor replied, "I have trained them for this very hour. They will fight and, if need be, die under the very shadow of the house of God."[6]

The village awoke, and the seventy or so men mustered at the church. As the sky turned from black to gray, hundreds of scarlet uniforms appeared. For a moment the two sides were frozen in silence. Then a gun fired—the shot heard round the world. After the battle seven of Pastor Clark's members lay dead under the windows of the church. Their innocent blood drenched the ground.

"The teachings of the pulpit of Lexington," it was said, "caused the first blow to be struck for American Independence."[7]

A year later, on the first anniversary of the Battle of Lexington, Clark preached a sermon from Joel 3:19–21, a passage in which the prophet condemned the nations of Egypt and Edom because they had attacked Judah and "shed innocent blood" in the land. To Clark, the attack of the British Army had been against innocent farmers and church members who wanted nothing more than peace and liberty. The American Colonies faced the same kind of hostile treatment Joel had condemned long ago, but the same God who helped Judah would help America. Clark went on to reassure his people that God was still in control. In the eloquent language employed by the colonial New England clergy, he said,

> To be impressed with a sense of the divine providence, to realize that God is Governor among the nations, that His government is wise and just, and that all our times and changes are in His hands and at His disposal, will have the happiest tendency to [produce] the most grateful acknowledgments of His goodness in prosperity, the most cordial resignation to His paternal discipline in adversity, and equanimity of mind in all the changing scenes of life.
>
> Inspired with this divine principle, we shall contemplate with grateful wonder and delight the goodness of God in prosperous events, and devoutly acknowledge and adore His sovereign hand in days of darkness and perplexity and when the greatest difficulties press. . . .
>
> Yea, however dark and mysterious the ways of providence may appear; yet nothing shall overwhelm the mind or destroy the truth and hope of those that realize the government of heaven . . . that an all-wise God is seated on the throne and that all things are well appointed for His chosen people—for them that fear Him.[8]

In our days of sound bites and tweets, I find this old language refreshing. Apply these thoughts to your own life today—be impressed with a sense of God's providence and remember He is Governor among the nations. Remind yourself that your times are in His hands and at His disposal. This will have the "happiest tendency" to produce grateful acknowledgment in your heart when things go well, and cordial resignation when things don't go as you'd like. Nothing will overwhelm the mind of those who remember an all-wise God is still on His throne.

24

April 23, 1775

The Origin of America's Military Chaplains

Do not be afraid of them. Remember the Lord, great and awesome, and fight for your brethren, your sons, your daughters, your wives, and your houses.

—NEHEMIAH 4:14

News of the Battles of Lexington and Concord flashed through New England like electricity, reaching every town and village as fast as horses could gallop. When a rider raced into the hamlet of Gaysboro, Vermont, nobody was more agitated than David Avery, the town's young pastor who had been converted under the preaching of George Whitefield.

When parishioners gathered for Sunday's service on April 23, 1775, Avery shocked them by preaching a farewell sermon; he was joining the Revolutionary Army. After the service he stood on the church steps and gave another address, appealing for volunteers to go with him.

It was a noble, soul-stirring spectacle, that earnest servant of God calling on his parishioners to leave wives and children and parents and follow him to the field of battle. His burning words fell on hearts already on fire with patriotism, and that quiet Sabbath day among the hills became a scene of thrilling excitement. Twenty of his parishioners responded to his call, and shouldering their muskets, started on foot with him for Boston.[1]

Avery's band arrived at Cambridge on Saturday, April 29, and the next day took part in outdoor services at the college. A rum barrel was turned upside down, and Avery stood on it and preached from Nehemiah 4:14. It was an apt choice. In the biblical reference, Nehemiah had been trying to help the residents of Jerusalem build a wall to defend their city from attack. Local enemies, however, were doing all they could to hinder and halt the construction. The citizens of Jerusalem were discouraged, so Nehemiah spoke rousing words of truth to encourage them. "Do not be afraid of them. Remember the Lord, great and awesome, and fight for your brethren, your sons, your daughters, your wives, and your houses."

Hardly a text in the Bible could have been a better choice for his sermon that day.

Avery went on to become one of the Revolutionary Army's first chaplains.[2] He preached, visited the soldiers tent to tent and cot to cot, listened to their distresses, tended their wounds, and prayed with them. One biographer has said: "The camp and bustle of war were strange to these men—they had come from quiet homes in the valleys and on the hillsides, and from the family altar and the house of God; and the presence of such a minister was a comfort and a blessing that at this day we cannot appreciate."[3]

In the Battle of Bunker Hill, Avery stood on the hilltop watching the fighting unfold on Breed's Hill, and there in the open he lifted his arms like Moses and appealed for divine aid amid the bloodshed. These words went into his diary:

I stood on [Bunker Hill] with hands uplifted, supplicating the blessings of Heaven to crown our unworthy arms with success. To us infantile Americans, unused to the thunder, the carnage of battle, the flames of Charlestown before our eyes—the incessant play of cannon from their shipping—from Boston, and their wings in various cross directions, together with the fire of musketry from more than four times our number, all heightened the majestic terrors of the field, exhibiting a scene most awful and tremendous. But amid the perils of the dread encounter, the Lord was our rock and fortress.[4]

Avery was there in Boston when George Washington arrived to take control of the army. He stood in the ranks of Dorchester Heights on the morning the Americans took their brave stand; and when the British retreated, he exclaimed, "Give God the praise, for He hath done it."

Avery was with Washington during the retreat from New York, and he crossed the Delaware River with Washington during the attack on Trenton, later writing, "We were greatly distressed with a very cold storm of rain, hail, and snow which blew with great violence. . . . I was extremely chilled and came near to perishing before I could get to a fire."[5]

Washington later said that David Avery was the embodiment of all those qualities he wished in a chaplain.

After the War, Avery returned to the pastorate, married, had ups and downs with his churches, and persevered in ministry until his death by typhus fever at age seventy-one. But he is most remembered in history as one of America's first chaplains.

The US Army Chaplain Corps, officially inaugurated by the Continental Congress on July 29, 1775, is virtually as old as the army itself. Since the first days of the American Revolution, chaplains like David Avery have been preaching, praying, and ministering among the troops, risking their lives on behalf of those who are risking their lives for us.

What would America have done without them?

June 17, 1775

The Boy Who Saw the Battle of Bunker Hill

Trust in Him at all times, you people;
Pour out your heart before Him;
God is a refuge for us.

—Psalm 62:8

After the Boston Tea Party, the British issued punitive measures against Boston, which prompted the Colonies to convene the First Continental Congress in 1774. John Adams of Massachusetts traveled to Philadelphia, leaving his wife, Abigail, and their children in Braintree, near Boston, which was quickly becoming a battle zone. British troops began swarming the area, and shots were fired at nearby Lexington and Concord.

Abigail was the daughter of a minister and a force to be reckoned with, but she grew increasingly anxious for her children's safety. On June 15, she wrote her husband, "We now expect our seacoast to be ravaged; perhaps the very next letter I write will inform you that I am driven away from our yet quiet cottage . . . We live in continual expectation of alarms.

Courage, I know we have in abundance . . . but powder—where shall we get a sufficient supply?"[1]

Seven-year-old John Quincy felt the strain, too, later writing, "My mother with her infant children dwelt every hour of the day and of the night liable to be butchered in cold blood or taken and carried into Boston as hostages by any foraging or marauding detachment of men."[2]

On June 17, Abigail and her children heard the guns and cannons that marked the beginning of the Battles of Bunker Hill and Breed's Hill. As the British started up the slopes, a command reportedly passed through the American lines: "Don't shoot until you see the white of their eyes."

When the guns began firing, the sound traveled for miles. Hearing the roar of the cannons and the sounds of the battle, Abigail took John Quincy and hiked to the top of Penn Hill, where they watched the battle unfold across the bay. The Boston neighborhood of Charlestown went up in flames, and the winds blew the heat and smoke into their faces. Waves of British soldiers fell while charging up Bunker's hill. The Patriots were driven back, and it was the bloodiest battle thus far in the War. The next morning Abigail wrote John, and in the middle of her letter, she burst into the cherished scriptures sustaining her, especially a passage from Psalm 62:

> The day—perhaps the decisive day—is come, on which the fate of America depends. My bursting heart must give vent at my pen. I have just heard that our dear friend, Dr. Warren, is no more, but fell gloriously fighting. . . . "The race is not to the swift, nor the battle to the strong; but the God of Israel is He that giveth strength and power to His people. Trust in Him at all times, ye people, pour out your hearts before Him; God is a refuge for us." Charlestown is laid in ashes. The battle began upon our intrenchments upon Bunker's Hill, Saturday morning about three o'clock, and has not ceased yet. . . . It is expected they will come out over the Neck tonight, and a dreadful battle must ensue. Almighty God, cover the heads of our countrymen, and be a shield to

our dear friends! How many have fallen, we know not. The constant roar of the cannon is so distressing that we cannot eat, drink, or sleep.[3]

John Quincy Adams never forgot the carnage that filled his seven-year-old eyes as he stood transfixed by the cannons, gunfire, charging soldiers, dying troops, burning city, and unfolding history. He later said it made an impression on his mind that haunted him the rest of his life. Even in old age he couldn't bring himself to attend celebrations associated with the events of that day.[4]

"I saw with my own eyes the fires of Charlestown and heard Britannia's thunders in the battle . . . and witnessed the tears of my mother and mingled them with my own," he wrote.[5]

Abigail finally turned and left the bloody panorama, leading her son back home where she made him promise to repeat the Lord's Prayer every morning before rising from bed, a practice he kept the rest of his life.[6]

Thus the little family watched, prayed, trusted God, poured out their hearts to Him—and melted Abigail's collection of pewter spoons into musket balls for the Patriots.[7]

January 21, 1776

The Fighting Parson of the Revolution

A time for war and a time for peace.

—ECCLESIASTES 3:8 NIV

This story is about a man with three biblical names—John Peter Gabriel Muhlenberg, who was born in Pennsylvania in 1746 and began pastoring a Lutheran church in Woodstock, Virginia, in 1772. Muhlenberg had a military bent to his mind, and he followed the unfolding drama between the Colonies and the mother country with keen interest. When his community formed a local militia, he was elected its chairman.

The news of the Battle of Bunker Hill cut into Muhlenberg's heart like a sword, and on January 21, 1776, he preached a dramatic sermon with a surprise ending. His text was Ecclesiastes 3:1–8: "To everything there is a season, a time for every purpose under heaven: A time to be born, and a time to die; a time to plant, and a time to pluck up what is planted; a time to kill, and a time to heal; a time to break down, and a time to build up" (verses 1–3).

According to a nephew, when Muhlenberg came to verse 8, he read the words with great feeling: "A time to love, and a time to hate; a time of war, and a time of peace."

"The Bible tells us there is a time for all things," the preacher said, "and there is a time to preach and a time to pray; but for me the time to preach has passed away." Raising his voice like a trumpet, he called out, "And there is a time to fight, and that time has now come."[1]

Some accounts say he went into a side room, removed his clerical gown, and put on the uniform of a soldier. Others claim he threw off his clerical gown before the congregation, revealing a soldier's uniform beneath. In any event, the church was stirred as he walked down the aisle, strode out the door, and signaled a drum to beat as he appealed for volunteers.

The congregation spilled onto the lawn while others from the village, hearing the drum, rushed to the scene. "The sight of the pastor in uniform, standing at the door and calling for recruits, kindled the most unbounded enthusiasm, and before night nearly three hundred men had joined his standard."[2]

Muhlenberg was with George Washington at Valley Forge. He fought battle after battle, and after the War was promoted to major general. He never returned to the pulpit, though his faith in Christ remained strong. Instead, Muhlenberg felt God's guidance to devote himself to affairs of state. He was elected from Pennsylvania to the first Congress and, in 1801, was elected a United States senator. President Thomas Jefferson appointed him Supervisor of Revenue for Pennsylvania, and Muhlenberg served in that post until he died on his sixty-first birthday.

To someone who had questioned whether Muhlenberg should have left the ministry for the military, he wrote:

> You say, as a clergyman nothing can excuse my conduct. I am a clergyman, it is true, but I am a member of society as well as the poorest layman, and my liberty is as dear to me as any man. Shall I then sit

still and enjoy myself at home when the best blood of the continent is spilling. Heaven forbid it!

Do you think if America should be conquered, I should be safe? Far from it. And would you not sooner fight like a man than die like a dog? I am called by my country to its defense. The cause is just and noble. Were I a bishop, even a Lutheran one, I should obey without hesitation, and so far am I from thinking that I am wrong, I am convinced it is my duty so to do, a duty I owe to my God and to my country.[3]

Today a statue of John Peter Gabriel Muhlenberg stands in the United States Capitol; a memorial to him is located on Connecticut Avenue in Washington, DC; Muhlenberg County in Kentucky is named for him; another memorial to him stands behind the Philadelphia Museum of Art; two statues of him are located in Woodstock, Virginia; and Muhlenberg College in Allentown, Pennsylvania, is named for him—the man known as the Fighting Parson of the American Revolution.

March 5, 1776

Dorchester Heights

Let us flee from the face of Israel, for the LORD fights for them against the Egyptians.

—EXODUS 14:25

In March 1776, an unusual set of weather patterns in Boston saved the Continental Army, propelled the Colonies onward toward the momentous events of July, and shifted the War from New England to the Middle Atlantic region.

Here's what happened. The Siege of Boston in April 1775 represented the opening chapters of the Revolutionary War, with battles at Lexington and Concord, then at Bunker and Breed's Hills. George Washington, the new commander of the Continental Army, arrived in Boston to assess the threat. Gazing down from Prospect Hill, he saw the British fleet anchored in the harbor and the city occupied by Redcoats. Washington was up against the strongest military force in the world, and his own army was little more than an untrained mob.

To the south, Dorchester Heights was a low hill with commanding views of Boston and its harbor. In a risky gambit, Washington decided to seize this ground. On the evening of March 4, 1776, his troops began moving into place, using haystacks to shield their movement. Eight hundred men led the way, followed by wagons packed with spades, crowbars, hatchets, hammers, and nails. Behind there were three hundred oxcarts of materials and twelve hundred men, followed by cannons and heavy siege guns brought from Fort Ticonderoga.[1]

The weather conditions were perfect for the Americans. On the Heights, they found mild temperatures and the moon "shining in its full luster," but at the lower elevations a deep smoky haze fell across the bay, hiding them from the British.[2] The wind blew from the southwest, carrying the sound of their work away from the city. And the frozen ground became an asset once ruts were made for the wagons, giving them solid ground instead of muddy paths.

When the sun rose the next morning, March 5, the British were stunned to see Dorchester Heights occupied and fortified by the Americans as if by magic. General Howe reportedly swore and said, "The rebels have done more in one night than my whole army would have done in months." Another British officer felt the defenses had been "raised with an expedition equal to that of the Genii belonging to Aladdin's Wonderful Lamp."[3]

British cannon fire couldn't reach the elevation of the American positions, but British ships were vulnerable to American cannonballs from the Heights.

The British, with superior training and numbers, made plans to storm the Heights, and throughout the day Washington watched with apprehension, riding up and down the lines, reminding the soldiers that March 5 was the anniversary of the Boston Massacre. Meanwhile, his men kept strengthening the fortifications as General Howe prepared his attack.

Suddenly the weather shifted dramatically. The balmy day became blustery, and then tempestuous. What was later described as something of a hurricane lashed the harbor, with gale-force winds strong enough to break windows in the city and blow down fences in the countryside.[4] British boats and ships were tossed like driftwood and unable to mount an offensive. Fierce snow and blowing sleet made it impossible to scale the Heights. Unable to attack, the British had no choice but to evacuate Boston, leaving large caches of weapons and ammunition behind. When news reached Philadelphia, celebrations broke out, augmenting the energy that led to July's Declaration of Independence.

The British evacuation day was March 17, 1776—St. Patrick's Day. From his vantage point on Dorchester, Washington watched the eleven thousand British troops depart and ordered an extra gill of whiskey for his soldiers with Irish roots. Washington, however, wasn't in a mood for celebrating but for worshipping. He and his officers rode over to Cambridge to attend a thanksgiving service where Rev. Abiel Leonard, chaplain of the Continental Army, preached from Exodus 14:25: "Let us flee from the face of Israel, for the LORD fights for them against the Egyptians."[5] Exodus 14 is the story of the parting of the Red Sea. As the Egyptian soldiers saw the children of Israel marching safely through the waters, while the waves came crashing down on Pharaoh's troops, they were filled with panic, for they saw the hand of God fighting for Israel. Even at this early stage of the Revolution, the American Patriots sensed God was fighting for them.

Washington felt that way too. A few days later, contemplating the moonlight on the mountain, the fog in the bay, the storm from nowhere, and the marvel of a strategy that achieved success without bloodshed, he wrote his brother, John, saying: "That this most remarkable interposition of Providence is for some wise purpose, I have not a doubt."[6]

28

May 17, 1776

When Politics Got into the Pulpit

Surely the wrath of man shall praise You;
With the remainder of wrath You shall gird
Yourself.

—Psalm 76:10

In 1768, the small Presbyterian College of New Jersey (later Princeton), needed a president. They hired a hardheaded, strong-hearted clergyman from Scotland, John Witherspoon, who brought his family to America to assume the task. Arriving on campus, Witherspoon was shocked at the fledgling state of the school. He immediately loaned his books to the library and began raising funds. He was successful. From his students came twelve members of the Continental Congress, five delegates to the Constitutional Convention, twenty-eight senators, forty-nine congressmen, three Supreme Court justices, one secretary of state and several other cabinet members, a vice president—and one president: James Madison, the Father of the Constitution.[1]

Yet we remember Witherspoon more as a Founding Father than as an educator. Soon after arriving in America he began advocating liberty. On May 17, 1776, following the news from Boston, he preached one of the most important sermons in the lead-up to the Declaration of Independence. Delivered at Princeton and printed for distribution on both sides of the Atlantic, Witherspoon's message, "The Dominion of Providence over the Passions of Men," was based on Psalm 76:10, and it stoked the colonies for independence. He began:

> There is not a greater evidence either of the reality or the power of religion than a firm belief in God's universal presence and . . . the influence and operation of His providence. It is by this means that the Christian may be said, in the emphatical Scripture language, to walk with God and to endure as seeing Him who is invisible.

Witherspoon then moved to his text in Psalm 76, giving the context and explaining that verse 10 tells us God can bring good out of the ravings of one's opponents. The Lord knows how to work everything for the good of His cause. Witherspoon continued:

> To apply it more particularly to the present state of the American colonies and the plague of war—the ambition of mistaken princes, the cunning and cruelty of oppressive and corrupt ministers, and even the inhumanity of brutal soldiers, however dreadful, shall finally promote the glory of God, and in the meantime, while the storm continues, His mercy and kindness shall appear in prescribing bounds to their rage and fury.

In his closing application, Witherspoon urged his listeners to commit themselves to Jesus Christ for the salvation of their souls, and then he said:

> You are all my witnesses, that this is the first time of my introducing any political subject into the pulpit. At this season, however, it is not

only lawful but necessary; and I willingly embrace the opportunity of declaring my opinion without any hesitation, that the cause in which America is now in arms, is the cause of justice, of liberty, and of human nature. . . . Be of good courage and let us behave ourselves valiantly for our people . . . and let the Lord do that which is good in His sight.

Witherspoon closed with words designed to arouse the nation:

I beseech you to make a wise improvement of the present threatening aspect of public affairs, and to remember that your duty to God, to your country, to your families, and to yourselves is the same. True religion is nothing else but an inward temper and outward conduct suited to your state and circumstances in providence at any time. . . . In times of difficulty and trial, it is in the man of piety and inward principles that we may expect to find the uncorrupted patriot, the useful citizen, and the invincible soldier. God grant that in America, true religion and civil liberty may be inseparable, and that the unjust attempts to destroy the one may in the [end] tend to the support and establishing of both.[2]

Witherspoon was elected to the Continental Congress and appointed Congressional chaplain by John Hancock. During his tenure in congress, he signed the Declaration of Independence (the only clergyman or college president to do so), served on countless committees, helped draft the Articles of Confederation, advocated the adoption of the Constitution, rebuilt Princeton after the War—and lost a son during the Battle of Dutchtown in 1777.

29

August 29, 1776

The Fog of War

The effective, fervent prayer of a righteous man avails much.

—JAMES 5:16

After their humiliation in Boston, the British fleet retired to Canada to lick their wounds and repair their vessels, then sailed straight for New York City. Washington also moved his troops to New York and began building siege works along Brooklyn Heights. A handful of residents in New York, still loyal to England, plotted to assassinate him. His army was ragged and undisciplined, and his troops suffered illness and disease, including dysentery and smallpox.

When British ships, carrying thirty-two thousand troops, sailed into New York, their masts tilting with the tides, they looked like a forest of trees swaying in the wind. One observer said, "I thought all London was afloat."[1] It was "the largest, most powerful force ever sent forth from Britain or any nation."[2]

Washington didn't stand a chance.

The British invasion began before dawn on Thursday, August 22, and within days the Revolutionary Army was trapped in Brooklyn across the East River from Manhattan and facing annihilation, which would have ended the War less than two months after the signing of the Declaration of Independence.

Late on the afternoon of August 29, Washington gave the order to retreat. The escape of nine thousand weary, rain-soaked troops across a mile-wide river was a desperate gamble. If the British caught on, the entire army would be decimated. Many of the men wrote their last wills and testaments on the spot. Just after nightfall the weakest warriors headed for the ferry landing as the retreat began.

Immediately the weather became an ally. A strong northeast wind kept British ships from venturing into the area; yet at about 11:00 p.m. the wind died down, allowing Washington's hastily assembled armada to cross the river without danger. Sympathetic New York sailors and fishermen mobilized, loading soldiers, horses, wagons, cannons, and all manner of equipment onto boats.

Wagon wheels were wrapped in cloth to muffle their sounds on the cobblestones and not a word was spoken. The soldiers were told not to cough or make any sounds, and orders passed through the ranks by whispers. Campfires were kept burning to deceive the enemy.

All night, boats silently ferried the army back and forth across the river, yet when the sun arose, a large portion of the army was still trapped. But a fog had rolled in during the night, thick as velvet, shielding the remaining evacuees, and it remained until the evacuation was completed. One soldier wrote:

> In this fearful dilemma fervent prayers went up to Him who alone could deliver. As if in answer to those prayers, when the night deepened, a dense fog came rolling in, and settled on land and water. . . . Under cover of this fog . . . Washington silently withdrew his entire army across to New York.[3]

Another eyewitness said:

> It was one of the most anxious, busy nights that I ever recollect, and being the third in which hardly any of us had closed our eyes to sleep, we were all greatly fatigued. As the dawn of the next day approached, those of us who remained in the trenches became very anxious for our own safety, and when the dawn appeared there were several regiments still on duty. . . . At this time a very dense fog began to rise off the river, and it seemed to settle in a peculiar manner over both encampments. I recollect this peculiar providential occurrence perfectly well, and so very dense was the atmosphere that I could scarcely discern a man at six yards distance. . . . We tarried until the sun had risen, but the fog remained as dense as ever. . . . In the history of warfare, I do not recollect a more fortunate retreat. After all, the providential appearance of the fog saved a part of our army from being captured, and certainly myself among others who formed the rear guard.[4]

When the fog lifted, the Americans were gone. Historian David McCullough wrote, "The immediate reaction of the British was utter astonishment. That the rebel army had silently vanished in the night under their very noses was almost inconceivable."[5]

The evacuation occurred near the current site of the Brooklyn Bridge and has been called the Colonial Dunkirk, referring to the similar, almost miraculous evacuation of the British Army from France during World War II. The "fervent prayers" of the army were answered. Thirteen years later, General Washington took the presidential oath of office at the old Federal Building in lower Manhattan, just a few moments' walk from the spot he had stepped ashore in 1776, divinely shielded by the fog of war.

America was forged by men and women who believed in *fervent* prayer. That adjective has largely been lost to us today. It means earnest, warm, persistent prayer. Imagine the silent but strong prayers rising to heaven from Washington's desperate army. The Lord responds to prayers like that, for the Bible says, "The prayer of a righteous person is powerful and effective" (James 5:16 NIV).

30

May 28, 1777

The Prayers That Turned the Tide

"Enough, O princes . . . ! Remove violence and plunder-
ing, execute justice and righteousness, and stop dispos-
sessing My people," says the Lord GOD.

—EZEKIEL 45:9

S amuel Webster graduated from Harvard in 1737 and enjoyed a
ministry of nearly fifty-five years, dying on July 18, 1796, at age
seventy-eight. It was said of him, "In his preaching he was remarkably
clear and plain. There was an earnestness in his manner which convinced
his hearers that he himself felt what he delivered. . . . He possessed a happy
talent in visiting his people, and could adapt himself to their circumstances, and, in a pleasing manner, give them instruction."[1]

Webster was among the Revolutionary War preachers whose pulpit
ministry did much to strengthen the hearts of Americans before and
during the drive for independence. Joel Headley, in his 1864 book about
the chaplains and clergy of the Revolution, lamented (even in his day) the

failure of historians to recognize the role of Scripture in the success of the conflict, writing, "Notwithstanding the numberless books that have been written on the American Revolution, there is one feature of it which has been sadly overlooked. I mean the religious element. . . . He who forgets or underestimates the moral forces that uphold or bear on a great struggle, lacks the chief qualities of a historian."[2]

Headley described the clergy of America as being like Aaron and Hur on the mountaintop, holding up the hands of Moses as he prayed for Joshua's battle in the valley below.

Samuel Webster provides a prime example. In the spring of 1777, after a series of disasters for the colonial forces—the defeat at Long Island, the fall of New York and Fort Washington, and the disorganized retreat of Washington's troops through New Jersey—Webster preached a sermon on May 28, 1777, before the Massachusetts House of Representatives. His text was Ezekiel 45:8–9, and he appealed to the lawmakers to trust in One greater than Washington—the Lord of hosts "who was always able to deliver Israel in the most discouraging circumstances," and, he said, would deliver America if she leaned on more than "the arm of flesh."

His message centered Ezekiel's thundering words against the kind of enemy that plundered and dispossessed people from their houses and places of worship, as the occupying British troops had done. British leaders knew the role sermons had played in the American Revolution, and they often seized church buildings and turned them into barns for their horses or depots for their ammunitions. Webster decried this desecration, and then he offered a prayer—the kind of plainspoken prayer that turned the tide of the Revolution.

Speaking to God about the invading British forces who, while occupying Boston, destroyed church buildings or turned them into armories and horse stables, Webster prayed:

They have vented a particular spite against the houses of God, defaced and defiled Thy holy and beautiful sanctuaries where our fathers worshipped Thee, turning them into houses of merchandise and receptacles of beasts, and some of them they have torn in pieces and burned with fire.

Therefore we humbly pray that Thou wilt hedge up their way and not suffer them to proceed and prosper. But put them to flight speedily, if it be Thine holy will, and make them run fast as a wheel downward, or as fast as stubble and chaff is driven before the furious whirlwind.

As a fire consumes wood, and sometimes lays waste whole forests on the mountains, so let them be laid waste and consumed if they obstinately persist in their bloody designs against us.

Webster continued on with his prayer, heaping metaphor after metaphor, asking God to raise up a "dreadful tempest" against the enemy, to "pursue them with Thine arrow, till they are brought to see that God is with us." He prayed the British would return to their own land "covered with shame and confusion" to humble themselves before God and seek repentance for their plundering ways. Then he ended on a high note, bringing his entire congregation into the final amen:

That so all nations, seeing Thy mighty power and Thy marvelous works, may no more call themselves supreme, but know and acknowledge that Thou art God alone, the only supreme Governor among men, doing whatsoever pleaseth Thee. And so let Thy glorious name be magnified in all the earth, till time shall be no more. And let all the people say amen and amen.[3]

31

September 30, 1777

A Speech to Bewildered Men

The name of the LORD is a strong tower. The righteous run to it and are safe.

—PROVERBS 18:10

A blanket of discouragement fell across America in September 1777, following the retreat of Washington's army from New York and his defeat at Brandywine, where two hundred American troops were killed, five hundred were wounded, and four hundred captured. The British invaded Philadelphia, and the Continental Congress fled the city. Washington headed toward Valley Forge. What remained of his ammunition was soaked, and what remained of his army was destitute. Most observers considered the War as good as over. John Adams wrote: "The prospect is chilling on every side; gloomy, dark, melancholy, and dispiriting."[1]

It was the darkest period of the Revolution.[2]

But one man was undaunted—John's cousin, Samuel Adams, fifty-five. Historians call Adams the "moral conscience of the American

Revolution"[3] and "the greatest single personal force in bringing on and maintaining the struggle for independence."[4] Jefferson referred to him as "the patriarch of liberty."[5]

Adams was the brains behind the Sons of Liberty. He was an open rabble-rouser against British taxation, a member of the first Continental Congress, a signer of the Declaration of Independence, and later the governor of Massachusetts. Throughout the War, the British had a price on his head, and he was often just a step away from the scaffold.

His zeal came from his faith. Adams was a devoted follower of Christ who anchored his soul in God's Word. While on the run, he wrote his wife, Betsy, saying, "I pray God to . . . protect you in these perilous times from every kind of evil. The name of the Lord, says the Scripture, is a strong tower, thither the righteous flee and are safe. Let us secure His favor, and He will lead us through the journey of this life and at length receive us to a better."[6]

Samuel Adams truly believed Proverbs 18:10. The name of the Lord is a strong tower—a place of security and watchfulness, a place of refuge. Everything else may go wrong, but God's name never loses its power or its protective care over His people. Though all else may crumble, the Lord Himself remains a beacon of personal safety and perpetual strength.

Armed with this conviction, Adams became the man whose face never betrayed defeat. His countenance encouraged others.

As the Continental Congress fled Philadelphia and tried to reconvene in York in late September 1777, only about twenty members showed up—all of them bewildered men. As they spoke, their faces betrayed gloom and their words were grave and desolate. Sam spoke last, and his words may be the greatest pep talk of all time:

> Gentlemen, your spirits appear oppressed with the weight of the public calamities. Your sadness of countenance reveals your disquietude. A patriot may grieve at the distress of his country, but he will never despair. . . . If we wear long faces, long faces will become fashionable.

The eyes of the people are upon us. The tone of their feelings is regulated by ours. If we despond, public confidence is destroyed, the people will no longer yield their support to a hopeless contest, and American liberty is no more. But we are not driven to such narrow straits. . . . We have appealed to Heaven for the justice of our cause, and in Heaven we have placed our trust. Numerous have been the manifestations of God's providence in sustaining us. In the gloomy period of adversity, we have had our cloud by day and pillar of fire at night. We have been reduced to distress, and the arm of Omnipotence has raised us up. Let us still rely in humble confidence on Him who is mighty to save. Good tidings will soon arrive. We shall never be abandoned by Heaven while we act worthy of its aid and protection.[7]

Sam Adams positioned himself in Christ, trusted God for strength and safety, and kept his morale strong even when times were darkest. His confidence spread into the hearts of his compatriots, for he was as certain as sunrise that the name of the Lord is a tower of refuge.

October 26, 1777

Watchman, What of the Night?

> *"Watchman, what of the night?"*
> *The watchman said,*
> *"The morning comes."*
>
> —ISAIAH 21:11–12

I n the fall of 1777, British general John Burgoyne led a large invasion force from Canada, intending to isolate New England, merge
with southern British forces, and end the rebellion. The invasion left the
Northeast population "in a state of the most painful suspense. The next
breeze that swept from the north might bring the news of the overthrow
of the American army."[1]

No other subject occupied the thoughts, conversations, or prayers
of New England villagers, especially because many of their husbands,
sons, and fathers were on the battlefield. In this atmosphere of fear
and foreboding, Rev. Cotton Mather Smith stepped into his pulpit on
October 26, 1777, in the town of Sharon, Connecticut, population two

thousand. He took his text from Isaiah 21:11–12: "'Watchman, what of the night? Watchman, what of the night?' The watchman said, 'The morning comes.'"

In this passage, Isaiah pictures a guard on the walls of Edom, watching through the night, waiting for the enemy's approach. Someone calls to him for a report, and his comment was, "The morning comes." Truthfully, Smith took this verse somewhat out of context, but he was grasping the eloquence of Isaiah's language. Smith acknowledged the constant mental agony that had preoccupied every heart.

> He did not attempt to conceal or lessen the calamities that had befallen the country, nor deny that a fearful crisis was at hand. He confessed that to human appearance "clouds and darkness were round about God's throne," but he said that the eye of faith could pierce the gloom. The throne was there, though wrapped in impenetrable darkness, and he told them, "Man's extremity is God's opportunity."[2]

As Smith pursued his subject, a change came over his expression. To the astonishment of all, he told the congregation he believed they were "on the point of hearing extraordinary news of victory to our arms." He reminded them that Isaiah has asked the watchman, "What of the night?" to which the watchman replied, "The morning comes."

Pausing, the preacher declared, "The morning now cometh. I see its beams already gilding the mountain tops, and you shall soon behold its brightness bursting over all the land."

He ceased his sermon, closed his Bible, and exclaimed, "Amen! So let it be."[3]

A silence filled the room, and the audience sat without moving. Somehow a solemn feeling pervaded every heart, and observers later said a sense of premonition hung over the assembly. Suddenly the silence was broken by the distant clatter of horse's hoofs, echoing from the end of the street. The rider was evidently racing, as though he had important news that must be delivered at once. Everyone knew instinctively it was about the threatened invasion, and everyone felt as if their life and death, their homes and family members, rested on the news racing toward them.

As the hoofbeats grew louder, the suspense became nearly unbearable. The rider pulled up to the church, leaped from his saddle, left his foam-covered horse untended, opened the doors, and marched down the aisle toward the pulpit, his boots sounding like a hammer to an anvil.

> As he passed along, a sudden paleness spread over the crowd of faces turned with a painful eagerness towards him. But looking neither to the right hand nor the left, the dread messenger passed on, and mounting the pulpit stairs handed the pastor a letter.
>
> Notwithstanding the good man's faith, his hand trembled and an ashy hue overspread his face as he reached out to receive it. "BURGOYNE HAS SURRENDERED" were the first words that met his eye. He staggered under them as under a blow. The next moment a radiance like that of the morning broke over his countenance, and he burst into tears. Rising to read the incredible tidings, such a tide of emotion flooded his heart that he could scarcely utter them aloud. The audience sat for a moment overwhelmed, then, as their pastor folded his hands and turned his eyes toward heaven in thankful prayer, they fell like one man on their knees and wept aloud. Sobs, sighs and fervidly murmured "amens" were heard on every side, attesting the depth of their gratitude and the ecstasy of their joy. The morning had come.[4]

One writer from yesteryear said, "The arrival of such news at the close of that sermon was a strange coincidence, but the Revolution is a history of just such coincidences."[5]

Scenes like that from American history should never be forgotten.

33

December 31, 1777

How Prayer Funded the Army at Valley Forge

Then everyone came whose heart was stirred, and everyone whose spirit was willing, and they brought the LORD's offering for the work.

—EXODUS 35:21

When we study the conditions of Washington's tattered army at Valley Forge during the winter of 1777–1778, we can try to imagine their misery, but it was beyond words. The son of one veteran said,

I have often heard my father, who was one of the number, describe the situation of himself and companions in arms, who after a fatiguing and forced march during an inclement day, many of them in this condition, suffering cold and hunger, and leaving the ground over which they marched, marked with the blood that flowed from their almost naked feet. In this situation when night had overtaken them, they have lain down on the bare ground, with no other canopy but the shades of night, with their knapsacks for pillows; and wrapping themselves in their blankets, they have lain down, and awoke covered with snow.[1]

After the defeats at Brandywine, Paoli, and Germantown, the twelve thousand or so soldiers were dejected as they wintered in the snow about twenty miles from occupied Philadelphia. Smallpox and other diseases spread through the camp, and more than twenty-five hundred of them died from illness or exposure. Others deserted. Washington's army needed $50,000 to survive the winter, but America was broke, and Congress was not forthcoming.

It was at this critical hour that George Washington resorted to prayer, as we often see portrayed in the paintings, where he is kneeling in a grove of trees, his horse behind him, pleading with God for help. But Washington wasn't the only one praying.

On New Year's Eve, St. George's Methodist Church in Philadelphia held an all-night prayer meeting for the soldiers and for the American cause. St. George's is called "the Cradle of American Methodism" and is the nation's oldest standing Methodist church edifice. In 1777, it was only a few years old, and on this evening it was packed with those who had come to pray throughout the night that "God would open up the hearts of the people to furnish the money they needed to pay the troops at Valley Forge that the Army might be saved."[2]

That prayer was based on the great offering needed in Exodus 35 for the building of the tabernacle. When the nation of Israel left Egypt, it entered the desert with lots of gold and silver and precious fabrics; the Egyptians, devastated by the plagues of Moses, had paid them to leave. Now Moses wanted to build an expensive and elaborate worship complex for the nation—the portable tabernacle. He appealed for funds, and "everyone came whose heart was stirred, and everyone whose spirit was willing . . . brought the LORD's offering for the work."

That evening in St. George's, prayers ascended to heaven for people's hearts to be stirred so that everyone whose spirit was willing might provide for the cause for their naked, sick, and starving army in the snows of Valley Forge.

Among the worshippers that night was Robert Morris, a Philadelphia businessman who had migrated from Liverpool in 1747 to be an apprentice at a shipping and banking firm. Over the years, he had become a prosperous merchant and an advocate of the Revolution. As a member of the Continental Congress, he had signed the Declaration of Independence.

As Morris prayed that evening, a conviction came over him. His own heart must be willing, and he must act at once. Getting up and leaving the service, he went door-to-door waking his wealthy friends and telling them he had just come from the prayer service and their help was desperately needed to keep the cause alive.[3] Within hours Morris had convinced Philadelphia's richest men and women to donate large amounts of their fortunes to the freezing soldiers of Washington's army, and within hours the General learned he would have the provisions he needed.[4]

"Morris, with his extensive international fortune, had been able to secure funds through his own personal credit that the fledgling Continental government could not. Washington, exasperated by the states' inability or unwillingness to support his rabble army, came to view Morris as the sole force keeping his troops on the field."[5]

The all-night prayers at the Methodist church were answered, and the Revolution Army got their provisions from heaven through Robert Morris.

And Morris? Sadly, in the latter years of his life he ended up personally bankrupt and in debtor's prison. When Congress passed the Bankruptcy Act of 1800, he was able to declare bankruptcy and reach a final settlement on his debts before his death in 1806.

34

September 26, 1780

The Sword of the Lord and of Gideon

> *Then the three companies blew the trumpets and broke the pitchers . . . and they cried, "The sword of the LORD and of Gideon!"*
>
> —JUDGES 7:20

My small hometown of Elizabethton, Tennessee, played its part in winning the American Revolution. Just before the War, a migration of Scotch-Irish settlers filtered into northeast Tennessee and began populating the hills and hollows. When the British government ordered them to leave, the settlers proved stubborn. They met at Sycamore Shoals (in present-day Elizabethton) and established the Watauga Association, the first independent American constitutional government west of the Alleghenies. When the Revolutionary War broke out, these backwoods settlers expected a British invasion, so they formed a militia, readied their Deckard rifles, and prepared for war.

It took a while for the War to reach them, but when word came that the British Redcoats were ready to invade North Carolina, they knew it was time for action. On September 25, 1780, more than a thousand Overmountain Men mustered at Sycamore Shoals.

A young Presbyterian preacher was there too—Samuel Doak. He was an educated man, having gone to school at Princeton and taught at Hampden-Sydney College. After being licensed to preach, he was sent to Abingdon, Virginia, to do evangelistic work in the mountains. He became the first Presbyterian minister to settle in Tennessee, and he reportedly organized twenty-five churches in East Tennessee and many of the first schools in the mountains.[1] He had deep blue eyes, sandy hair, and a voice that roused the attention of his hearers.

He used that voice to great effect on the morning of September 26, 1780, as the Overmountain Men prepared for battle. With the thousand or so men gathered around him in rings and leaning on their rifles, Doak lifted up his voice and proclaimed:

> My countrymen, you are about to set out on an expedition which is full of hardships and dangers, but one in which the Almighty will attend you. The Mother Country had her hands upon you, these American Colonies, and takes that for which our fathers planted their homes in the wilderness—our liberty. Taxation without representation and the quartering of soldiers in the homes of our people without their consent are evidence that the Crown of England would take from its American subjects the last vestige of freedom. Your brethren across the mountains are crying like Macedonia unto you for help. God forbid that you shall refuse to hear and answer their call.[2]

Doak went on to warn the Overmountain Men that the battle was no longer in New England or along the Eastern Seaboard. "The enemy is marching hither to destroy your own homes," he said. He reminded the men of the struggles they had already encountered in their attempts to settle in the mountains of East Tennessee, western North Carolina, and southwestern Virginia. Up and down the hollows and hills, farms and houses had been carved out of dense forests. They had faced many hardships, but now a greater threat was headed straight for them. Should they wait until the enemy showed up on their doorstep?

"No," shouted Doak, "it shall not be. Go forth then in the strength of your manhood to the aid of your brethren, the defense of your liberty, and the protection of your homes. And may the God of Justice be with you and give you victory." Then, looking over the motley group of mountaineers, he shouted, "Shall we pray?"

Almighty and gracious God! Thou hast been the refuge and strength of Thy people in all ages. In the time of sorest need we have learned to come to Thee—our Rock and our Fortress. Thou knowest the dangers and snares that surround us on march and in battle. Thou knowest the dangers that constantly threaten the humble but well-beloved homes Thy servants have left behind them. Oh, in Thine infinite mercy, save us from the cruel hand of the savage and the Tyrant. . . . Thou, who promised to protect the sparrow in its flight, keep ceaseless watch by day and by night, over our loved ones. . . . Oh, God of Battle, arise in Thy Spirit. Avenge the slaughter of Thy people. Confound those who plot for our destruction. Crown this mighty effort with victory and smite those who exalt themselves against liberty and justice and truth. Help us as good soldiers to wield the *sword of the Lord and of Gideon*. Amen![3]

There was something about the cry of "the sword of the Lord and of Gideon" that raised the upcoming battle to an almost biblical level in the souls of the Overmountain Men. They knew the story in Judges 7, when the soldiers of Israel were called upon to save their families from their Midianite enemies. Gideon's army numbered only three hundred men, but they were all brave and ready to follow their leader. They also knew God was with them and they were fighting under His banner and with the aid of an unseen sword. Standing on the ridge of the mountain overlooking the Midianites, the three hundred had broken their pitchers, exposed their torches, blown their trumpets, and shouted, "The sword of the Lord and of Gideon!"

The enemy turned on itself in confusion and fled.

Now that ancient battle cry burned in the hearts of the Overmountain Men. They marched to Roan Mountain and then across the hills to Kings Mountain. There the British major Patrick Ferguson, who had claimed God Himself could not drive him from the place, met his match.

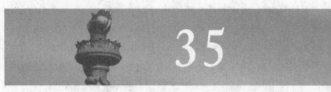

35

October 19, 1781

The Victory Sermon at Yorktown

Thus far the LORD has helped us.

—1 SAMUEL 7:12

The Battle of Yorktown effectively ended the American Revolution. British General Charles Cornwallis, badly outnumbered and isolated, sent out a white flag and surrendered to George Washington.

Israel Evans was there to preach a sermon of victory to the American forces. A native of Pennsylvania, Evans had served as a chaplain throughout the War. His sermons had strengthened George Washington at Valley Forge, and he was standing beside Washington at Yorktown when they were both nearly hit by a cannonball. On October 20, 1781, the day after the victorious battle, Evans preached to the euphoric troops from 1 Samuel 7:12, which is a quotation from the prophet Samuel after a battlefield victory over the Philistines. Samuel wanted to commemorate the victory, so he established a monument and called it Ebenezer, which meant, "Thus far has the Lord helped us."

"I now beg your further attention, my dearly beloved hearers, while I attempt to illustrate the meaning of the words, which I have chosen for the assistance of your devotions on this joyful day," said Evans in his victory sermon.

> By these words we are called to a devout consideration of our dependence on the Almighty God, and to a recollection of the many instances of help and relief with which He has condescended to bless us.... This is a truth which cannot be justly contradicted; and this is a truth from which America ought to learn her happiness as a nation.... Hitherto hath the Lord helped us![1]

Evans went on to say that everyone in the new nation—all the Patriots and brothers and sisters, should form one great concert of praise to "Him who has aided us." Historians would look back on the struggle, he said, and see the "ways of God" in allowing the oppressed of the land to gain their freedom. God had made the new nation like the "apple of His eye" or like a vine that is planted. God had raised up the warriors needed, and He had ordained statesmen to assist the cause. He had established a new nation to praise Him and to thank Him for their liberty.

"Praise the Lord, who hath redeemed us from our enemies, for His mercy endureth forever!" Evans shouted to the generals and all the troops gathered before him. He also reminded them of the twists of providence and the rather miraculous moments that had saved America from expected disaster. That the colonial army, ragtag and unproven and outmatched, should defeat the greatest military power in the world was a remarkable exhibition of providence, virtually unseen since the days of Samuel.

> No expedition which depended, in the first plan of it, upon forces so much disjoined and events so precarious, was ever blessed with a more seasonable and harmonious junction of prosperous circumstances or ended with more substantial glory and complete success.... O! All ye

inhabitants of the United States, let your thankfulness appear by the piety of your hearts and the purity of our lives. . . . Bless the Lord, O my soul, and all that is within me. . . . Methinks if men uttered no songs of praise to their Deliverer, this continent itself would reprove their ingratitude.[2]

Israel Evans's sermon on October 20 looked backward at God's providential hand over the course of the War. But later he preached another victory sermon in New York City, in which he looked ahead and painted a picture of what America could be. His words were almost prophetic, and they picture America as she should be.

> The great Continent of America . . . is now free and independent! The blood and treasure of the sons of freedom have purchased these privileges. . . . Oh, blessed day which brings us to the possession of all we have been contending for and enables us to erect the standard of liberty and glory upon one of the four great divisions of earth! Hail auspicious morning of the rising empire. Hail arts and sciences, America is the new theatre of your improvements. . . . Commerce and trade shall spread their sails and waft the riches of distant lands to this great continent. Now, without fear of an insulting enemy, the industrious husbandman shall sow his enlarged fields and reap his rich and joyful harvests. Here the oppressed shall find a secure retreat from all the poverty and misery of merciless tyranny. Religion and learning shall raise their drooping heads and flourish again. Now shall the brave soldier claim the honor of being a free and independent citizen of the United States of America. The blessed soil of independence shall strive to reward him for his persevering valor. . . . May peace and love and human affection be once more planted in the human mind, and there grow and flourish till time shall be no more.[3]

The Revolutionary leaders of America understood the meaning of *Ebenezer*—hitherto has the Lord helped us! There wasn't a better word in the dictionary to describe their feelings on that day of final victory. And those among them who understood the role of providence knew that the God who had helped them thus far was needed now more than ever for the future.

We all have Ebenezer moments in our lives. Looking back, we can see God's help; and looking forward we can see God's hand. Hitherto has the Lord helped us.

36

December 11, 1783

God's Instructions to a New Nation

He has shown you, O man, what is good; and what does
the LORD require of you but to do justly, to love mercy,
and to walk humbly with your God?

—MICAH 6:8

In his book *Reading the Bible with the Founding Fathers*, Daniel L. Dreisbach observes that the leaders of the American Revolution repeatedly referred to Micah 6:8. "The literature of the founding era has numerous references and allusions to this biblical text," he wrote.[1] John Winthrop referred to this passage in his "City on the Hill" sermon. John Adams quoted it frequently. George Washington alluded to it in his farewell letter when resigning as commander in chief of the Continental Army.

It was also a key text used by George Duffield, a Presbyterian minister in Philadelphia who served as chaplain of the Continental Congress.

Duffield's story is interesting. He was appointed pastor of the Pine Street Presbyterian Church in Philadelphia in 1771, but when he arrived at his church on his first Sunday the door had been locked by a group opposed to his appointment. His supporters pushed him into the sanctuary through an open window, and thus he began his ministry.[2]

The Colonies were in turmoil, trying to decide whether to sever their ties with England, and Duffield became a vocal advocate for independence. So many of the Founding Fathers crowded into his pews that Pine Street became known as the Church of the Patriots.

During the Revolutionary War, the British put a price on Duffield's head, and when Philadelphia was occupied, his church was converted into a hospital and the pews were burned to keep the wounded British soldiers warm. Duffield put his gifts to work as chaplain of the Continental Congress and chaplain of the Pennsylvania regiment. He also counseled and comforted General George Washington at Valley Forge.

After the War was won and peace established, Congress appointed December 11, 1783, as a Day of Thanksgiving, and Duffield gave a powerful sermon praising God for His providence:

Who indeed hath heard such a thing? Who, but a few years back, would have believed the report, had a prophet himself declared it? . . . Who since time began, hath seen such events take place so soon? The earth has indeed brought forth, as in a day. A nation has indeed been born, as at once. . . . Let us look back, on what God hath done; and contemplate the prospect He opens before us.

Duffield went on to quote verse after verse in his Day of Thanksgiving sermon, verses that were on the lips of thousands of new American citizens, such as "This is the Lord's doing; it is marvelous in our eyes" (Psalm 118:23) and "Not unto us, O LORD, not unto us, but to Your name give glory, because of Your mercy, because of Your truth" (Psalm 115:1).

The verses rolled off his tongue like boulders down a hill, and he exhorted his audience to "Praise, therefore, Thy God, O America, praise the Lord, ye His highly favored United States."

He also exhorted his listeners to make sure their thanksgiving was not confined to an appointed day but radiated from their hearts all the time. "Let every heart glow with gratitude: And every life, by a devout regard to his holy law, proclaim his praise. It is this, our God requires, as that wherein our personal, and national good and the glory of his great name consist. And without which, all our professions will be but an empty name."

Then, like so many other early American preachers, he referenced Micah 6:8 and reminded us of our greatest obligations as citizens of a great nation and as followers of God:

> It is, that we love the Lord our God, to walk in his ways, and keep his commandments, to observe his statutes and his judgments. That a sacred regard be maintained to righteousness and truth. That we do justice, love mercy, and walk humbly with our God. Then shall God delight to dwell amongst us. And these United States shall long remain, a great, a glorious, and a happy people. Which may God, of his infinite mercy, grant. Amen.[3]

To Duffield, Micah 6:8 represented God's instructions to the new nation.

In a world adrift with moral confusion and ethical lapses, there's no better instruction for any nation—or for any of us as individuals—than the proclamation of the prophet Micah. God isn't as interested in our rituals as He is in our righteousness. "The LORD has told you what is good, and this is what he requires of you: to do what is right, to love mercy, and to walk humbly with your God" (Micah 6:8 NLT).

P.S. You might be interested to know it was George Duffield's grandson, George Duffield Jr., who, in 1858, wrote the hymn "Stand Up, Stand Up for Jesus."

June 28, 1787

The Prayer That Saved the Constitution

Unless the LORD builds the house,
They labor in vain who build it.

—PSALM 127:1

After the British surrender, the American Colonies had a nation but needed a constitution. The old Articles of Confederation were inadequate. In May 1787, delegates gathered in Philadelphia for a convention to draft a constitution that would establish an effective federal government. They appointed George Washington as chair, but that's about all they agreed on. From the beginning, the delegates quarreled over deeply held disagreements as to the extent and form of the new government.

That's when venerable Benjamin Franklin, eighty-one, rose to make a motion:

> In this situation of this assembly, groping, as it were, in the dark to find political truth, and scarce able to distinguish it when presented to

113

us, how has it happened, sir, that we have not hitherto once thought of humbly applying to the Father of Lights to illuminate our understandings? In the beginning of the contest with Britain, when we were sensible of danger, we had daily prayers in this room for the divine protection. Our prayers, sir, were heard—and they were graciously answered. All of us, who were engaged in the struggle, must have observed frequent instances of a superintending Providence in our favor. To that kind Providence we owe this happy opportunity of consulting in peace on the means of establishing our future national felicity. And have we now forgotten that powerful friend? . . . I have lived, sir, a long time; and the longer I live, the more convincing proofs I see of this truth, *that God governs in the affairs of men!* And if a sparrow cannot fall to the ground without his notice, is it probable that an empire can rise without his aid? We have been assured, sir, in the sacred writings, that "except the Lord build the house, they labor in vain that build it."[1]

Ben Franklin was quoting here from Psalm 127. His entire remarkable speech, short as it was, was filled with biblical quotations and allusions, but this psalm was at the heart of what he wanted to say. Unless the Lord is in any enterprise, it has a limited future. Even building a house without His aid is perilous. Raising a family or a home without His strength is hazardous. Guarding a city without His blessings is futile. Working hard to gain wealth without putting Him first is vain.

How much more the establishing of a new nation, one unlike any ever seen on the earth. Surely such an undertaking requires the help of almighty God.

Franklin continued:

I firmly believe this; and I also believe, that without his concurring aid, we shall succeed in this political building no better than the builders of Babel: we shall be divided by our little partial local interests, our projects will be confounded, and we ourselves shall become a reproach. . . .

I therefore beg leave to move, that henceforth prayers, imploring the assistance of heaven, and its blessings on our deliberations, be held in this assembly every morning before we proceed to business; and that one or more of the clergy of the city be requested to officiate in that service.[2]

Even this motion failed because, perhaps, the convention had no money to hire a chaplain. But a few days later, on July 4, 1787, General Washington led the delegates to a prayer service at Philadelphia's Reformed Calvinist Lutheran Church, where Rev. William Rogers offered these words:

As this is a period, O Lord, big with events, impenetrable by any human scrutiny, we fervently recommend to Thy Fatherly notice that august Body, assembled in this city, who compose our Federal Convention; will it please Thee, O Thou Eternal I AM, to favor them from day to day with Thy immediate presence; be Thou their wisdom and their strength! Enable them to devise such measures as may prove happily instrumental for healing all divisions and promoting the good of the great whole . . . that the United States of America may furnish the world with one example of a free and permanent government, which shall be the result of human and mutual deliberation, and which shall not, like all other governments, whether ancient or modern, spring out of mere chance or be established by force. . . .

We close this, our solemn address, by saying, as our Lord and Savior Jesus Christ hath taught us—Our Father, who art in Heaven . . .[3]

The delegates joined in the Lord's Prayer, then went back to work. Soon they had a document that began: "We the People of the United States, in Order to form a more perfect Union."

James Madison, writing about the event later, said, "It is impossible for the man of pious reflection not to perceive in it a finger of that Almighty Hand, which has been so frequently and signally extended to our relief in the critical states of the revolution."[4]

38

October 26, 1788

Kindling the Second Great Awakening

I did not believe the words until I came and saw with my own eyes; and indeed the half was not told me.

—1 Kings 10:7

Evangelical Christianity crashed after the American Revolution. Church attendance dropped to near nothing, and French rationalism swept over colleges, which became hotbeds of atheism. Thomas Paine's anti-Christian ravings demoralized the church, and the reorganization of society and its westward expansion left little time for spirituality. Chief Justice John Marshall worried that the church was too far gone to be redeemed.[1]

But a Second Great Awakening was on its way, kindled by students at Virginia's Hampden-Sydney College.[2] The First Great Awakening, remember, had stirred the American Colonies with spiritual vitality and zeal. And now America needed a second dose.

A Hampden-Sydney student named Cary Allen had embraced Christ in September 1787. Another, William Hill, began secretly reading Joseph Alleine's book *Alarm to the Unconverted*, which he kept locked in his trunk. One day a third student, James Blythe, found him reading it and broke out in sobs, under deep conviction. These three students met secretly for prayer in a thick forest about a mile from the college and determined to meet the next Saturday on campus. Their secrecy was due to other students' animosity toward Christians. Fundamentalist secularism harbors a deep intolerance for the Christian faith. That was as true in the early 1800s as it is today. As Hill later recounted:

> Although we sung and prayed with suppressed voices, not wishing it should be known what we were about, we were overheard by some of the students, when it was noised about through every room in College, and a noisy mob was raised, which collected in the passage before our door, and began to thump at the door, and whoop, and swear, and threaten vengeance. . . . We had to cease, and bear the ridicule and abuse of this noisy riot, which could not be quietened until two of the Professors intervened and ordered them all to their rooms. Information of this riot was given to [President Robert Blair] Smith . . . [who] demanded the cause of the riot, and who were the leaders in it. Some of the most prominent leaders stepped forward and said, there were some of the students, who had shut themselves up in one of the rooms in College, and began singing and praying and carrying on like the Methodists, and they were determined to break it up. . . .
>
> The President's eyes filled with tears. . . . After a short pause he said—And has it come to this! Is it possible! Some of my students are under religious impressions!—and determined to serve their Savior! And is it possible that there are such monsters of iniquity . . . in College, who dare set themselves against such things![3]

Turning to the Christians, Smith said, "I rejoice, my young friends, that you have taken the stand you have. You shall not be interrupted in your meetings for the future. Your appointment next Saturday afternoon shall be held in my parlor; and I will be with you."

A sense of conviction swept over the college, and the next week the parlor was filled with praying students. A spirit of revival overspread the campus and penetrated into Virginia, spreading through churches and schools.

President Blair's father, who had been converted during the First Great Awakening, came to investigate the matter. On October 26, 1788, he wrote to a friend:

> The half was not told me of the display of God's power and grace among them; no, not the tenth part. I have seen nothing equal to it for extensive spread, power, and spiritual glory since the years '40 and '41. The word has spread for a hundred miles. . . . The blessed work has spread among many people of every description, high and low, rich and poor, learned and unlearned, orthodox and hetero-dox, sober and rude, white and black, young and old; especially the youth.[4]

The elder Blair was using biblical language when he said the half had not been told him. That was the reaction of the Queen of Sheba when she visited the kingdom of Israel in Solomon's time and saw the great wealth, education, public works, and unity of the land. She said she didn't believe the earlier reports she heard "until I came and saw with my own eyes; and indeed the half was not told me" (1 Kings 10:7).

That's how observers described the revival that erupted on university campuses at the beginning of the period known as the Second Great Awakening—the series of revivals that swept over the new United States of America, starting among students at places like Hampden-Sydney College.

One of the marvels of American history is how the country was born between two of the greatest revivals in history. The First Great Awakening prepared the Colonies for independence, and the Second solidified her moral and spiritual foundation for the future. Today our nation's problems are not primarily political but spiritual. And the answers are not found in our politics but in the hope of another spiritual return to God.

39

September 26, 1789

The Founder Who Walked with God

And Enoch walked with God; and he was not, for God took him.

—GENESIS 5:24

D o you know this man?

He drafted New York's first constitution in 1777. He served in the Second Continental Congress from 1774 to 1777, and as its president from 1778 to 1779. During the War's dark days after the fall of New York, he rallied spirits by advocating the righteousness of the effort, declaring,

> You may be told that your forts have been taken, your country ravaged, and that your armies have retreated, and therefore that God is not with you . . . [But] if we turn from our sins, he will turn from his anger—then will our arms be crowned with success. . . . The Holy Gospels are yet to be preached to those Western regions, and we have the highest reason

to believe that the Almighty will not [allow defeat] and the Gospel to go hand in hand. It cannot, it will not.[1]

From 1779 to 1782, he served as ambassador to Spain (and was nearly shipwrecked on one of the voyages). He helped negotiate the Treaty of Paris and signed it, ending the Revolutionary War. He became secretary of foreign affairs and later secretary of state. He coauthored the *Federalist Papers*, and on one occasion during the debate was wounded when struck by a stone during a riot.[2]

On September 21, 1789, he was confirmed as the first chief justice of the US Supreme Court, and he ended his political career as governor of New York, where he enacted laws for the emancipation of slaves.

John Adams wanted to reappoint him to the Supreme Court, but this man had other things in mind—to advance the gospel. He became president of the American Bible Society, saying, "No human society has ever been able to maintain both order and freedom . . . apart from the moral precepts of the Christian Religion. Should our Republic ever forget this fundamental precept of governance, we will then be surely doomed."[3]

Who was this man? He was John Jay.

After retiring from public life, Jay and his wife, Sarah, moved to their farm in Westchester, New York. Their son, William, wrote of his mother and father:

In less than twelve months after her removal to Westchester, she was seized with a severe illness, which in a few days terminated fatally. Mr. Jay, calm and collected, was watching by her side when she expired. Immediately on perceiving that the spirit had taken its flight, he led his children, who were with him, into an adjoining room, and with a firm voice but glistening eye, read to them the fifteenth chapter of First Corinthians [the Resurrection Chapter of the Bible]; thus leading their thoughts to that day when the lifeless but beloved form they had just left would rise to glory and immortality.[4]

In all his domestic habits [my father] observed great exactness and regularity. . . . Every morning immediately before breakfast, the family, including the domestics, were summoned to prayers; and the call was repeated precisely at nine at night, when he read to them a chapter in the Bible, and concluded with prayer.[5]

In 1827, Jay fell ill. The doctor told William that it was fatal, and William shared the diagnosis with his father. Jay took the news in good spirits and seemed "unusually raised . . . with cheerfulness and animation." Someone told him he should share with his family the reason for his joy, to which he concisely replied: "They have the Book."[6]

"When the tidings of his death came to us," said one American leader, "they were received through the nation, not with sorrow and mourning, but with solemn awe, like that with which we read the mysterious passage of ancient Scripture, 'And Enoch walked with God, and He was not, for God took Him.'"[7]

This is true of many of America's Founding Fathers. They were Enochs.

The biblical reference in the book of Genesis refers to a mighty servant of God, who began walking with God after the birth of his firstborn, a son named Methuselah. Genesis 5:14 says, "And Enoch walked with God; and he was not, for God took him." The book of Hebrews explains the meaning of this verse, saying, "By faith Enoch was taken away so that he did not see death, 'and was not found, because God had taken him'; for before he was taken he had this testimony, that he pleased God" (Hebrews 11:5). In other words, it seems that Enoch was such a delight to God that the Lord simply transported him to heaven before he died, as in the case of Elijah (2 Kings 2:11).

His friends viewed Jay's greatness and nobility in those terms—he walked with God.

Jay revealed his philosophy of life in a simple 1784 letter to his son Peter:

Your aunt informs me that you . . . love your books, and that you daily read in the Bible and have learned by heart some of the hymns in the book I sent you. These accounts give me great pleasure. . . . The Bible is the best of all books, for it is the Word of God, and teaches us the way to be happy in this world and in the next. Continue therefore to read it, and to regulate your life by its precepts.[8]

To retain its power and influence and ministry for good, America needs leaders who know what it is to walk with God. That's a privilege available to each of us through Jesus Christ our Lord.

November 26, 1789

An American Holiday Is Born

The LORD *reigns;*
Let the earth *rejoice.*

—PSALM 97:1

After the Constitution was adopted, the First Congress searched for a way for Americans to express gratitude to God. Special days of thanksgiving had been part of American history since Pilgrim times. Before and during the Revolutionary War, frequent days of fasting, prayer, and thanksgiving were appointed. But now, against all odds, America was a new nation with a new Constitution, a new president, and a new Congress. Should there not be a special day for praise and thanksgiving to God?

On September 25, 1789, Congress finished work on twelve proposed amendments to the Constitution—the Bill of Rights—and prepared to take a break. Before the session adjourned, Elias Boudinot rose to introduce a resolution calling on the president to issue a proclamation of public prayer and thanksgiving. Boudinot's motion was hotly debated. Some congressmen felt the custom was too "European." Others believed the federal government had no authority to issue national proclamations; that was the prerogative of the states. And those who still harbored unhappiness with the Constitution had no reason to thank God for it.

Roger Sherman of Connecticut—the only person to have signed all four of the great founding documents of the United States (the Continental Association; the Declaration of Independence; the Articles of Confederation; and the Constitution)—argued in favor of the resolution, saying the act of national thanksgiving is "warranted by a number of precedents" in the Bible, such as "the solemn thanksgiving and rejoicing which took place in the time of Solomon, after the building of the temple."[1]

The motion passed, and on October 3, 1789, George Washington set aside November 26 as a national day of prayer and thanksgiving, saying,

Whereas it is the duty of all Nations to acknowledge the providence of Almighty God, to obey His will, to be grateful for His benefits, and humbly to implore his protection and favor, and whereas both Houses of Congress have by their joint Committee requested me "to recommend to the People of the United States a day of public thanksgiving and prayer to be observed by acknowledging with grateful hearts the many signal favors of Almighty God especially by affording them an opportunity peaceably to establish a form of government for their safety and happiness." Now therefore I do recommend and assign Thursday the 26th day of November next to be devoted by the People of these States to the service of that great and glorious Being, who is the beneficent Author of all the good that was, that is, or that will be.[2]

On November 26, President Washington attended services at St. Paul's Chapel in New York City and donated beer and food to the imprisoned debtors of the city.[3] In his diary, he wrote, "November 26—Being the day appointed for a thanksgiving, I went to St. Paul's Chapel, though it was most inclement and stormy—but few people at Church."[4]

Other churches, however, saw greater success. Newspapers carried the proclamation, and churches conducted special worship services on that day. Thanksgiving Day was "widely celebrated throughout the nation."[5]

At First Presbyterian Church in Freehold, New Jersey, Rev. John Woodhull, who had been a Revolutionary War chaplain, preached "A Sermon for the Day of Publick Thanksgiving, Appointed by the President, On Account of the Establishment of the New Constitution, & c." His text was Psalm 97:1: "The LORD reigns; let the earth rejoice."

Psalm 97 is among the great psalms of praise that focus on the glory of the enthroned God who reigns forever. According to verse 2, clouds and darkness surround Him, and righteousness is the foundation of His throne. Verse 4 says vividly, "His lightnings light up the world." Verse 6 says, "The heavens declare His righteousness." And verse 12 admonishes us to rejoice in Him and give thanks at the remembrance of His holy name.

During his sermon, Woodhull said, "With respect to us in these United States, wise observers have, with grateful admiration, [noticed] a kind and powerful hand of Providence conducting us from the feeble state of infancy and dependence, through darkness—through dangers—and through a long and bloody contest, to our present state of greatness and glory."[6]

In following years other presidents offered similar resolutions; but not until 1863 did Thanksgiving Day become an annual federal holiday, established by President Abraham Lincoln during the dark days of the Civil War.

41

December 10, 1795

Invaluable Treasure

> *But sanctify the Lord God in your hearts, and always be*
> *ready to give a defense to everyone who asks you a rea-*
> *son for the hope that is in you.*
>
> —1 PETER 3:15

E lias Boudinot was a Founding Father thoroughly committed to Jesus Christ. He was born in Philadelphia, just down the street from Benjamin Franklin, on May 2, 1740, and baptized by George Whitefield. As a young man Boudinot wanted to go into the ministry, but his family couldn't afford to send him to college. So Boudinot studied law under his brother-in-law, Richard Stockton, who would later be a signer of the Declaration of Independence. Boudinot set up practice in New Jersey and soon became known as a gifted attorney and businessman.[1]

When the Revolutionary War broke out, Boudinot was named commissary-general of prisoners and superintended the intelligence department of the army as head of George Washington's ring of spies.[2]

In 1777, he was chosen as a member of the Continental Congress, and he was appointed its president in 1782. In this role, Boudinot signed the Treaty of Paris, ending the War of Independence. After the Revolution, Boudinot returned to private practice, but upon the adoption of the Constitution he was elected to the House of Representatives from New Jersey.

As a member of the First Congress, Boudinot proposed the first national Thanksgiving Day.

When Boudinot retired from Congress, Washington appointed him to be the director of the United States Mint. Boudinot also served as a trustee of Princeton College for fifty years, and he was active in promoting many Christian and evangelistic causes.[3]

In the days following the American Revolution, the new nation quickly abandoned its Christian heritage. Church attendance plunged, and colleges became seedbeds of atheism. The spiritual progress of the Great Awakening, which had helped fuel the American Revolution, dissipated. French rationalism and the Enlightenment captivated American minds, and much of the secularism was fueled by Thomas Paine's rabidly anti-Christian book *The Age of Reason*.

To counter Paine's arguments, Boudinot published *The Age of Revelation: Or the Age of Reason Shown to be an Age of Infidelity*, one of America's first books of Christian apologetics. He told his readers he had written the book, "knowing the importance of your being able to give a ready answer for the hope that is in you."[4] Boudinot was referring to 1 Peter 3:15, the Bible's key text on the subject of what is called "apologetics"—the defense of the Christian faith. Many people believe that faith is believing in something despite the evidence, but a valid faith is believing in something because of the evidence. The Lord never wants us to commit intellectual suicide to trust Him. He has given us copious amounts of proof—many infallible proofs, as we read in Acts 1:3—that the Christian faith is verifiable and true.

Because of that, the apostle Peter said in 1 Peter 3:15, "But sanctify the Lord God in your hearts, and always be ready to give a defense to everyone who asks you for a reason for the hope that is in you."

On the Bible, Boudinot also wrote:

For nearly half a century, have I anxiously and critically studied that invaluable treasure [the Bible]; and I still scarcely ever take it up, that I do not find something new—that I do not receive some valuable addition to my stock of knowledge; or perceive some instructive fact, never observed before. In short, were you to ask me to recommend the most valuable book in the world, I should fix on the Bible as the most instructive, both to the wise and ignorant. Were you to ask me for one affording the most rational and pleasing entertainment to the inquiring mind, I should repeat, it is the Bible. And should you renew the inquiry for the best philosophy, or the most interesting history, I should still urge you to look into your Bible. I would make it, in short, the Alpha and Omega of knowledge.[5]

In 1816, Boudinot gave $10,000 to establish the American Bible Society and served as its first president. He lived to age eighty-one, devoting his final years to writing about the hope that was within him. His dying words were, "Lord Jesus, receive my spirit."[6]

After providing for his daughter in his will, Boudinot bequeathed the remainder of his estate to Christian causes, including 4,000 acres for the Society for the Benefit of the Jews; $5,000 to the Presbyterian Church; 4,080 acres for theological students; more than 3,000 acres for the Hospital of Philadelphia; and over 13,000 acres to the city of Philadelphia for the benefit of the poor.[7] Every aspect of his life and death was devoted to expressing the hope that was within him—the certain hope of the gospel of Christ.

April 25, 1799

The Father of American Geography

If the foundations are destroyed,
What can the righteous do?

—PSALM 11:3

During the height of the Revolutionary War, Jedidiah Morse enrolled at Yale and soon came under a sense of his need for Christ. Writing his father, he said, "I have conversed with the President [Ezra Stiles] on the subject of religion. He gave me excellent advice and proposed my joining a church. I think it of the first importance to engage in religion in early life, while we have the promise of finding, and not to delay the duty to old age or a sick bed."

Shortly afterward, on February 20, 1781, he wrote, "I have now to tell you something of greatest importance to me . . . It is my purpose to make a solemn dedication of myself to God, my Creator . . . to enter into covenant with the living God. . . . I trust I can do so with the utmost willingness, and with a humble dependence on Jesus Christ, the Mediator."[1]

On March 4, 1781, Morse, twenty, made a public commitment of his life to Christ. By the time he graduated Yale, he had determined to enter the ministry to "preach the glad tidings of salvation."[2]

A church in Charlestown, Massachusetts, across the harbor from Boston, hired him as pastor for a salary of eleven dollars a week and "firewood sufficient for his study until married, and, when married, that he be furnished with a dwelling house and barn, and twenty cords of wood annually."[3]

Morse was installed as pastor on April 30, 1789, the same day and hour in which Washington was inaugurated president. Morse's first sermon was from 1 Corinthians 2:2: "For I determined not to know anything among you except Jesus Christ and Him crucified." He served as pastor for many years, preaching Christ crucified and battling anything that would erode the standards of biblical doctrine that he held dear.

Perhaps his best-known sermon was preached from Psalm 11:3 on April 25, 1799. Psalm 11 is a response written by King David to a crisis that had rattled his advisor. Some emergency had struck the king, and David's aid had told him to "flee as a bird to your mountain" (v. 1). In other words, David's counselors were advising him to run for his life. They were telling him that the wicked "bend their bow" and "make ready their arrow on the string" (v. 2). The foundations were being destroyed, and what could David do? What could any righteous person do?

David's response was to remind them that the Lord was in His holy temple. He was still on His heavenly throne (v. 4). In other words, don't panic. Our God is still in charge.

In his sermon marking Washington's inauguration, Jedidiah Morse declared:

In proportion as the genuine effects of Christianity are diminished in any nation . . . in the same proportion will the people of that nation recede from the blessings of genuine freedom. . . . I hold this to be a truth confirmed by experience. If so, it follows, that all efforts made to destroy the foundation of our holy religion, ultimately tend to the subversion also of our political freedom and happiness. Whenever the pillars of Christianity shall be overthrown, our present republican forms of government, and all the blessings which flow from them, must fall with them.[4]

Morse continued in Charlestown until the spring of 1820, when he resigned to write and pursue benevolent ministries, including foreign missions and evangelistic efforts among Native Americans. His health, which had never been strong, faltered and he passed away on June 9, 1826. His last words were, "A hope full of immortality—*that* expresses it."[5]

Today Morse is chiefly remembered as the Father of American Geography. His career as a geographer started during the winter of 1783, while he was studying theology. He became interested in the physical layout of the United States and actively researched "information from all the sources within his reach."[6] He traveled south to study the terrain, and he corresponded with prominent individuals across the country.

His biographer said, "The United States were now first assuming a fixed national character in the adoption of the Constitution; and it seemed especially desirable that some authentic and correct account of the country, including its territorial extent [and] its natural resources . . . should be given to the world."[7]

Morse developed a series of lectures and then crafted his lectures into a book—*Geography Made Easy*—the first geography textbook published in America. It was a bestseller, and in 1789 was enlarged and published as *American Geography* and later as *Universal Geography of the United States*. Morse's textbook went through many editions and became the means by which thousands of students learned about their nation. It was also published abroad, where it played a vital part in educating multitudes of immigrants coming to American shores.

Morse had eleven children, but eight died in infancy. The eldest son survived—Samuel Morse—and went on to invent the telegraph, but that's a story for later.[8]

43

June 6, 1799

Patrick Henry's Sealed Envelope

Righteousness exalts a nation, but sin is a reproach to any people.

—Proverbs 14:34

The Founding Fathers constantly quoted the Bible in their speeches, letters, and conversations; but some verses showed up more often than others. According to historian Daniel L. Dreisbach, one of the most ubiquitous biblical quotations was Proverbs 14:34.

For example, on April 30, 1776, Samuel Adams wrote his friend Richard Henry Lee, saying, "Should there be found a citizen of the United States so unprincipled as to ask what will become of us if we do not follow the corrupt maxims of the world? I should tell him that the strength of a republic is consolidated by its virtues, and that righteousness will exalt a nation."[1]

On October 25, 1780, when the Massachusetts constitution went into effect and John Hancock was sworn in as governor, Rev. Samuel Cooper preached before the dignitaries, saying, "Righteousness, says one of the greatest politicians and wisest princes that ever lived, 'Righteousness exalteth a nation.' This maxim doth not barely rest upon his own word but also on a divine authority; and the truth of it has been verified by the experience of all the ages."[2]

President John Adams issued a proclamation setting aside April 25, 1799, as a day of prayer and fasting, asking people to implore God's "pardoning mercy, through the Great Mediator and Redeemer, for our past transgressions, and that through the grace of His Holy Spirit we may be disposed and enabled to yield a more suitable obedience to His righteous requisitions in time to come; that He would interpose to arrest the progress of that impiety and licentiousness in principle and practice so offensive to Himself and so ruinous to mankind; that He would make us deeply sensible that 'righteousness exalteth a nation, but sin is a reproach to any people.'"[3]

Perhaps the most poignant use of Proverbs 14:34 came from the pen of America's greatest orator, Patrick Henry, who, by June 1799, was sixty-three years old and on his deathbed battling stomach cancer. On June 6, his doctor handed him a dose of liquid mercury. Henry took the vial in his hand, looked at it for a moment, and said, "I suppose, doctor, this is your last resort?"

"I am sorry to say, governor, that it is."

"What will be the effect of the medicine?"

"It will give immediate relief, or . . . ," and the doctor trailed off.

"You mean, doctor," said Henry, "that it will give relief or will prove fatal immediately."

The doctor answered, "You can only live a very short time without it, and it may possibly relieve you."

Henry said, "Excuse me, doctor, for a few minutes."

Drawing down over his eyes a silken cap which he usually wore, and still holding the vial in his hand, he prayed, in clear words, a simple childlike prayer, for his family, for his country, and for his own soul then in the presence of death. Afterward, in perfect calmness, he swallowed the medicine. Meanwhile Dr. Cabell, who greatly loved him, went out on the lawn, and in his grief threw himself down upon the earth under one of the trees, weeping bitterly.

Recovering his composure, Dr. Cabell returned to the sickroom to find Henry speaking words of comfort to his weeping family. He told them he was thankful for the goodness of God, who had blessed him all his life, and, seeing Dr. Cabell, he implored him to receive Christ as his Savior. With that, the statesman breathed his last.[4]

Shortly afterward, his executors found a small envelope sealed with wax near his last will and testament. On a single sheet of paper, the great orator had recorded some of his last thoughts, including these words about American independence:

Whether this will prove a Blessing or a Curse will depend upon the Use our people make of the Blessings which a gracious God hath bestowed on us. If they are wise, they will be great and happy. If they are of a contrary Character, they will be miserable. Righteousness alone can exalt them as a Nation. Reader!, whoever thou art, remember this; and in thy Sphere, practice Virtue thyself, and encourage it in others. P. Henry.[5]

June 4, 1800

Noah Webster and His Dictionary

*Festus said with a loud voice, "Paul, you are beside yourself!
Much learning is driving you mad!" But he said, "I am not mad,
most noble Festus, but speak the words of truth and reason."*

—ACTS 26:24–25

F ew American heroes were as eccentric, interesting, or brilliant as
Noah Webster. Often depressed, anxious, and obsessive-compulsive,
he published more words than any of America's founders and is called the
Father of American Scholarship and Education.[1] His *American Dictionary
of the English Language* would "succeed in forever unifying the world's
most ethnically diverse nation with a common language."[2]

Webster was born in 1758 and graduated from Yale during the
Revolutionary War. He tried teaching but failed. He opened a school, but
it closed. He became a lawyer but struggled to make a living. He fell in
love twice but was rejected. He longed to become Washington's official
biographer, but that job went to someone else.

To keep from starving, Webster assembled a spelling textbook, *The Blue-Backed Speller*, and he invented the concept of a "book tour" to promote it, stopping in every state capital to lobby for copyright laws to protect his resource. Webster's *Speller* taught generations of children to read, spell, and pronounce, and it gave him a trickle of sustained income. Except for the Bible, Webster's *Speller* became the most purchased book in America for a century.[3]

On October 26, 1789, Noah married Rebecca Greenleaf, a woman absolutely perfect for him. The only threat to their happiness was his massive debt and his failure to find a life's work. In 1793, they moved to New York City to start a newspaper, but for years it, too, failed. Just as the tide turned and the paper showed signs of success, Webster lost interest. His mind was seized by another dream—the compiling of a dictionary of American English.

Relocating to New Haven, Connecticut, Webster announced his project in the local paper on June 4, 1800, referring to himself in third person: "Mr. Webster of this city, we understand is engaged in completing . . . a Dictionary of the American Language."

Webster worked at a round table in his second-floor study from sunrise until four in the afternoon, usually standing while reading and writing, using a quill pen and pad, and surrounded by reference works. But the mental strain, financial worries, and constant criticism nearly broke him. That is, until he came to faith in Jesus Christ.

Rev. Moses Stuart, a local pastor, was a powerful preacher during the Second Great Awakening, and Webster's teenage daughters were converted under his preaching. Webster, disturbed, requested a meeting with Stuart. For several weeks, Webster struggled with the gospel message, but one morning in April 1808, "I instantly fell to my knees and confessed my sins to God, implored His pardon and made my vows to Him." Calling his family, Webster announced his decision to follow Christ, and his inner turmoil ceased. "From that time," he said, "I have had a perfect tranquility of mind."[4]

When his brother criticized him for "religious enthusiasm," Webster replied in a letter, which later became one of America's premier apologetic pamphlets. He recalled that when the apostle Paul was accused by King Agrippa of going insane because of his extreme intelligence, Paul had replied, "I am not mad, most noble Festus, but speak the words of truth and reason" (Acts 26:24).

Webster wrote:

These sentiments may perhaps expose me to the charge of *enthusiasm*. Of this I cannot complain, when I read in the Gospel that the apostles, when they first preached Christ crucified, were accused of being full of new wine; when Paul was charged by Felix with being a madman; and when Christ Himself was charged with performing miracles through the influence of evil spirits. If, therefore, I am accused of enthusiasm, I am not ashamed of the imputation. It is my earnest desire to cherish evangelical doctrines and no other . . . for nothing is uniform but truth; nothing unchangeable but God and His works. . . . To reject the Scriptures as forgeries is to undermine the foundation of all history; for no books of the historical kind stand on a firmer basis than the Sacred Books.[5]

Noah Webster published his dictionary in 1828, defining more than sixty-five thousand words, shaping American English for the lifetime of the nation, and making *Webster* a household name that has spanned the centuries.

Many secular critics accuse Christians of inferior intelligence and faulty reasoning; they think Christianity is untrue. But the evidence for the truthfulness of the Christian faith is greater than they realize, and it's as true today as in the days of Noah Webster: no other books in history can compare to the reliability and life-changing power of God's Word, the Bible.

August 6, 1801

America's Pentecost

Go into all the world and preach the gospel to every creature.

—MARK 16:15

After the Revolutionary War, the newly independent Americans were intent on building a nation. Christianity declined as French agnostics and Enlightenment scholars eroded the faith of thousands. One North Carolina Christian lamented that few people in the South had ever heard the name of Christ, except as a curse.[1] Another man wrote:

> At the close of the long and arduous struggle for independence large districts of the country were destitute of the Gospel, and the people in great measure seemed to be given over to intemperance and irreligion. The disbanded armies carried immorality of the camp into almost every community. The vices contracted there, the infidelity imbibed from French allies, were spread. . . . Religion and morals were at the lowest ebb they have ever reached in America.[2]

But things were changing. In the east, revival struck colleges like Hampden-Sydney; and on the frontier there were unmistakable stirrings of the Holy Spirit. In 1800 and 1801, large crowds showed up for a series of communion services conducted by Presbyterian James McGready of Logan, Kentucky. Among the attenders was Barton Stone, the pastor of two small churches west of Lexington. Stone went back to his church in Cane Ridge to report on what he had seen:

> I returned with ardent spirits to my congregations. I reached my appointment at Cane Ridge on Lord's Day. Multitudes had collected, anxious to hear the religious news of the meeting I had attended in Logan. I ascended the pulpit and gave a relation of what I had seen and heard; then opened my Bible and preached from these words: "Go ye into all the world and preach the Gospel to every creature."[3]

That verse struck a chord with the church in Cane Ridge, and the members decided to host a similar communion service for their area. They wanted to reach their region, their new nation, and, truly, the whole world. Their building was large and could hold five hundred people; they erected a tent for the overflow. But nobody expected the multitudes who showed up. Stone later described it:

> The roads were literally crowded with wagons, carriages, horsemen and footmen moving to the solemn camp. The sight was affecting. It was judged, by military men on the ground, that there were between twenty and thirty thousand collected. Four or five preachers were frequently speaking at the same time in different parts of the encampment without confusion. The Methodist and Baptist preachers aided in the work, and all appeared cordially united in it—of one mind and one soul, and the salvation of sinners seemed to be the great object of all. We all engaged in singing the same songs of praise—all united in prayer—all preached the same things—free salvation urged upon all by faith and

repentance. A particular description of this meeting would fill a large volume, and then the half would not be told. The numbers converted will be known only in eternity. Many things transpired there which were so much like miracles. . . . The meeting continued six or seven days, and would have continued longer, but provision for such a multitude failed in the neighborhood.[4]

Unexplainable things happened at Cane Ridge, and there were strange manifestations. The wave of emotions that swept over the crowds produced religious ecstasy, with people fainting, falling as if dead, jerking, dancing, running, laughing, and singing. It's estimated that as many as three thousand people were converted.

It's hard to comprehend what happened at Cane Ridge between August 6 and 12, 1801—the revival that began there and the impact it had. It effectively launched the Second Great Awakening, which means the United States of America was born between two great spiritual revivals— the First and Second Great Awakening. Coming as it did at the beginning of the 1800s, it established a basis for the greatest era of national and international missionary expansion hitherto in history—taking the gospel to every creature.

Dr. Paul Keith Conkin summed up the Cane Ridge Revival this way:

Never before in America had so many people attended this type of sacramental occasion. Never before had such a diversity of seizures or "physical exercises" affected, or afflicted so many people. The Cane Ridge sacrament has become a legendary event, the clearest approximation to an American Pentecost, prelude to a Christian century. It arguably remains the most important religious gathering in all of American history, both for what it symbolized and for the effects that flowed from it.[5]

July 11, 1804

The Death of Alexander Hamilton

> *Nor is there salvation in any other, for there is no other name under heaven given among men by which we must be saved.*
>
> —ACTS 4:12

Alexander Hamilton was born on a Caribbean island out of wedlock, was orphaned as a child, went to work at age eleven, and came to New York City as a teenager to enroll in King's College. The Revolutionary War disrupted his studies, and Hamilton ended up as George Washington's young aide. He was brilliant, ambitious, and gifted, and he argued for a strong central government. Washington appointed him America's first secretary of the treasury, and it was Hamilton who established the US Mint.

In 1804, Aaron Burr grew angry when Hamilton reportedly called him unfit and dangerous, and he challenged Hamilton to a duel. The conflict was occasioned by the election of 1804, in which Hamilton assisted Morgan Lewis in defeating Burr for the governorship of New

York. A newspaper reporter accused Hamilton of expressing a "despicable opinion" of Burr at a dinner party. Burr was livid, but Hamilton wanted no part in the clash, having earlier lost a son to a duel. Yet in keeping with the tenor of the times, he felt he had no choice.

On Wednesday morning, July 11, 1804, the two men met on the New Jersey shoreline opposite New York, near today's Lincoln Tunnel. When the men fired, Hamilton apparently didn't aim at Burr, but a bullet from Burr's gun struck Hamilton, lifting him off his toes and sending him to the ground.

Hamilton was carried unconscious to a barge and transported to a house in Greenwich Village. Rousing, he called for Dr. John Mason, a Presbyterian pastor, who rushed to his side. Hamilton asked for communion. The anguished pastor replied it was against the rules of his church to administer the Lord's Supper privately to an individual, but he spoke at length of the gospel. Mason quoted Acts 4:12, telling Hamilton no other name but Christ could give us eternal life. "He is able to save to the uttermost them who would come unto God through Him, seeing he ever liveth to make intercession for them. The blood of Jesus Christ cleanses from all sin."

The blood of Christ, said the pastor, could even wash away the sin of dueling. Hamilton agreed, saying, "It was always against my principles. . . . I went to the field determined not to take his life."

Mason told him about the richness of the grace that brings us salvation. Hamilton replied, "It is *rich* grace. I have a tender reliance on the mercy of the Almighty, through the merits of the Lord Jesus Christ." He closed his eyes, but at length opened them again to find Pastor Mason still by his side. Mason said tenderly, "The simple truths of the Gospel . . . are best suited to your present condition, and they are full of consolation."

"I feel them to be so," said Hamilton, and he asked the pastor to pray for him. Mason knelt in prayer, and when he finished, Hamilton said, "Amen, God grant it!" As Mason left the room, he heard Hamilton exclaim, "God be merciful to me a sinner."

The dying statesman, however, still longed for the Lord's Supper, and Dr. Benjamin Moore of Trinity Church was called. When he entered the room, Hamilton said, "My dear sir, you perceive my unfortunate situation, and no doubt have been made acquainted with the circumstances which led to it. It is my desire to receive the Communion at your hands."

Dr. Moore agreed, provided Hamilton renounce the sin of dueling, to which Hamilton assented. Moore asked, "Do you sincerely repent of your past sins? Have you a lively faith in God's mercy through Christ, with a thankful remembrance of the death of Christ? And are you disposed to live in love and charity with all men?"

Hamilton raised his hands toward heaven and said, "With the utmost sincerity of heart I can answer those questions in the affirmative. I have no ill-will against Colonel Burr. I met him with a fixed resolution to do him no harm. I forgive all that happened."

Moore handed him the sacrament. After partaking of the Lord's Supper, Hamilton wanted to see his family a final time. With his wife and children around his bed, he looked lovingly at each and closed his eyes. His last words were to his wife: "Remember, my Eliza, you are a Christian."

As an early biographer said: "Thus passed away from the earth one of the most gifted, powerful and illustrious spirits which has ever figured upon the great and wondrous stage of human affairs."[1]

47

June 27, 1810

The Haystack Prayer Meeting

Blessed are the dead who die in the Lord.... Their works follow them.

—REVELATION 14:13

In the early 1800s, most of the students in northeastern colleges were abusive to Christians, forcing believers to meet in virtual secrecy.[1] That began to change with the Second Great Awakening, and the spiritual life of Williams College in Williamstown, Massachusetts, took a decided turn in April 1806, when a student named Samuel Mills showed up.

Since he was a teenager Mills had been burdened for those overseas who had never heard the gospel.[2] Up to this point, no American group had done much to reach foreign fields, but Mills had been inspired by the stories of David Brainerd and John Eliot. As he told one friend, "Though you and I are very little beings, we must not rest satisfied till we have made our influence extend to the remotest corner of this ruined world."[3]

Mills and a handful of friends began meeting twice a week in a grove of trees near the college. One Saturday afternoon in August 1806, their prayer meeting was interrupted by a lightning storm, and they sought shelter in a nearby haystack. Though still exposed to the open sky, they were partially shielded from the rain and wind. As the storm passed over, the fellows were overwhelmed to pray for country after country.[4] Mills spoke passionately about taking the gospel to the ends of the earth, telling the others, "We can do it if we will."[5]

The students finished their prayer, sang a hymn, and returned to their rooms, knowing something special had happened. To this day, church historians point to the Haystack Prayer Meeting as "the birthplace of American foreign missions."[6]

After graduating from Williams, Mills enrolled in Andover Seminary, where he continued speaking up for international missions.

> He might always be found . . . engaged in conversations on this inter-
> esting topic. He made himself complete master of the subject; and daily
> might be seen arm in arm with one or more of his fellow students . . .
> pressing the obligation to missions upon their consciences, by consid-
> erations well nigh irresistible. There was a beautiful grove that spread
> itself in the rear of the college buildings, and "along that shady walk,"
> says one of his fellow-missionaries, "where I have often walked alone,
> Mr. Mills has at other times been my companion, and there urged the
> importance of missions to the heathen. And when he had reached some
> sequestered spot, where there was no fear of interruption, he would
> say—'Come, God only can guide us right; let us kneel down and pray,'
> and then he would pour out his soul."[7]

On June 27, 1810, Mills and his friends appealed to their Congregational denomination to establish a missionary society. Their petition said:

> The undersigned, members of the Divinity College, respectfully
> request the attention of their Reverend Fathers, convened in the

General Association at Bradford, to the following statement and inquires: They beg leave to state that their minds have been long impressed with the duty and importance of personally attempting a Mission to the Heathen . . . and . . . they consider themselves as devoted to this work for life, whenever God in His providence shall open the way. . . . The undersigned, feeling their youth and inexperience, look up to their Fathers in the Church and respectfully solicit their advice, direction, and prayers.

[SIGNED] ADONIRAM JUDSON, JR., SAMUEL NOTT, JR., SAMUEL J. MILLS[8]

The "Reverend Fathers" responded quickly, establishing the American Board of Commissioners for Foreign Missions. Mills became a missionary to the American frontier. Samuel Nott went to India. Adoniram and Ann Judson, along with Luther Rice and Samuel and Harriet Newell, sailed for Asia on February 19, 1812.

How incredible that America's great foreign missionary movement—the golden age of missions—was started by a handful of college students. When Mills contracted tuberculosis and died at sea at age thirty-five, he was eulogized with these words:

He found a grave in the ocean, leaving his worthy and reverend father and a bereaved community to mourn his loss. We knew not his worth till he left us. He stole silent through this world and kept himself unseen while he waked the energies of others . . . till, early ripe for heaven, he rested from his labors and his works do follow him.[9]

That verse from Revelation 14:13—"Blessed are the dead who die in the Lord. . . . Their works follow them"—has sustained missions for hundreds of years. The work of winning people to Jesus Christ is often slow and laborious. We don't always see immediate results. But our labor is never in vain in the Lord, and often, as in the case of David Brainerd, our greatest fruitfulness occurs after our deaths. The impact of our work reverberates in the echo chamber of time, and the pass-along effects of our witnessing multiplies through the ages, all the way to the return of Christ.

Never be discouraged in your efforts for the Lord. Our works will follow us to heaven.

April 19, 1813

The Father of American Medicine

Well done, good and faithful servant!

—MATTHEW 25:23

D r. Benjamin Rush is America's Forgotten Founding Father. He encouraged Thomas Paine to write *Common Sense*, which fueled the American Revolution. Paine wanted to call his work *Plain Truth*, but Rush suggested the title *Common Sense* and served as editor to the work. Rush was among the youngest signers of the Declaration of Independence and was appointed the surgeon-general of the Continental Army.

Rush was the personal physician to many of the other Founding Fathers and is known as the "Father of American Medicine" and as the "American Hippocrates." He wrote America's first chemistry textbook. He's also called the "Father of Public Schools Under the Constitution," advocating free public schools for all children. His studies into the nature of mental illness made him one of the founders of American psychiatry.

Among the first to champion the abolition of slavery, Rush was instrumental in founding America's first anti-slavery society. He crusaded for the reform of prisons and the end of cruel punishments as well as advocated the cause of the mentally ill. He established Bible societies and actively promoted the case of higher Christian education.

In 1790, he also helped organize the First Day Society, which started the Sunday School movement in the United States. He was also one of the founders of the Bible Society movement in America, which sought to make sure every citizen and every home had access to God's Word.

Rush helped start five colleges and universities, including the first college for women. He was an early supporter of women's rights, advocating education for women. He also believed education should include a thorough knowledge of Scripture. He became a sought-after college lecturer who trained three thousand American physicians.[1]

Regarding public education, he wrote:

Let the children who are sent to those schools be taught to read and write. Above all, let both sexes be carefully instructed on the principles and obligations of the Christian religion. This is the most essential part of education—this will make them dutiful children, teachable scholars, and afterwards, good apprentices, good husbands, good wives, honest mechanics, industrious farmers, peaceable sailors, and, in everything that relates to this country, good citizens.[2]

In 1791, Dr. Rush published one of his most popular works, *A Defense of the Use of the Bible as a Schoolbook*, writing, "The Bible contains more truth than any other book in the world."

His advice to physicians:

To no secular profession does the Christian religion afford more aid than to medicine. Our business leads us daily into the abodes of pain and misery. It obliges us likewise frequently to witness the fears with which our friends leave the world, and the anguish which follows in their surviving relatives. Here the common resources of our art fail us, but the comfortable views of the divine government and of a future state which are laid open by Christianity more than supply their place. A pious word dropped from the lips of a physician in such circumstances of his patients can often do more good.[3]

During the yellow fever epidemic in Philadelphia in 1793, Rush insisted on staying in the city while others were fleeing. At that time, Philadelphia was the nation's capital and the largest city, and President and Mrs. Washington left town along with many others. But many could not flee, and nearly one-tenth of the city's population died. The plague lasted for one hundred days with at least five thousand fatalities.

Calling together his medical students, Rush told them: "As for myself, I am determined to remain. I may fall a victim to the epidemic, and so may you, gentlemen. But I prefer since I am placed here by Divine Providence, to fall in performing my duty, if such must be the consequence of staying upon the ground, than to secure my life by fleeing from the post of duty allotted in the Providence of God. I will remain, if I remain alone."[4]

Rush survived and lived for many more years. When he died, his body was buried in the graveyard of Christ's Church in Philadelphia, along with seven other signers of the Declaration of Independence. His tombstone reads:

In memory of
Benjamin Rush, M.D.
Who died on the 19th of April
In the year of our Lord, 1813
Aged 68 years.
"Well done good and faithful servant;
Enter thou into the joy of the Lord." (Matthew 25:23)

49

August 24, 1814

The Tornado That Saved Washington

> *Every good gift and every perfect gift is from above, and comes down from the Father of lights.*
>
> —JAMES 1:17

Only a few years after the Battle of Yorktown, tensions between America and Britain again boiled over as England tried to hinder America's trading might and openly harassed her fledgling navy. A group of War Hawks in Congress pressured President James Madison to declare war against Britain, but British troops in Canada routed the American forces, and the British navy sailed into the Chesapeake Bay and headed to the nation's capital.

On August 19, 1814, British admiral George Cockburn (pronounced Co-burn) led 4,500 troops into Washington, intent on burning the city. President Madison was away with his war council, and First Lady Dolley Madison held forth in the President's Mansion, as the White House was then called.

On August 24, the invaders set fire to the Capitol building and its library, then headed down Pennsylvania Avenue to the President's Mansion. They barely missed Dolley, who stayed until the last minute. In a letter to her sister earlier that day, Mrs. Madison wrote:

> Since sunrise I have been turning my spy-glass in every direction, and watching with unwearied anxiety. . . . Two messengers, covered with dust, come to me to bid me fly. . . . I insist on waiting until the large picture of General Washington is secured, and it requires to be unscrewed from the wall. This process was found too tedious for these perilous moments; I have ordered the frame to be broken, and the canvas taken out. It is done! . . . And now, dear sister, I must leave this house.[1]

As Dolley Madison fled the city, the flames filled the skies behind her. But as the city burned, the weather began behaving oddly. A hurricane swept in from nowhere, triggering a tornado in the middle of the city that headed straight down Constitution Avenue toward the British soldiers, one of whom wrote:

> The most tremendous hurricane ever remembered by the inhabitants broke over Washington. . . . Roofs of houses were torn off and carried up into the air like sheets of paper, while the rain which accompanied it was like the rushing of a mighty cataract rather than the dropping of a shower. This lasted for two hours without intermission, during which . . . thirty of our men . . . were buried beneath the ruins. Two cannons standing upon a bit of rising ground were fairly lifted in the air and carried several yards to the rear.[2]

The rain doused the fires, and the British left as quickly as they had come. As Admiral Cockburn retreated, he reportedly snarled at a local woman, saying, "Great God, Madam! Is this the kind of storm to which you are accustomed in this infernal country?"

She replied, "No, Sir, this is a special interposition of Providence to drive our enemies from our city."[3]

In recent articles about the event, the *Smithsonian Magazine* called it "The Tornado That Saved Washington."[4] *Constitution Daily* dubbed it "The Tornado That Stopped the Burning of Washington."[5] The *Washington Post* referred to the same event as "The Thunderstorm That Saved Washington."[6]

After the war, James Madison called America to thanksgiving and prayer with a proclamation that said, in part:

> No people ought to feel greater obligations to celebrate the goodness of the Great Disposer of events, and of the Destiny of Nations, than the people of the United States. . . . To the same Divine Author of every good and perfect Gift, we are indebted for all those privileges and advantages, religious as well as civil, which are so richly enjoyed in this favored land. . . . It is for blessings, such as these, and more especially for the restoration of the blessings of peace, that I now recommend . . . a day on which the people . . . may, in their solemn assemblies, unite their hearts and their voices in a free will offering to their Heavenly Benefactor, of their homage of thanksgiving, and of their songs of praise.[7]

In his proclamation of thanksgiving, Madison quoted James 1:17 to remind America that if anything good happens to our nation it is from God, for He is the Father of Lights—the God of the sun, moon, and stars—who sends down every good and perfect gift needed for our care. We all love to receive gifts, but the best ones of all are good and perfect, sent from heaven, and distributed by the heavenly Father.

Understanding that gives us a different perspective on life. Dolley Madison, for example, was an extraordinary First Lady whose grace, wit, and charm delighted the nation. In her later years, she lived in a house on Lafayette Square. A few days before her death, a niece complained about some problem or burden. "My dear," Dolley replied, "do not trouble about it; there is nothing in *this* world worth really caring for. Yes, . . . believe me, I, who have lived so long, repeat to you there is nothing in this world here below worth caring for."

These last days she was very fond of having the Bible read to her and invariably asked for the gospel of Saint John. It was at one of these times that her last sleep came upon her.[8]

50

March 31, 1816

Circuit Riders Who Tamed the Frontier

*For this purpose the Son of God was manifested, that He
might destroy the works of the devil.*

—1 JOHN 3:8

The Cane Ridge Revival was started by Presbyterian Barton Stone, but its combustion fired up the Methodists, whose circuit riders tackled the frontier—Kentucky, Tennessee, Ohio, Illinois, and points beyond. Two names top the list of those riders, and they were as different as lightning and thunder.

Bishop Francis Asbury was lightning. John Wesley appointed him to oversee the Methodist work in America, and for nearly half a century Asbury traveled three hundred thousand miles by horse and carriage, preaching more than sixteen thousand sermons.[1] He began his work in America in 1771, at age twenty-two, and he became part of the Second Great Awakening. His journals are an American classic.

Sunday, December 23, 1788

I had very little life in preaching to a few dead souls at Pope's. On Monday, at Hutt's it was nearly the same both in preaching and sacrament. In the evening, at brother Cannon's the Lord powerfully broke into my soul and the cloud disappeared. That night while sleeping, I dreamed I was praying for sanctification, and God very sensibly filled me with love, and I waked shouting glory, glory to God! My soul was all in a flame. I had never felt so much of God in my life. . . . I rode to the Widow Wollard's and preached on, "For this purpose was the Son of God manifested, that He might destroy the works of the devil." During the last five days, we have ridden one hundred and forty miles.[2]

This verse from 1 John 3 gave itinerant evangelists like Asbury their sense of godly militancy. They saw themselves in a battle, not against the wild frontier they were seeking to tame but against the Devil, who was destroying the souls of those they were seeking to reach. The eighteenth-century circuit riders were big-hearted and loud-voiced, and they were not easily intimidated or silenced. They were fighting Satan and claiming the victory Christ had gained over the works of the Devil.

When Francis Asbury arrived in America, there were fewer than six hundred Methodists in the country. By the time he died, the number had grown to two hundred thousand. By the middle of the 1800s, one in every thirty-six Americans was Methodist.[3]

If Asbury was lightning, the thunder belonged to Peter Cartwright, a rough-and-tumble preacher who wasn't afraid to leave the pulpit and scuffle with hecklers. His seventy-one-year ministry began shortly before Asbury died on March 31, 1816; his autobiography is filled with remarkable stories. For example, one evening he stopped for lodgings in a tavern in the Cumberland Mountains, where most settlers had never heard a gospel sermon. A party was in full swing, and Cartwright sat in the corner of the room.

A beautiful, ruddy young lady walked gracefully over to me . . . and invited me to take a dance with her. I can hardly describe my thoughts or feelings on that occasion. However, in a moment I resolved on a desperate experiment. . . . I grasped her right hand with my right hand while she leaned her left arm on mine. In this position we walked on the floor. . . . I then spoke to the fiddler to hold a moment, and added that for several years I had not undertaken any matter of importance without first [asking] the blessing of God upon it . . . .

Here I grasped the young lady's hand tightly and said, "Let us all kneel down and pray," and then instantly dropped on my knees and commenced praying with all the power of soul and body that I could command. The young lady tried to get loose from me, but I held her hand tight. Presently she fell on her knees. Some of the company kneeled, some stood, some fled, and some sat still. . . . The fiddler ran off into the kitchen . . . .

While I prayed, some wept . . . and some cried for mercy. I rose from my knees and commenced an exhortation, after which I sang a hymn. The young lady who invited me on the floor lay prostrate, crying earnestly for mercy. I exhorted again, I sang and prayed nearly all night. About fifteen of that company professed religion, and our meeting lasted next day and next night, and as many more were powerfully converted. I organized a society, took 32 into the church, and sent them a preacher. . . . That was the commencement of a great and glorious revival . . . in that region.[4]

51

May 11, 1816

"Give Me That Book!"

The Lord gave the word: great was the company of those that published it.

—PSALM 68:11 KJV

In 1849, William Strickland authored a history of the American Bible Society, putting Psalm 68:11 on the title page: "The Lord gave the word: great was the company of those that published it" (KJV). He began by pointing back to the Puritans, saying, "The Bible was the star that guided them across a wintry ocean upward of two hundred years ago, and when they landed upon these shores and laid the foundations of this great republic, they labored assiduously to incorporate its principles with the elements of government."[1]

Strickland then recalled some incredible facts about the printing of the first English Bibles in America. As tensions grew with England, the importation of Scripture became impossible. In 1777, the Continental Congress voted to order twenty thousand Bibles "from Holland, Scotland, or elsewhere," but no Bibles arrived. Copies of Scripture were hard to find.

In 1781, publisher Robert Aitken petitioned Congress for permission to publish an edition of the Bible, and Congress voted to endorse Aitken's plan, leading to the first English Bibles printed in America.

> Resolved, That the United States in Congress assembled highly approve the pious and laudable undertaking of Mr. Aitkin, as subservient to the interest of religion as well as an influence of the progress of arts in this country and being satisfied from the above report [by the congressional chaplains] . . . recommend this edition of the Bible to the inhabitants of the United States and hereby authorize him to publish this recommendation in the manner he shall think proper.[2]

Aitken's Bible became the Bible of the American Revolution.[3]

Still, after the War, Bibles were in short supply. On May 11, 1816, a *who's who* of statesmen and clergymen met in New York City and formed the American Bible Society to publish and distribute Bibles across the new nation. Elias Boudinot, who had been president of the Continental Congress, gave $10,000 to launch the society and served as its president until his death in 1821, whereupon John Jay, the first chief justice of the US Supreme Court, became president. Francis Scott Key, author of the National Anthem, was vice president until his death in 1843.

The mayor of New York helped procure office space, and the society began collecting funds from business leaders and churches.[4] Soon Bibles were being printed and distributed to homes, schools, Native Americans, prisons, and "the two great arms of national defense, the army and navy."[5]

> Away from home and kindred, no companion is so valuable to the sailor as the Bible. . . . Hundreds have been awakened and converted to God solely through its instrumentality. The soldier has borne it in his knapsack on his weary marches and in the deadly strife of battle. Wounded and dying, he has pillowed his aching head upon this sacred treasure.[6]

In 1829, the American Bible Society undertook one of the most astounding missions in American church history—to provide every family in the United States with a Bible. In 1839, the society envisioned supplying Scriptures to the entire world, and millions of copies of God's Word went abroad in many languages.

Dr. Robert Newton, a Methodist leader in England, told the delegates at one of its early conventions:

> The Bible is a divine book, and the religion it unfolds is from Heaven, and not of men, and . . . this revelation is duly attested and authenticated. The Bible is based on the rock of eternal truth. It stands like the cerulean arch and cannot be overturned. . . . The Bible is THE BOOK, it being the foundation of all other books that are worthy [of] the attention of men. . . . The Bible has not only God for its author, but truth for its matter and salvation for its end. . . . I remember the words of an eminent saint of a past age: "I am as an arrow flying through the air; a spirit come from God and must return to God. A few moments I have on earth, to be seen no more. I want to learn one thing, the way to heaven. I hear God has caused this to be written in a book. Give me that book!"[7]

Psalm 68:11 is often now translated as "proclaimed" rather than "published." God gave us His Word, and great is the company of those who proclaim it. But the old King James Version used the word "publish," and it struck America's first Bible societies as a mission they could embrace. The Bible is the most distributed, impactful book in human history, yet millions of people around the world and in the United States do not have a copy of their own. Recently I gave my own well-worn Bible to a sailor on an airplane who had just finished boot camp and who promised to read it every day.

You can be your own one-person Bible society. Let's keep distributing the Word of God.

52

December 30, 1823

Preaching in Sodom

> *Get up, get out of this place; for the LORD will destroy this city!*
>
> —GENESIS 19:14

The Second Great Awakening pulsated throughout the 1800s, as various regions experienced revival, often in the wake of unusual preachers such as Charles Finney. A lawyer by trade, Finney was dramatically converted in 1821, and licensed to preach on December 30, 1823. Early in his ministry, he toured upstate New York and came to the town of Antwerp.

> In passing around the village I heard a vast amount of profanity. I thought I had never heard so much in any place that I ever visited . . . I felt as if I had arrived on the borders of hell. I had a kind of awful feeling. . . . Sabbath morning I arose and left my lodging in the hotel; and in order to get alone, where I could let out my voice as well as my

heart, I went up into the woods at some distance from the village and continued for a considerable time in prayer. . . . I found it was time for the meeting, and went immediately to the school-house. I found it was packed to the utmost capacity. I had my pocket Bible in hand and. . . . preached and poured out my soul and my tears together . . . .

On the third Sabbath I preached there, an aged man came to me . . . and asked me if I would go and preach in a school-house in his neighborhood about three miles distant, saying they had never had any services there. . . . I appointed the next day, Monday, at five o'clock in the afternoon.

Arriving at the schoolhouse in the outlying community, Finney found it so full he could barely get in. As he made his way to the pulpit, he decided he would preach from Genesis 19:14, "Get up, get out of this place; for the LORD will destroy this city!" He described the city of Sodom with its wickedness, and how Lot, a righteous man, was grieved, and how the city faced the fires of God's judgment.

I observed the people looking as if they were angry. Many of the men were in their shirt sleeves; and they looked at each other and at me as if they were ready to fall upon me and chastise me on the spot. I saw their strange and unaccountable looks and could not understand what I was saying that had offended them. . . . Their anger rose higher and higher as I continued the narrative. . . . All at once an awful solemnity seemed to settle down upon them; the congregation began to fall from their seats in every direction and cried for mercy. . . . Indeed, nearly the whole congregation were either on their knees or prostrate, I should think, in less than two minutes . . . .

I was obliged to stop preaching, for they no longer paid any attention. . . . I said to them, "You are not in hell yet; and now let me direct you to Christ . . . ." I turned to a young man close to me, laid my hand on his shoulder and preached in his ear Jesus. As soon as

I got his attention to the cross of Christ, he believed, was calm and quiet for a minute or two, and then broke out praying for the others. I turned to another and took the same course . . . and then another and another. . . . There was too much interest and too many wounded souls to dismiss the meeting; and so it was held all night. . . . .

When I went down the second time, I got an explanation of the anger manifested by the congregation during the introduction of my sermon the day before. I learned the place was called Sodom, but I knew it not; and that there was but one pious man in the place, and they called him Lot. This was the old man that invited me there. The people supposed I had chosen my subject . . . because they were so wicked as to be called Sodom. This was a striking coincidence; but so far as I was concerned, it was altogether accidental.[1]

The revivals of the 1800s were not coincidence or accidental; they were produced by the Holy Spirit to establish a spiritual foundation for a new nation dedicated to goodness and liberty.

53

July 4, 1826

Benjamin Rush's Amazing Dream

Blessed are the peacemakers, for they shall be called sons of God.

—MATTHEW 5:9

M any people know that John Adams and Thomas Jefferson had a falling out, which turned them into bitter enemies for decades. In the early years of the American Revolution, the two were close friends. They had met for the first time in the Congress of 1775, and they became fellow advocates of liberty. But during the Washington administration, the two disagreed about the role of the federal government. Jefferson worried about a strong central government while Adams thought it necessary. Nor were things helped by Jefferson's persistent support of the French Revolution, even after it turned violent.

The election of 1800, which pitted the two men against each other, was among the most bitter in American history. When Jefferson won, outgoing President Adams didn't even stay for his inauguration. The two men remained enemies for years.

Few people know the amazing story of how a dream restored their friendship.

No one was more distressed by the enmity between Adams and Jefferson than their mutual friend Dr. Benjamin Rush, America's forgotten Founding Father. On October 17, 1809, Rush described a vivid dream that came to him during the night. Writing to John Adams, he said he dreamed Jefferson and Adams would renew their friendship. Rush dreamed that Adams was going to write a letter congratulating Jefferson on his successful life and to extend good wishes for his welfare. He also dreamed that Jefferson, receiving the letter, would respond with affection and esteem. This, Rush dreamed, would lead to a resumption of their correspondence and friendship.

Adams replied that he had no objection to Rush's dream but considered it "history," not "prophecy." Rush then wrote to Jefferson, encouraging him to revive "a friendly and epistolary intercourse" with Adams.

For a while, nothing happened. But on December 5, 1811, Jefferson wrote to Rush about his continued warm and deep feelings for the memories of his friendship with Adams, and Rush immediately passed on the news to Adams, imploring the two men to "embrace each other" and "bury in silence all the causes of your separation."

On January 1, 1812, Adams sent Jefferson a polite letter expressing New Year's greetings, and Jefferson responded with a note fondly recalling their earlier labors for the cause of liberty. Soon Adams and Jefferson were writing to each other—they did so for the next fourteen years—and their letters were later published as "one of the most celebrated epistolary conversations in American history, one that continued until the last year of both men's lives."[1]

Dr. Rush was elated, having fulfilled the words of Jesus, "Blessed are the peacemakers." In a letter dated February 17, 1812, Rush wrote to John Adams:

> I rejoice in the correspondence which has taken place between you and
> your old friend Mr. Jefferson. I consider you and him as the North and

South poles of the American Revolution. Some talked, some wrote—
and some fought to promote & establish it, but you, and Mr. Jefferson
thought for us all.[2]

According to historian David Barton,

The accuracy and future fulfillment of several parts of this dream are
absolutely astounding. Recall that at the time this letter was written,
Jefferson and Adams were still opponents. None of what was described
in this letter had even begun to come to pass—nor did it seem likely
that it ever could. However, as accurately described in this letter, they
did again become close friends, and there did indeed follow the "correspondence of several years" described in the dream.[3]

Seventeen years later in different parts of the east, Adams, ninety, and
Jefferson, eighty-two, passed away on the same day—July 4, 1826—on the
fiftieth anniversary of Independence Day.

54

April 23, 1833

The Nation's Schoolmaster

Therefore, whatever you want men to do to you, do also to them.

—Matthew 7:12

D r. William Holmes McGuffey was born in 1800 in Pennsylvania and grew up in Ohio. He had a remarkable ability to memorize Scripture, learning whole books by heart. Much of his education occurred at his mother's knees, and he was only fourteen when he started teaching school, beginning with a class of forty-eight pupils in Calcutta, Ohio. But he and his mother longed for him to gain a better education.

One summer day in 1818, Rev. Thomas Hughes was riding his horse down the road when he heard Mrs. McGuffey in a garden and out of his sight, plaintively praying that her son could receive a better education. Hughes stopped at the next log cabin to inquire as to the woman's identity. He retraced his steps and invited William to enroll at his Old Stone Academy.

McGuffey thrived on education, and in 1826, he was named professor of languages at Miami University in Oxford, Ohio, and soon became known for his lectures on moral values and biblical themes. On April 23, 1833, he made an agreement with Cincinnati publishers Truman & Smith to produce a set of textbooks for America's schoolchildren.[1]

He initially produced a series of four Readers, which were published in 1836 and 1837, and in the Fourth Reader he wrote, "From no source has the author drawn more copiously, in his selections, than from the sacred Scriptures. . . . That man is to be pitied, who at this day, can honestly object to imbuing the minds of youth with the language and spirit of the Word of God."[2]

According to John H. Westerhoff III, "McGuffey's interest in teaching children to read is directly related to his conviction that knowing the contents of the Scriptures is of ultimate significance."[3]

For decades the *McGuffey Readers* were America's textbooks for the first six years of grade school, with 120 million copies landing on children's desks between 1836 and 1960—and they are still in print. They dominated schools from their publication until the beginning of the twentieth century, and one scholar ranks the *McGuffey Readers* alongside Thomas Paine's *Common Sense* and Alexander Hamilton's *The Federalist* as "books that changed the course of U.S. history."[4]

One biographer said, "For many common folk, McGuffey represents 'the most important figure in the history of American public education—the schoolmaster of the nation!'"[5] Another writer suggested that, except for the Bible, *McGuffey Readers* represent the most significant force in the framing of our national morals and tastes, saying, "For seventy-five years his system and his books guided the minds of four-fifths of the school children of the nation in their taste for literature, in their morality, in their social development, and next to the Bible, in their religion."[6]

In his book *William McGuffey: Mentor to American Industry*, Quentin R. Skrabec Jr. wrote:

As I researched and wrote biographies on presidents such as William McKinley and industrialists such as George Westinghouse, Henry Clay Frick, Henry Ford, Andrew Carnegie, Edward Libbey, Michael Owens, and H. J. Heinz, the name William Holmes McGuffey kept popping up. William McGuffey was clearly the mentor of many of America's greatest capitalists. Almost all had used the *McGuffey Reader*, and developed their belief systems in one-room schoolhouses.[7]

Here is a sample from *McGuffey's Eclectic Second Reader*, in which he taught children to read using the golden rule of Matthew 7:12:

My little reader, have you brothers and sisters? Then love them with all your heart. Do all you can for them. Help them when in need; and wait not to be asked. Add to their mirth. Share their grief. Vex them not. Use no cross words. Touch not what is not your own. Speak the truth at all times. Do no wrong; but do as you would be done by. So shall you make the hearts of your parents rejoice. So shall you have the blessings of the great God who made you.[8]

It's remarkable that in His first public sermon, the Carpenter from Nazareth gave the world the Beatitudes, the Lord's Prayer, the golden rule, and the greatest system of ethics ever devised. Pity a student who is educated without ever learning those things. McGuffey made sure America's schoolchildren knew the golden rule from their earliest days in the classroom.

P.S. If you're interested in copies of the *McGuffey Readers*, it's important to know there are three editions. The original editions are dated 1836–1837. A revision occurred in 1857, and another revision in 1879, and with each revision the distinct biblical nature of the contents was reduced.

December 4, 1833

The Tappan Brothers

For no other foundation can anyone lay than that which is laid, which is Jesus Christ.

—1 CORINTHIANS 3:11

Arthur Tappan was born into a godly family in Northampton, Massachusetts, and moved to Boston at age fifteen to apprentice at an importing company. He lived a moral life but was not a Christian. His mother wrote to him, saying:

My Dear Son:

I cannot feel willing you should leave me without saying more to you than I have; and, as I have not the opportunity to speak, I think it best to write. Your happiness, as that of all my children lies near my heart. . . . It is your happiness I seek, and fain would I assist you in building it on a sure foundation. *"Other foundation can no man lay that is laid*, which is Jesus Christ." 1 Cor 3.11. Build on Christ Jesus, as the chief cornerstone. I fear you have imbibed some errors, from what you dropped last night respecting the new birth. There are many loose writers, and it is to be feared, unsound preachers in our day. But the word of God is plain. . . . Study it attentively, with sincere and fervent prayer for the outpouring of the Holy Spirit to enlighten your darkened understanding and make your path of duty plain. God is a prayer-hearing God. . . . Oh, seek first the kingdom of God, and all other things shall be added unto you.[1]

When he was about thirty, Arthur did as his mother suggested and gave himself fully to Christ. His silk import business in New York City thrived, and he gave vast sums of money to ministries like the American Bible Society, the American Sunday School Union, the American Missionary Association, and the American Tract Society. He established programs for the destitute and for prisoners, and he paid the tuition of many ministerial students.[2] He served as president of the New York Magdalen Society to help prostitutes escape their circumstances.[3] He also helped finance the starting of Oberlin, a fully integrated college in Ohio.

One day in 1828, Arthur's brother, Lewis, visited. Lewis had embraced Unitarianism, rejecting the doctrine of the Trinity. The Unitarian beliefs at the time devalued the roles of Jesus Christ as God the Son and of the Holy Spirit as part of the Godhead. Arthur challenged Lewis about these things, and Lewis was solidly converted to Christ, recognizing His biblical role as both God and human. Moving to New York, Lewis joined Arthur in a growing portfolio of business enterprises.

While the Tappan brothers supported many causes, they are most remembered for their roles in the fight against slavery. Their philosophy was, "God has made of one blood all men, black and white; and Christ . . . died for all."[4]

On October 2, 1833, the brothers announced the formation of a society in New York calling for the immediate emancipation of all slaves. About fifty people gathered, but they were surrounded by thousands of agitators, banging on the gates. Undeterred, the abolitionists formed the New York Anti-Slavery Society, with Arthur as president and Lewis serving as a manager.[5]

Shortly afterward, Arthur issued a call for a national anti-slavery society; on December 4, 1833, delegates from across the country met in Philadelphia to form the American Anti-Slavery Society, with Arthur Tappan as president. Theodore Weld became a lecturing agent of the society and one of the most effective voices for the immediate emancipation of slavery in America. Weld's book, *American Slavery As It Is: Testimony of a Thousand Witnesses*, opened the eyes of the nation to the horrors of human bondage and aided Harriet Beecher Stowe in writing *Uncle Tom's Cabin*.[6]

Both Arthur and Lewis suffered during the 1834 anti-abolitionist riots in New York, and Lewis's home was attacked by a mob who trashed his house and threw his furniture into the street. But the brothers would not be denied. They backed the slaves who had taken over the ship *Amistad*, and they donated money for the Underground Railroad. Arthur and Lewis spent the rest of their days fighting the slave trade in the name of Christ, and they lived long enough to see the Emancipation Proclamation.

Near the end of his life, Arthur wrote his brother, saying, "I agree with you in rejoicing to see the day of universal freedom in our country, and feel ready to say now, 'Lord, let Thy servant depart in peace, for I have seen the Divine blessing resting on the efforts of Thy servants, the poor slaves.'"[7]

56

June 21, 1834

Better Make It a Hundred

Yet in all these things we are more than conquerors through Him who loved us.

—ROMANS 8:37

Cyrus McCormick grew up on a Virginia farm where cutting grain with scythes and sickles was slow and laborious. His father, Robert, dreamed of inventing a mechanical reaper to harvest crops quickly, but his contraptions always failed. As a teenager, Cyrus began tinkering alongside his dad. One day in July 1831, Cyrus called his family into the field, put a horse between the shafts of his reaper, and cut a swath through the grain. For the first time in history, grain was effectively harvested mechanically. His machine was placed in the public square where a college professor inspected it and announced, "This machine is worth a hundred thousand dollars."[1]

Cyrus began thinking about that, and one day as his horse stopped to drink in the middle of a stream and he gazed across the laden fields, he thought, "Perhaps I may make a million dollars from this reaper."[2]

About that time he found something far more valuable. In 1834, an evangelistic meeting was held in a nearby stone church, and a challenge was given to those wanting to receive Christ. Cyrus, twenty-five, refused to stand. That night his father came to his bedside and gently said, "My son, don't you know that your silence is a public rejection of your Savior?"

Instantly smitten, Cyrus jumped out of bed and dressed. "I'll go and see old Billy McClung," he said. He went down the road and woke up the man, who led him to saving faith. The next Sunday Cyrus stood in church, making public his decision.

On June 21, 1834, McCormick took out a patent on his reaper and began offering them for fifty dollars each, but no one bought one—not for years. Rather than being a millionaire, McCormick began drowning in debt. "If it were not for the fact that Providence has seemed to assist me," he said, "I would almost sink . . . but I believe the Lord will help us out."[3] His favorite Bible passage was Romans 8, with its great verse 37: "Yet in all these things we are more than conquerors through Him who loved us."

Romans 8 serves as the climax for Paul's great discussion of the truth of Jesus Christ as our Savior. From Romans 1 through Romans 8, the apostle lays out his case that only Christ Himself can provide us with peace with God, forgiveness of sin, and an eternal hope in heaven. The entire last half of Romans 8 is a great shout of triumph. It's well worth memorizing, for it reminds us that regardless of our perils and problems in life, we are not just victorious through Christ—we are more than conquerors.

This great truth fueled McCormick's resiliency. It was said he "was at his best when the situation was at its worst."[4]

One day a stranger named Adam Smith rode up and said he would risk fifty dollars on a reaper. Then another customer came. McCormick raised the price to one hundred dollars and sold seven reapers in 1842. As word spread, he noticed how many demands were coming from the Midwest. At age thirty-eight he moved to Chicago, built a factory, and indeed became a millionaire.[5]

As McCormick crisscrossed the Midwest selling his machines, he noticed the lack of churches, and he donated his funds to establish a seminary for training ministers. He established a Christian magazine and heavily supported Presbyterian ministries. When evangelist D. L. Moody began his campaigns, McCormick became a chief backer.

When Moody decided to establish a school (now the Moody Bible Institute), McCormick offered $50,000 to help him. Moody, who was equal to McCormick in every way, said, "Better make it a hundred." Moody got his $100,000.

By 1884, the year McCormick died, more than a half million of his reapers were being used somewhere on earth, and the average acre of American farmland was producing more than twice the harvest of before.[6]

An early biographer said that Cyrus McCormick "fed his country as truly as Washington created it and Lincoln preserved it. . . . He did more than any other member of the human race to abolish the famine of cities and the drudgery of the farm—to feed the hungry and straighten the backs of the world."[7]

Both spiritually and agriculturally, McCormick devoted his life to bringing in the sheaves.

November 7, 1837

Freedom of the Press

*I found it necessary to write to you exhorting you to con-
tend earnestly for the faith.*

—JUDE 1:3

Elijah Lovejoy began reading his Bible at the age of four, and while
very young memorized all of Psalm 119, along with twenty hymns.
He later graduated at the top of his class and decided to move "west"—to
St. Louis. His parents, concerned for his spiritual well-being, prayed
earnestly for him. Their prayers were answered when he wrote home,
telling them he had found the Lord during a revival and was entering the
Presbyterian ministry.

Within a year, Lovejoy was licensed to preach, but he didn't confine
his sermons to the pulpit. He also became editor of a weekly Christian
publication, the *St. Louis Observer*. The first issue rolled off the press
on November 22, 1833. In his opening editorial, Lovejoy wrote that his
paper "will seek no controversy, and it will decline none, when by so

doing it might compromise the purity of that 'faith once delivered to the saints.'"

Lovejoy understood the message of the book of Jude—that not every opinion in the world is equally valid. Objective truth exists because God exists. There is, therefore, a basis for objective truth and moral absolutes. False teachers are to be judged by biblical truth, and Lovejoy's dedication to journalism stemmed from this commitment to truth.

He added, "Opinions honestly entertained will be fearlessly declared."

The *Observer* became a vehicle for teaching Scripture, relating the news of the day, and interpreting the latter by the former. His editorials were must-reads, and sparks began to fly when he set forth the biblical facts and brutal truths about slavery.

On April 16, 1835, he wrote prophetically:

While Christians have been slumbering over it, the eye of God has not slumbered, nor has His Justice been an indifferent spectator of the scene. The groans, and sighs, and tears, and blood of the poor slave have gone up as a memorial before the throne of Heaven. In due time they will descend in awful curses upon this land, unless averted by the speedy repentance of us all.

Lovejoy's drumbeat against slavery sparked an uproar in St. Louis. Mobs formed, threatening his newspaper and life. Officials sought to silence him, demanding he "pass over in silence everything connected with the subject of slavery." In fiery public meetings, citizens demanded he cease writing. Crowds marched in the streets chanting, "Down with the *Observer*." Lovejoy was threatened with whipping.

"I cannot surrender my principles," he wrote in his next editorial, "though the whole world besides should vote them down." Asserting his freedom of speech, he fired off another series of blistering editorials condemning slavery with all its horrors. He compared himself to his namesake, Elijah, who stood before Ahab rebuking his sins, and he refused to be silenced.

I do, therefore, as an American citizen, and Christian patriot, and in the name of Liberty, and Law, and Religion, solemnly PROTEST against all these attempts, howsoever or by whomsoever made, to frown down the liberty of the press and forbid the free expression of opinion. Under a deep sense of my obligations to my country, the church, and my God, I declare it to be my fixed purpose to submit to no such dictation.

Writing to his brother, he said, "Men came to me and told me I could not walk the streets of St. Louis by night or by day. . . . I was alone in St. Louis, with none but God of whom to ask counsel. But thrice blessed be His name; He did not forsake me. I was enabled, deliberately and unreservedly, to surrender myself to Him."

When it became impossible for Lovejoy to dwell in St. Louis, he moved thirty miles away to Alton, Illinois. His printing press, transported by boat up the Mississippi, was destroyed by a mob on arrival. He ordered another press from Cincinnati, and the paper resumed publishing on August 17, 1837. Another mob surrounded him, shoved him around, and destroyed his new press. Lovejoy ordered a third.

About 10:00 p.m. on November 21, in the light of a full moon, a mob of about thirty men, armed with rocks and pistols, left local taverns and began marching toward Lovejoy's house. Church bells rang, and by midnight the whole town had assembled. The mob broke into his house, and one of the rioters shot Lovejoy. Three bullets struck his chest, another his stomach, and another his left arm. His new printing press was destroyed and thrown into the Mississippi River, and his hearse was hissed in the streets on the way to the cemetery.

He was buried on his thirty-fifth birthday, the first white martyr for the cause of abolition; a fearless publisher who gave his life for the freedom of the press; and a preacher of the gospel who once said, "I can die at my post, but I cannot desert it."[1]

58

March 1, 1841

The Friend of Both Washington and Lincoln

You crown the year with Your goodness.

—Psalm 65:11

No one in American history can match the résumé of John Quincy Adams, who served in the government of George Washington and in Congress with Abraham Lincoln. He was:

- The son of an American Founding Father and Mother, John and Abigail Adams
- An eyewitness at the Battle of Bunker Hill
- At age fourteen, the personal secretary and translator for the ambassador to Russia
- A friend of the likes of Benjamin Franklin and Charles Dickens, engaging them in conversations when just a teenager

- A graduate of Harvard and a professor there
- The eldest son of an American vice president and of an American president
- An ambassador to six different European nations
- A secretary of state
- A jurist who argued cases before the Supreme Court
- A senator from Massachusetts
- The diplomat who negotiated the end of the War of 1812
- The mind behind the Monroe Doctrine
- A negotiator who acquired Florida for the United States and pushed for the territories of the West Coast
- The sixth president of the United States
- The only ex-president to return to Congress
- A diarist whose journal, begun at age ten, provides fourteen thousand pages of eyewitness accounts of American history from the eve of the Revolutionary War to the eve of the Civil War
- And "America's first champion of human rights . . . who stunned Congress—and the nation—by demanding that Congress extend constitutional liberties to Americans of African descent by abolishing slavery."[1]

John Quincy Adams was also a man devoted to his Bible. In a letter dated June 22, 1838, he wrote:

The first and almost the only book deserving universal attention is the Bible. . . . The Bible is the book of all others, to be read at all ages, and in all conditions of human life; not to be read once or twice or thrice through, and then laid aside, but to be read in small portions of one or two chapters every day, and never to be intermitted unless by some overruling necessity. I speak as a man of the world to men of the world; and I say to you, "Search the Scriptures."[2]

To his son, he wrote, "I have myself, for many years, made it a prac-tice to read through the Bible once every year. My custom is to read four or five chapters every morning, immediately after rising from my bed. It employs about an hour of my time and seems to be the most suitable manner of beginning the day."[3]

Adams was also a hymn writer. He paraphrased all 150 Psalms for singing; and once attended a church service where his version of Psalm 65 was sung. Afterward he wrote:

> Were it possible to compress into one pulsation of the heart the pleasures which, in the whole period of my life, I have enjoyed in praise from the lips of mortal man, it would not weigh a straw to balance the ecstasy of delight which streamed from my eyes as the organ pealed and the choir of voices sung the praise of Almighty God from the soul of David, adapted to my native tongue by me.[4]

Adam's version of Psalm 65 became popular in many hymnbooks, and it expresses the joy and reverence of all creation for its Maker. It seems to me John Quincy Adams lived such a long and productive life because of his understanding of God's crowning the years with goodness. In his hymn based on Psalm 65, here is the way Adams worded his final stanza, based on Psalm 65:11–12:

> Thy goodness crowns the circling year,
> The wilderness repeats Thy voice;
> The mountains clad with flocks appear,
> The hills on every side rejoice.

As the circling years passed, Adams never stopped, especially in his campaign for African-American rights. Adams fiercely represented the slaves aboard the *Amistad*, arguing successfully on their behalf before the Supreme Court. At the end of the case, he grew nostalgic about the many times he had stood before the court over the decades. This was his final appearance, and he had a message for the justices:

> I stand before the same Court, but not before the same judges. . . . As I cast my eyes along those seats of honor and of public trust, now occupied by you, they seek in vain for one of those honored and honorable persons whose indulgence listened then to my voice. Marshall—Cushing—Chase—Washington—Livingstone—Todd—Where are they? . . . Where are they all? Gone! Gone! All gone! . . . I humbly hope and fondly trust that they have gone to receive the rewards of the blessedness on high. In taking, then, my final leave of this . . . honorable Court, I can only [offer] a fervent [prayer] to Heaven that each member of [this Court] may go to his final account with as little of earthly frailty to answer for as [possible] . . . and that you may, every one [of you], after the close of a long and virtuous career in this world, be received at the portals of [Heaven] with the approving sentence, "Well done, good and faithful servant; enter thou into the joy of the Lord."[5]

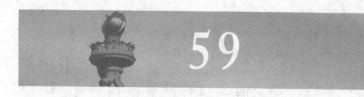

May 24, 1844

The Artist Who Struck Lightning

What hath God wrought!

—NUMBERS 23:23 KJV

I magine coming to the apex of your career, to the breakthrough that would immortalize your name, only to face catastrophic rejection and the collapse of your dream. Where can you find comfort? Only in the Lord, who turns disappointments into *His* appointments. That's what happened to Samuel Morse, the son of the "Father of Geography," Jedidiah Morse.

Jedidiah and his wife, Sarah, raised their firstborn to follow Christ. "Rise early in the morning," Jedidiah told him, "read a chapter in the Bible and say your prayers. . . . After a serious performance of these religious duties, comb your head and wash your face, hands, and mouth in cold water, not hastily and slightly, but thoroughly."[1]

After graduating from Yale, Samuel announced his decision to be an artist. He traveled to London and Paris to study, and he longed to show

Americans what he was seeing. Working on huge canvases, Samuel created massive works of stunning beauty, including his masterpiece, *Gallery of the Louvre*, in which he reproduced a room in the Louvre, bedecked with thirty-eight paintings, including the *Mona Lisa*. In this way, Samuel brought the treasures of the world's greatest museum to American eyes. He also painted many patriotic moments and was called the American Leonardo.[2]

Along the way, he fell in love with Lucretia Walker, whom he led to Christ. "I feel the dawning of religious joy in my soul," she wrote him, "and that my only hope of acceptance is through the merits of my Redeemer.... Your letters, dearest love, first awakened my attention."[3]

The pinnacle of Samuel's professional life approached in 1837, when he applied for the appointment to fill the vast panels of the Rotunda of the United States Capitol with historical panoramas. Everything in his life had prepared him for this moment, and he seemed the perfect candidate. But Congress chose another artist, and Samuel was so devastated that he lost all interest in painting.[4]

He turned his attention to his other preoccupation—electricity and the transmission of electrical signals, which developed into an obsession. He spent years stringing wires hither and yon, creating a mechanism and a code for long-distance communication.

On May 24, 1844, Samuel unveiled his invention before a crowd of wide-eyed dignitaries in the chambers of the US Supreme Court, which met in the Capitol. An associate waited on the other end of the line in Baltimore. Samuel tapped out a quotation from Numbers 23:23: "What Hath God Wrought." The message flew across the wires like lightning, the response came back, and the age of instant long-distance communication was born. Samuel explained his choice of Numbers 23:23 this way: "It baptized the American telegraph with the name of its Author"—God.[5]

He later said, "That sentence was divinely [prescribed], for it is in my thoughts day and night. 'What hath God wrought!' It is *His* work, and He alone carried me thus far through all my trials and enabled me to triumph over the obstacles, physical and moral, which opposed me."[6]

Late in life he wrote his grandson, "The nearer I approach the end of my pilgrimage, the clearer is the evidence of the divine origin of the Bible, the grandeur and sublimity of God's remedy for fallen men are more appreciated, and the future is illumined with hope and joy."[7]

To his brother, he said, "The Savior daily seems more precious; His love, His atonement, His divine power are themes which occupy my mind in the wakeful of the night."[8]

His biographer, John Trowbridge, opened the story of Samuel's life this way:

> I invite the attention of the reader to the record of a man who spent the first half of his life as an artist and the last half as an electrician. The vast storehouse of Nature was opened to him, and he was given honors and gold. He changed the world more than Caesar or Napoleon. . . . He bound together the states of this great continent with bands of iron. While an artist, no canvas seemed to him large enough upon which to express his ideas; and as an electrician, he was given the whole surface of the globe whereon to inscribe his name. . . . Samuel Findley Bresse Morse was selected by the Ruler of the universe to give the world a method of communication of thought and ideas which was destined to create a greater revolution than any military hero has caused among the nations.[9]

60

June 8, 1845

Old Hickory's Firm Foundation

Exceedingly great and precious promises.

—2 PETER 1:4

A fter leaving the White House, Andrew Jackson returned to the Hermitage, his home east of Nashville, aged and ill. During an 1838 Presbyterian revival meeting, he gave his life to the Lord and joined a nearby church. The change in him was enormous, and he spent hours reading and studying his Bible, commentaries, and hymnbooks.[1]

One day in September 1843, a group of visitors came, and Jackson said, "There is a beautiful hymn on the subject of the exceeding great and precious promises of God to His people. It was a favorite hymn with my dear wife until the day of her death. It begins thus: 'How Firm a Foundation, ye saints of the Lord.' I wish you would sing it now."[2]

That hymn, based on 2 Peter 1:4, devotes its verses to various biblical promises, and these were very precious to Jackson. When his son-in-law, John Donelson, faced crippling problems, Jackson told him, "Go, read the

Scriptures. The joyful promises it contains will be a balsam to all your troubles, . . . a consolation to your troubled mind that is not to be found in the hurry and bustle of this world."[3]

At the beginning of 1845, Jackson's condition deteriorated. Jesse Elliott offered to send a sarcophagus that had been excavated in Palestine. Jackson wrote back, declining the tomb, saying, "I have prepared a humble depository for my mortal body beside . . . my beloved wife, where . . . we, I hope, shall rise together, clothed with the heavenly body promised to all who believe in our glorious Redeemer, who died for us, that we might live, and by whose atonement I hope for a blessed immortality."[4]

On Sunday, May 24, 1845, Jackson told his family, "Death has no terrors for me. . . . The Lord will take me to Himself; but what are my sufferings compared with those of the blessed Savior, who died on the accursed tree for me?"[5]

The following Thursday he told a visiting pastor, "Sir, I am in the hands of a merciful God. I have full confidence in His goodness and mercy. My lamp of life is nearly out, and the last glimmer has come. I am ready to depart. . . . The Bible is true. . . . Upon that sacred volume I rest my hope for eternal salvation through the merits and blood of our blessed Lord and Savior, Jesus Christ."[6]

That night, Jackson spoke of the comfort he received from the hymns, and from memory he recited a verse of "How Firm a Foundation."[7]

> When through the deep waters I call them to go
> The rivers of sorrow shall not thee overflow.

On Sunday, June 8, Dr. John Esselman entered Jackson's room and saw him in a chair, near death. As the attendants picked Jackson up, he lost consciousness, and Dr. Esselman pronounced, "He is gone." They laid Jackson's emaciated body on the bed.[8]

But Jackson jolted them all by opening his eyes and asking to see his grandchildren. They filed into the room, and he blessed each one, telling them "they must all keep holy the Sabbath Day and read the New Testament."[9]

"My dear children," he said, "do not grieve for me; it is true I am going to leave you; I am well aware of my situation; I have suffered much bodily pain, but my sufferings are but as nothing compared with that which our blessed Savior endured upon that accursed cross, that we might all be saved who put their trust in Him."[10]

Dr. Esselman wrote:

He delivered one of the most impressive lectures on the subject of religion that I have ever heard. He spoke for nearly half an hour, and apparently with the power of inspiration; for he spoke with calmness, with strength, and, indeed, with animation. . . . In conclusion, he said: "My dear children, and friends, and servants, I hope and trust to meet you all in heaven, both white and black."[11]

Everyone in the room burst into tears, and Jackson, rousing once more, said, "What is the matter with my dear children? Have I alarmed you? Oh, do not cry. Be good children and, we will all meet in heaven."[12] His eyes closed, and he fell asleep.

At his funeral three thousand people joined their voices to sing:

How firm a foundation, ye saints of the Lord
Is laid for your faith in His excellent word.[13]

61

February 23, 1848

Death in the House

Jesus said to her, "I am the resurrection and the life."

—JOHN 11:25

After his one-term presidency, John Quincy Adams, fit and feisty, ran for Congress and was elected to the House of Representatives, where, based on his Christian convictions, he fought slavery tooth and nail. His last public appearance in Boston was to preside over an injustice committed against an African-American slave.[1]

Adams traveled and spoke and worked like a man half his age. He had always exercised and kept himself fit, and he was famous for his early-morning skinny-dipping in the Potomac River. But, in 1846, he began suffering bouts of paralysis. This didn't keep him from his duties in the House of Representatives, where he served alongside a new congressman named Abraham Lincoln.

On Sunday, February 20, Adams went to church both morning and afternoon, and that evening his wife read him a sermon about redeeming the time. The next morning he rose early and ascended the steps of the Capitol, cheerfully and jauntily.

As the House conducted its business, the Speaker rose for an item of business when a cry rang out in the House chamber: "Mr. Adams is dead! Stop! Stop! Mr. Adams!"

The former president had been about to rise from his seat when he keeled over and was caught by a fellow congressman. Several nearby colleagues rushed to his side, shouting, "What's the matter? Has he fainted?"

Adams was lifted onto the clerk's table as the House quickly adjourned. Someone fetched a sofa, and his friends carried him into the Rotunda where the entire Congress gathered around him while five members who were physicians attended him. From the Rotunda, he was carried to the office of the Speaker of the House, where he rallied enough to ask about his wife before lapsing into unconsciousness. A few minutes later he rallied again and spoke his final words: "This is the last of earth! I am content!"

There in the Speaker's office, John Quincy Adams remained through Washington's birthday, passing away on February 23.[2]

The next day the Speaker of the House, Robert C. Winthrop, rose before a somber Congress to say,

> On Monday, the 21st instant, John Quincy Adams sunk in his seat, in presence of us all, by a sudden illness, from which he never recovered; and he died, in the Speaker's room, at a quarter past seven o'clock last evening, with the officers of the House and the delegation of his own Massachusetts around him. . . .
>
> After a life of eighty years devoted from its earliest maturity to the public service, he has at length gone to his rest. He has been privileged to die at his post; to fall while in the discharge of his duties; to expire beneath the roof of the capitol; and to have his last scene associated forever, in history, with the birthday of that illustrious patriot, whose just discernment brought him first into the service of his country.[3]

The federal government paused for Adams's funeral at noon on Saturday, February 26, in the Capitol. President Polk, the cabinet, the members of Congress, the justices of the Supreme Court—all were there. Rev. R. R. Gurley, chaplain of the House of Representatives, gave the sermon. The verse that came to his mind and rang from his voice in the hallowed chambers of the Capitol that day was John 11:25. Considering how Adams was one of the last alive to have known George Washington, I cannot help wondering if Gurley chose this verse in part because it was the verse Martha Washington had inscribed on the tomb of the nation's first president. Whether intentional or not, it's remarkable how the words of John 11:25 link the deaths of Washington and Adams and bring to a full-circled close a most unique era of American history.

Gurley preached:

Hear, then, the great announcement of the Son of God: "I am the resurrection and the life, and whosoever believeth in me, though he were dead yet shall he live, and whosoever liveth and believeth in me shall never die." Is it strange that he . . . whose virtues and memory we now pay this sad, final, solemn tribute of honor and affection, should, in the last conversation I ever had with him, have expressed both regret and astonishment at the indifference among too many of our public men to the truths and ordinances of our holy religion? Is it to affect our hearts that he has been permitted to fall in the midst of us, to arouse us from this insensibility, and cause us to press towards the gates of the eternal city of God? Let us bless God for another great example to shine upon us, that another star (we humble trust) is planted amid the heavenly constellations to guide us to eternity![4]

62

September 17, 1849

Go Down, Moses

The LORD God of the Hebrews has sent me to you, saying,
"Let My people go."

—EXODUS 7:16

For the first twenty-five years of her life, Harriet Tubman was a slave in Maryland and spent much of her time behind oxen, loading and unloading wood and carrying heavy loads, which gave her the endurance of an athlete.[1] She was whipped in childhood, and as a young person she was injured when her owner threw a metal weight at her. Soon afterward, she began praying for God to convert him.

> I groaned and prayed for old master: "Oh Lord, convert master! Oh Lord, change that man's heart." Appears I prayed all the time, about my work, everywhere, I prayed and I groaned to the Lord. When I went to the horse trough to wash my face, I took up the water in my hand and I said, "Oh Lord, wash me, make me clean." Then I take up something

193

to wipe my face, and I said, "Oh Lord, wipe away all my sin . . . ." I prayed . . . for master till the first of March; and all the time he was bringing people to look at me and trying to sell me. Then we heard that some of us was going to be sold to go with the chain-gang down to the cotton and rice fields, and they said I was going, and my brothers and sisters. Then I changed my prayer. First of March, I began to pray, "Oh Lord, if You ain't never going to change that man's heart, kill him, Lord, and take him out of the way." Next thing I heard, old master wad dead.[2]

On September 17, 1849, Harriet mounted a daring escape, traveling to Pennsylvania and to freedom. But she couldn't escape the burden she felt for her oppressed family and friends: "I was free, and they should be free. I would make a home in the North and bring them there, God helping me. Oh, how I prayed then. I said to the Lord, 'I'm going to hold steady on to You, and I know You'll see me through.'"[3]

Harriet traveled silently and secretly, back and forth, escorting slaves to the North. Rewards for her capture ranged from $12,000 to $40,000. But her pursuers never caught her. They simply knew she was in their area when black men, women, and children began disappearing from the plantations. She was called Moses, and her great song—the Song of the Underground Railroad—was "Go down, Moses . . . tell old Pharaoh, 'Let my people go.'"

Harriet made nineteen trips back and forth from North to South, each with narrow escapes and heart-stopping drama. She never lost a passenger on the Underground Railroad, but neither would she let a passenger turn back. Her biographer said:

By night she traveled, many times on foot, over mountains, through forests, across rivers, mid perils by land, perils by water, perils from enemies, perils among false brethren. Sometimes members of her party would become exhausted, foot-sore, and bleeding, and declare they could not go on, they must stay where they dropped down, and die; others would think a voluntary return to slavery better than being overtaken and carried back . . . then there was no remedy but force; the revolver carried by this bold and daring pioneer would be pointed at their heads. "Dead [Negros] tell no tales," said Harriet; "Go on or die." And so she compelled them to drag their weary limbs on their northward journey.[4]

When asked how it was possible for her to keep traveling back and forth without fear, she said, "Why, . . . it wasn't me. 'Twas the Lord. I always told him, 'I trust to you. I don't know where to go or what to do, but I expect you to lead me, and he always did.'"[5]

During the Civil War, Tubman served as a Union spy, at one point leading an assault in the Combahee River Raid to free seven hundred slaves. After the war she made her home in Auburn, New York. When she died at age ninety-three, she was hailed a hero and buried with military honors.

63

June 5, 1851

Book of the Century

*I have called you friends, for all things that I heard from
My Father I have made known to you.*

—JOHN 15:15

As a child, Harriet Beecher Stowe loved her father's study and his "great writing-chair, on one arm of which lay open always his Cruden's Concordance and his Bible. Here I loved to retreat and niche myself down in a quiet corner with my favorite books around me. I had a kind of sheltered feeling as I thus sat and watched my father writing, turning to his books, and speaking from time to time with himself in a loud, earnest whisper."[1]

When she was a young teenager, Harriet made the greatest decision of her life. Her father, Rev. Lyman Beecher, preached from John 15:15 about Jesus as our friend. Harriet later said that her father

spoke in direct, simple, and tender language of the great love of Christ and His care for the soul. He pictured Him as patient with our errors, compassionate with our weaknesses, and sympathetic for our sorrows. He went on to say how He was ever near us, enlightening our ignorance, guiding our wanderings, comforting our sorrows with a love unwearied by faults, unchilled by ingratitude, till at last He should present us faultless before the throne of His glory with exceeding joy.

I sat intent and absorbed. Oh! how much I needed just such a friend. . . . Like a flash it came over me . . . I would trust Him . . . As I left the church to walk home, it seemed to me as if Nature herself were hushing her breath to hear the music of heaven.

As soon as father came home and was seated in his study, I went up to him and fell in his arms saying, "Father I have given myself to Jesus."[2]

Jesus spoke John 15:15 on the last night of His natural life as He walked through the darkened streets of Jerusalem toward the Garden of Gethsemane. His disciples had been His students, His followers, and His messengers, but now they were about to become the recipients of the grace He was gaining for them by dying on their behalf. That level of love raised them to the status of friends—friends of God Himself. The same is true for Christ's followers of all the ages, and it was this awareness that changed Harriet's life and led her on the path that helped change history.

In 1832, Harriet, twenty-one, moved to Cincinnati and married a seminary professor, Calvin Ellis Stowe, and the two became involved in aiding fugitive slaves escaping from Kentucky. Harriet also began writing, and her devotional materials, Bible studies, and fiction became popular throughout the nation.

When family friend, newspaper publisher Elijah Lovejoy, was murdered for his abolitionist views, the Beecher family reacted in horror. Harriet's brother, Edward, wrote her, saying, "Now, Hattie, if I could use a pen as you can, I would write something that would make this whole nation feel what an accursed thing slavery is."

Reading the letter, Harriet said, "I will write something. I will if I live."[3] Shortly afterward, as she attended a communion service at church, scenes for a book unfolded in her mind. Returning home, she began working on *Uncle Tom's Cabin*.

On June 5, 1851, the first segment of her book was published in the *National Era* as part of a forty-week serial. The story seized the nation's heart, and Harriet credited its success to the Lord. "I was but the humblest of instruments in His hand," she said. "To Him alone should be given all the praise."[4]

On March 13, 1852, a Boston publisher turned the serial into a book, which sold for fifty-six cents a copy.[5] A whopping three thousand copies of her book flew from the shelves the first day, and a second edition came out within a week. In its first year, three hundred thousand copies were sold in America and over a million copies in Great Britain. People stayed up all night reading the story, and Harriet became "the most talked-of woman in the world."[6] *Uncle Tom's Cabin* became the best-selling book of the century, apart from the Bible, and so inflamed the nation against slavery that social critics credit it with setting the stage for the Civil War.

Harriet Beecher Stowe went on to write many books and undertake many ministries, but she was always known as "the little woman who wrote the book that made this great war."[7]

Late in her life, Harriet wrote her son, Charlie, after she had been sorting through her lifetime of correspondence. She wanted to give him perspective for life:

> It is affecting to me to recall things that strongly moved me years ago, that filled my thoughts and made me anxious when the occasion and emotion have wholly vanished from my mind. But I thank God there is *one* thing running through all of them from the time I was thirteen years old, and that is the intense unwavering sense of Christ's educating, guiding presence and care. It is all that remains now.[8]

64

July 5, 1852

Frederick Douglass and the Fourth of July

Your hands are full of blood.

—ISAIAH 1:15

Frederick Douglass was done with the lash. As a spirited black teenager, he'd been sent by his master to face the wrath of Edward Covey, whose specialty was breaking slaves like a cowboy would break a horse. Covey's four-hundred-acre farm was called Mt. Misery, and for months the sixteen-year-old experienced hell on earth. Then one day, Douglass decided to fight back. He wrapped his hands around Covey's throat and the two men fought hand to hand for two hours until the torturer limped away from exhaustion. Douglass was never whipped again. As soon as he found half a chance, he escaped bondage and arrived in the North with a Bible in his hand. At age twenty-two, he was licensed to preach by the Quarterly Conference of the African Methodist Episcopal (A.M.E.) Zion Church in New Bedford, Massachusetts.[1]

One of Douglass's biographers points out that his relationship with Christianity was complicated.[2] Douglass never got over his revulsion that some Christians defended the institution of slavery. He knew that a true reading of both the Bible and the American Constitution stuck a knife into the heart of human trafficking, and he often quoted from both. His ringing declarations for abolition and liberty were based on the freedom proclaimed by Christ in Scripture, and today Douglass is known as the Father of the Civil Rights Movement.

Perhaps his most famous sermon was "What to a Slave Is the Fourth of July," delivered on July 5, 1852, to the Rochester Ladies' Anti-Slavery Society in Rochester, New York, quoting extensively from Isaiah 1:12–17, the passage in which God decried Judah for their sins against one another. The Lord told His people He was tired of their religious festivals, Sabbath days, and sacred gatherings, for there was no love or righteousness in the land. He was done with hearing their prayers, for they were treating one another with cruelty and prejudice. The Lord condemned the violence of Jerusalem, telling the residents,

> Your hands are full of blood.
> Wash yourselves, make yourselves clean;
> Put away the evil of your doings from before My eyes.
> Cease to do evil,
> Learn to do good;
> Seek justice,
> Rebuke the oppressor;
> Defend the fatherless,
> Plead for the widow.
>
> —ISAIAH 1:15–17

A true celebration of the Fourth of July, Douglass knew, would involve all these things. Looking at the crowd, he acknowledged that July 4 was "the birthday of your National Independence," but he added, "I am not included within the pale of this glorious anniversary! Your high independence only reveals the immeasurable distance between us."

We can hear Douglass's soaring voice in this paragraph as though we were there:

> Standing with God and the crushed and bleeding slave on this occasion, I will, in the name of humanity which is outraged, in the name of liberty which is fettered, in the name of the constitution and the Bible, which are disregarded and trampled upon, dare to call in question and to denounce, with all the emphasis I can command, everything that serves to perpetuate slavery—the great sin and shame of America!

"What, to the American slave, is your 4th of July?" Douglass asked. "I answer: a day that reveals to him, more than all other days in the year, the gross injustice and cruelty to which he is the constant victim."

Then Douglass was ready to go straight to the Bible, to the prophet Isaiah, and to remind Americans they are not excused from the truths proclaimed by God in the Bible:

> In the language of Isaiah, the American church might be well addressed, "Bring no more vain ablations; incense is an abomination unto me: the new moons and Sabbaths, the calling of assemblies, I cannot [endure]; it is iniquity even the solemn meeting. Your new moons and your appointed feasts my soul hateth. They are a trouble to me; I am weary to bear them; and when ye spread forth your hands I will hide mine eyes from you. Yea! when ye make many prayers, I will not hear. Your hands are full of blood; cease to do evil, learn to do well; seek judgment; relieve the oppressed; judge for the fatherless; plead for the widow."

Then Douglass made a prediction and quoted once more from the ancient prophet, this time from Isaiah 59:1 about the power of God's arm, saying, "There are forces in operation, which must inevitably work the downfall of slavery. 'The arm of the Lord is not shortened,' and the doom of slavery is certain."[3]

Christianity at its best stands up for the oppressed—victims of sexual trafficking, the homeless, the fatherless, the prisoner, the poor, the hurting, the unborn. As Isaiah said long ago:

> Cease to do evil,
> Learn to do good;
> Seek justice,
> Rebuke the oppressor;
> Defend the fatherless,
> Plead for the widow.
> "Come now, and let us reason together,"
> Says the LORD,
> "Though your sins are like scarlet,
> They shall be as white as snow."

—ISAIAH 1:16–18

September 23, 1857

Revival Sweeps the Country

Let us therefore come boldly to the throne of grace, that we
may obtain mercy and find grace to help in time of need.

—HEBREWS 4:16

In the mid-1800s, a tailor named Jeremiah Lanphier moved to Manhattan and established a clothing business. When a local ministry organization wanted to engage him for evangelistic work, he closed his shop and became a lay missionary on the streets of New York, headquartered in lower Manhattan near the present 9/11 Memorial.[1]

He began his new ministry on July 1, 1857, and began working up and down the streets of New York City, visiting the poor and needy. A financial panic was confounding Wall Street, and Lanphier noticed throngs of businessmen hurrying along their way, their faces careworn and their eyes glazed. He began to envision a noontime prayer meeting where men and women of commerce and business might come even if they could drop in for only a few minutes. "Perhaps they would find strength and guidance there," Lanphier thought.[2]

Lanphier developed and distributed a leaflet to announce these noontime prayer meetings, which were to commence on Wednesday, September 23, 1857. The purpose, wrote Lanphier, was "to give merchants, mechanics, clerks, strangers, and businessmen generally, an opportunity . . . to lift up their hearts and voices to the throne of grace."

The phrase "the throne of grace" comes from Hebrews 4:16. The writer of Hebrews was discussing the ascension of Jesus Christ into heaven following His death and resurrection. Having finished His work on earth, Jesus had ascended back to the throne of God where He now serves as our great high priest. He was tempted in every way, but He never sinned, so by His righteous life and conquering resurrection, He is able to advocate for us on the throne. We should think of prayer, then, as the act of confidently approaching the "throne of grace" where we can find mercy and grace to help us in our times of need.

This was exactly what the business community of New York needed, but when the day came for the first prayer meeting, no one showed up. At least, not at first. For a half hour Lanphier prayed alone. But at 12:30 p.m. he heard footsteps. Eventually six people gathered. The next week twenty showed up and the week after that he had forty.

After that the floodgates broke. Soon churches were overflowing with daily prayer meetings across the city. Fire departments and police stations opened their facilities for prayer, and local businesses set aside rooms for their employees to pray. Thousands came to Christ, with newspapers reporting hundreds of incidents from the revival. The *New York Tribune* devoted entire editions to the revival, and the headline in the *New York Press* was: "Revival Sweeps the Country."

And it did! The movement swept the Eastern Seaboard and pushed westward into the frontier. One man reported, "I am from Omaha, Nebraska. On my journey east I have found a continuous prayer meeting all the way. It was a prayer meeting two thousand miles long."[3]

In Chicago multitudes were converted. "The religious interest now existing in this city is very remarkable," one man said. "The Metropolitan

Hall is crowded to suffocation. The interest in [the revival] is beyond anything ever known in this city, and exceeds anything I have ever seen in my life. Some who have come to the city on business have become so distressed about their condition as sinners before God that they have entirely forgotten their business in their earnestness of their desire for salvation."[4]

One Chicago citizen, a twenty-one-year-old fellow, was so galvanized by the revival he entered evangelistic work: D. L. Moody.

Citywide awakenings struck Cincinnati, Louisville, Cleveland, Detroit, Indianapolis, St. Louis, and innumerable smaller cities and towns. In New Haven, nearly all the students of Yale College were converted, though some had been "very bitter scoffers."[5]

New England was transformed as businesses shut down at noon, and bars and taverns became houses of prayer. In Washington, President Franklin Pierce joined the daily prayer meetings.

One historian said, "A canopy of holy and awesome revival influence—in reality the presence of the Holy Spirit—seemed to hang like an invisible cloud over many parts of the United States."[6] From the United States the revival spread to Ireland, Scotland, Wales, and England.

For two years approximately fifty thousand people a week came to Christ. Within a year of the start of the Fulton Street Prayer Meetings, over a million new converts joined America's churches, and thousands of existing church members were born again—all at a time when the total population of the United States was about thirty million.[7]

It's remarkable that no great evangelists accentuated this revival, and it wasn't sustained by massive evangelistic meetings or famous preachers. Except for the largely unknown layman Jeremiah Lanphier, no prominent names are attached to this movement. The revival of 1857–1858 is often called the Third Great Awakening or the Prayer Revival, for it was sparked by "merchants, mechanics, clerks, strangers, and businessmen generally" who lifted up their hearts and voices to the throne of grace.

January 1, 1863

The Day the Nation Felt Clean

Alleluia! For the Lord God Omnipotent reigns!

—REVELATION 19:6

New Year's Day 1863 was a bright, sunny, and chilly Tuesday along the Eastern Seaboard. In Washington, Abraham Lincoln's staff brought him a draft of the Emancipation Proclamation, and he suggested a change in the superscription. While the correction was made, he hosted a large reception, and it wasn't until midafternoon that he entered his office to sign the document. As he picked up the pen, he noticed his hand was trembling. Puzzled at first, he recalled he had just shaken hands with hundreds of people. Relaxing his arm, he affixed his signature and by evening the news was traveling by wire across the land.

Civil Rights activist Frederick Douglass was among three thousand people—mostly African-Americans—who gathered at the Tremont (Baptist) Temple in Boston. The crowd's attitude was, "I'll believe it when I see it." Douglass described the excited tension of the crowd as everyone was waiting for "the first flash of electric wires" with news of Lincoln's proclamation. Many in the crowd, he said, were pessimistic and cynical. They were ready to stage a demonstration and speak their mind because they had been disappointed before. But others were hopeful and truly believed the day of liberation had come.

"Every moment of waiting chilled our hopes and strengthened our fears," Douglass recalled.

> A line of messengers was established between the telegraph office and the platform of Tremont Temple, and the time was occupied with brief speeches. . . . But speaking or listening to speeches was not the thing for which the people had come together. The time for argument was passed. It was not logic, but the trump of jubilee which everybody wanted to hear. We were waiting and listening as for a bolt from the sky, which should rend the fetters of four million slaves. We were watching, as it were, by the dim light of the stars, for the dawn of a new day. We were longing for the answer to the agonizing prayers of centuries. . . . We wanted to join in the shout of freedom and in the anthem of the redeemed.

For some reason, the news was delayed. Eight o'clock came with no word. Still, the people waited. Nine o'clock. Shadows and sadness began to intrude on the spirit of the night. Ten o'clock came, "when patience was well-nigh exhausted, and suspense was becoming agony."

Suddenly a man—"I think it was Judge Russell," recalled Douglass—pushed his way through the crowd and shouted, "It is coming! It is one of the wires!" The crowd went wild, shouting, weeping, praying, singing, roaring with joy and gladness until every voice was exhausted. Then a great old African-American preacher came to the stage and began leading the crowd in an old spiritual, which said: "Sound the loud timbrel o'er Egypt's dark sea, Jehovah has triumphed, His people are free."[1]

In another part of town, additional thousands had filled the Boston Music Hall, where officials had hastily planned a concert to celebrate "the day of affirmation of the President's Emancipation Proclamation, whereby the nation suddenly felt clean before God and the world."[2]

The hall echoed with the music of orchestras and choirs performing Beethoven, Mendelssohn, and Handel, along with "The Star-Spangled Banner" and "The Battle Hymn of the Republic." Ralph Waldo Emerson made a surprise appearance. The hall, bedecked with flags and banners, was taut with the tension and unbearable anticipation.

Finally someone ascended the platform with news the proclamation was coming over the wire, and the crowd erupted in pandemonium—a "demonstration of uncontainable enthusiasm, such cheers, and waving of handkerchiefs, and throwing up of hats, as was scarcely ever seen. . . . It lasted many minutes." The music resumed at last, "and in the Hallelujah Chorus, the joy and praise and confidence of the occasion reached their climax."[3]

The Hallelujah Chorus, a climactic part of George Frederic Handel's oratorio *Messiah*, which was composed in 1741, is based on the passage in Revelation 19 that predicts how the angelic choirs of heaven will erupt in peals of "Hallelujah" at the moment of Christ's return to earth. The recurring, driving crescendo of "Hallelujah" expressed the joy felt that night. As one group sang "Jehovah has triumphed; His people are free," another group a few miles away joined their voices in:

Hallelujah, Hallelujah, Hallelujah, Hallelujah, Hallelujah!
Hallelujah, Hallelujah, Hallelujah, Hallelujah, Hallelujah!
For the Lord God omnipotent reigneth!

July 5, 1863

Wrestling in Prayer for Gettysburg

He is always wresting in prayer for you.

—COLOSSIANS 4:12 NIV

Brigadier General James Fowler Rusling, a dedicated Christian and a Methodist, wrote a fascinating book, *Men and Things I Saw in Civil War Days*, in which he related his encounter with Abraham Lincoln following the Battle of Gettysburg. The meeting took place on Sunday, July 5, 1863, which was the Sunday after Gettysburg and Vicksburg.

Rusling was visiting his superior, General Daniel E. Sickles, who had been wounded at Gettysburg and was recovering in a private home in Washington on F Street. Sickles was a strange character whose reputation was clouded and unsavory. But at Gettysburg he had fought bravely, and as a result of his injuries had lost his right leg—it had been amputated above the knee.

Rusling arrived about three in the afternoon and found his general resting in a hospital stretcher on the first floor. As the two men conversed,

Abraham Lincoln strode into the room with his son, Tad. Hearing of Sickle's wound, they had come by horseback, escorted by a squad of cavalry. Rusling wrote:

> Mr. Lincoln dropped into a chair, and crossing his prodigious arms and legs, soon fell into questioning Sickles as to all the phases of the combat at Gettysburg. He asked first, of course, as to General Sickles' own ghastly wound; when and how it happened, and how he was getting on, and encouraged him; then passed next to our great causalities there, and how the wounded were being cared for; and finally came to the magnitude and significance of the victory there.

General Sickles, reclining on his stretcher, puffed away on a cigar and answered Lincoln's questions, giving a full account of the battle from his perspective. Occasionally, he winced in pain as an orderly treated his fevered stump. "But he never dropped his cigar nor lost the thread of conversation."

Finally Lincoln's questions ended, and for a moment there was silence in the room. General Sickles took a puff on his cigar, looked at Lincoln, and said, "Well, Mr. President, I beg pardon, but what did you think about Gettysburg? What was your opinion of things while we were campaigning and fighting up there?"

To the surprise of all in the room, Lincoln said he hadn't been very worried about the outcome of the battle.

"You were not?" Sickles exclaimed, amazed. "Why, we heard that you Washington folks were a good deal excited, and you certainly had good cause to be. For it was nip and tuck with us a good deal of the time!"

"Yes, I know that," said Lincoln. "And I suppose some of us were a little rattled. Indeed, some of the cabinet talked of Washington's being captured and ordered a gunboat or two here, and even went so far as to send some government archives abroad, and wanted me to go too, but I refused. . . . No, General Sickles, I had no fears of Gettysburg!"

"Why not, Mr. President? How was that? Pretty much everybody down here, we heard, was more or less panicky."

Lincoln's remarkable reply harkened back to the concept of wrestling in prayer, which is described in Colossians 4:12. The apostle Paul told the Colossians that their friend Epaphras was "always laboring fervently for you in prayers." The term "laboring fervently" means intense, ardent, and heartfelt. It conveys the idea of "wrestling in prayer" (NIV).

> General Sickles, I had no fears of Gettysburg, and if you really want to know I will tell you why. Of course, I don't want you and Colonel Rusling here to say anything about this—at least not now. People might laugh if it got out, you know. But the fact is, in the very pinch of the campaign there, I went to my room one day and got down on my knees and prayed Almighty God for victory at Gettysburg. I told Him that this was His country, and the war was His war, but that we really couldn't stand another Fredericksburg or Chancellorsville. And then and there I made a solemn vow with my Maker, that if He would stand by you boys at Gettysburg, I would stand by Him. And thus after wrestling with the Almighty in prayer, I don't know how it was, and it is not for me to explain, but somehow or other, a sweet comfort crept into my soul, that God Almighty had taken the whole business there into His own hands, and we were bound to win at Gettysburg. And He *did* stand by you boys at Gettysburg, and now I will stand by Him. No, General Sickles, I had no fears of Gettysburg, and that is the *why*![1]

This record seems plausible to me because I've had similar experiences—nothing, of course, compared to a Civil War battle but battles of my own—and, like all God's children, I've had to learn about wrestling in prayer, pleading fervently, and casting my burdens on the Lord. We sometimes face problems we cannot solve, challenges we cannot meet, and hurts we cannot heal. But we can wrestle in prayer and somehow—we don't know quite how it is—a sweet comfort comes to us. The psalmist said, "Cast your burden on the LORD, and He shall sustain you" (Psalm 55:22), and Peter told us to humble ourselves under the mighty hand of God, "casting all your care upon Him, for He cares for you" (1 Peter 5:6–7).

As Lincoln said on another occasion: "I have been driven many times upon my knees by the overwhelming conviction that I had nowhere else to go. My own wisdom and that of all about me seemed insufficient for that day."[2]

September 6, 1863

Revival in the Ranks

*That whoever believes in Him should not perish but have
eternal life.*

—JOHN 3:15

The Civil War was the bloodiest in American history, and experts have revised upward their estimates of fatalities to as many as 750,000.[1] The unspeakable carnage drove soldiers of both sides to Christ, and the resulting spiritual revival among both Union and Confederate forces is one of the most underreported aspects of the War.

Between 100,000 and 200,000 Union soldiers acknowledged Christ during the War, and approximately 150,000 Confederate troops did the same. Additional thousands were revived in their faith.[2] Among the converts were generals Braxton Bragg, Joseph E. Johnston, and John Bell Hood.[3]

Chaplains stayed busy day and night: preaching, soul-winning, distributing tracts and Bibles, baptizing, comforting, and burying. Young Dwight

L. Moody served as a Union chaplain. After the Battle of Murfreesboro, he visited a wounded soldier who asked him to help him die. Moody tried to share Christ, but the man replied, "He can't save me; I have sinned all my life."

Moody began reading from John 3 and came to the words, "And as Moses lifted up the serpent in the wilderness, even so must the Son of Man be lifted up, that whoever believes in Him should not perish but have eternal life" (verses 14–15). The soldier interrupted, saying, "I never knew that was in the Bible. Read it again." Moody read it again as the wounded man leaned forward on his elbow, his troubled expression giving way to peaceful calm. Lying back on his cot, he began repeating the words over and over, dying with those words on his lips.[4]

This was Moody's constant theme, and later it would set the tone of his great evangelistic ministry. God loves us, and He designed a plan in which He Himself would become a human—fully righteous in every way—and die on the cross for our sins. In the Old Testament this was foreshadowed by an event in which—during an outbreak of poisonous snake bites—Moses hung a bronze serpent on a pole, and everyone who looked at it was healed. In a similar way, Jesus became sin for us, was slain on a pole, and all who look to Him are saved from the sickness of sin and thereby have eternal life.

This message rang up and down the ranks of both armies during the Civil War. Confederate chaplain John Williams Jones described a meeting on Sunday, September 6, 1863, in which eighty-two soldiers were baptized in the river while five thousand soldiers, from the general to privates, lined the banks. That evening Jones traveled to another spot:

> When I got up to preach, the light of the fire-stands revealed at least 5,000 men seated on the rude logs, or on the ground, and with upturned, eager faces, ready to drink in every word the preacher had to say. . . . I tried to tell in simple, earnest worlds the old, old story of Jesus and His love. I could see in the dim light the intense interest and the starting

tear. At the close of the service, those interested in their souls' salvation and desiring an interest in the prayers of God's people were invited to come and give us their hand, and they continued to press forward until we had counted over 600.[5]

Later Jones added this poignant account:

In the summer of 1864, I preached a good deal in Wright's Georgia Brigade, where we had a precious revival and a large number of professions of conversion. The brigade was stationed at the point where the opposing lines were some distance apart, and I used to stand on a plat of grass in front of the trenches while the men would gather close around me. . . . One night, with a full moon shedding its light upon us, we had an unusually large congregation and a service of more than ordinary interest and power. A large number came forward for prayer . . . and at the close of the service I received nine for baptism, and had just announced that I would administer the ordinance in a pond nearby at 9 o'clock the next morning, when the "long roll" beat, the brigade formed at once, and in a few minutes were on the march to one of the series of bloody battles which we had that summer. Several days later the brigade returned to its quarters, and I went back to resume my meetings and look up my candidates for baptism. I found alas! That out of the nine received, three had been killed, two were wounded, and one was a prisoner, so that there were only three left for me to baptize.[6]

August 16, 1864

Providence Spring

*Moses lifted his hand and struck the rock twice with his
rod; and water came out abundantly.*

—Numbers 20:11

When the Civil War erupted, a Michigan teenager named John L. Maile enlisted with the Union, served bravely, and rose to the rank of lieutenant. During the Battle in the Wilderness, he was captured and shipped in a cattle car to the infamous POW camp at Andersonville, deep in the heart of Georgia, arriving on May 23, 1864.

The prison was an open meadow of twenty-six acres, surrounded by a fifteen-foot-high stockade fence. Pigeon roosts were manned by guards ready to shoot prisoners who crossed the dead line that framed the interior of the stockade.

The fort was built to house ten thousand prisoners, but Maile found himself crammed among thirty-three thousand starving, exposed men. The only source of water was a small brook that ran through the meadow, and this was where the prisoners drank, washed, and used the latrine. It was downstream from the Confederate camp, and the creek "became a vast cesspool on which boundless swarms of flies settled down and laid their eggs," Maile wrote. "The odor could be detected miles away. . . . A terrible water famine set in, with the result that many of the ailing ones became insane with thirst."[1]

Soon hundreds were dying of disease.

One evening Maile heard a group of prisoners singing the doxology, and he joined them around a pine stump. An emaciated cavalry sergeant named Shepherd from Columbus, Ohio, who had been an honored preacher of the gospel before the War, was sitting on the stump. The others recognized Shepherd as a spiritual leader among them, despite his physical weakness. He frequently led prayers when POWs died and did what he could to encourage the living.

On this occasion, Sergeant Shepherd had led those nearby in singing the doxology in order to gather a crowd. About twenty-five "unkempt, starving men" gathered and joined the song, and its strains reminded them of home and family and the worship services they had enjoyed before the War.[2]

As the singing died down, Sergeant Shepherd said something to this effect: "I have today read in the book of Numbers of Moses striking the rock from which water gushed out for the ample supply of man and beast. I tell you God must strike a rock in Andersonville or we shall all die of thirst. And if there is no rock here, He can smite the ground and bring forth water to supply our desperate needs. Of this I am sure; let us ask Him to do this."

The story from Numbers was an apt text for this thirsty group of men, dying for lack of fresh water at Andersonville. When the Israelites needed water in the desert, Moses struck the rock and the water gushed forth. Sergeant Shepherd was desperate enough to ask God for a similar miracle inside the walls of the stockade.

Pointing to an uncombed, unwashed, ragged comrade close by, he said, "Will the brother from Chicago pray?" One man after another prayed for water, asking God, as it were, to strike the rock again and provide needed water for the people. The impromptu prayer meeting lasted for about an hour, and the men concluded by again singing the doxology. As they dismissed, Shepherd admonished them, "Boys, when you awake during the night offer to God a little prayer for water. Do the same many times tomorrow, and let us meet here in the evening to pray again for water."[3]

Prayers went up among the prisoners for several days. Then one morning as they awoke, "an ominous stillness pervaded nature." By midmorning, black clouds began rolling in, and the camp was deluged by a long-lasting cloudburst. As Maile vividly recalled,

> Crashes of thunder broke over our heads and flashes of lightning swished around us as if the air was filled with short circuits. . . . As the mighty deluge swept through the clearing west of the prison, we bowed our heads in preparation of submersion. . . . When it came upon us the sensation was as if a million buckets of water were being poured upon us at once.[4]

When the storm finally ended, a prisoner near the north gate began shouting, "A spring! A spring!"

Maile later wrote in his memoirs, *Prison Life in Andersonville*, he saw "the vent of a spring of purest crystal water, which shot up into the air in a column, and, falling in a fanlike spray, went babbling down the grade."[5]

Some nearby prisoners described how, during the storm, a lightning bolt had struck inside the deadline, releasing the underground spring.[6] It was as dramatic as Moses striking the rock. A trough was built, bringing the endless supply of water to the prisoners, and the spring still gurgles to this day.

If you visit Andersonville, you can tour the National Prisoner of War Museum, then walk over to a stone shelter and see Providence Spring and its inscription: "God smote the hillside and gave them drink—August 16, 1864."[7]

April 14, 1865

Lincoln's Last Words

Have faith in God.

—MARK 11:22

Abraham Lincoln was born near the Kentucky camp meetings that helped spark the Second Great Awakening, but Lincoln's heart was not warmed by revival fire. He rejected frontier religion and the faith of his parents. As a young man he became a skeptic, an agnostic, maybe an atheist, and he was an avid reader of anti-Christian books. In the mid-1830s, Lincoln wrote a book disparaging the Bible and attacking the divinity of Christ. "The book was an attack upon the whole grounds of Christianity, and especially was it an attack upon the idea that Jesus was the Christ, the true and only-begotten Son of God, as the Christian world contends."[1]

Lincoln's friend Samuel Hill, fearing the book would doom Lincoln's political career, snatched it up and burned it in a stove "heated as hot as a furnace; and so Lincoln's book went up to the clouds in smoke."[2]

In 1849, Lincoln's father-in-law, Robert Todd, died of cholera. Lincoln traveled to Lexington to deal with the man's estate, and in Todd's impressive library he found a book on Christian apologetics: *The Christian's Defense, Containing a Fair Statement and Impartial Examination of the Leading Objections Urged by Infidels Against the Antiquity, Genuineness, Credibility, and Inspiration of the Holy Scriptures.*

Lincoln was gripped by the book and sought out its author, Dr. James Smith, a Presbyterian pastor in Lincoln's hometown of Springfield. Lincoln later told his brother-in-law, "I have been reading a work of Dr. Smith on the evidences of Christianity, and have heard him preach and converse on the subject, and I am now convinced of the truth of the Christian religion."[3]

Lincoln became an incessant student of the Bible and began drawing strength and insights from it. According to Stephen Mansfield, "He worked phrases from Scripture into his daily conversations with such ease that often his listeners did not realize until later he had mentioned a dozen verses from the Bible in a single visit with friends."[4]

After moving to Washington, Lincoln began attending services at a Presbyterian church near the White House. The pastor, Dr. Phineas Gurley, became Lincoln's spiritual advisor. "I like Gurley," Lincoln said. "He don't preach politics. I get enough of that through the week, and when I go to church I like to hear the Gospel."[5]

Gurley's pastoral care bore Lincoln through the horrors of the Civil War and the tragic death of his son Willie. Gurley later said, "I have had frequent and intimate conversations with him on the subject of the Bible. . . . In the latter days of his chastened and weary life, after the death of his son Willie and his visit to the battlefield of Gettysburg, he said, with tears in his eyes, that he had lost confidence in everything but God, and that he now believed his heart was changed and that he loved the Savior."[6]

On Good Friday, April 14, 1865, Abraham and Mary were sitting in Ford's Theatre, watching a production of "Our American Cousin." Lincoln leaned over and whispered that after the War, he didn't want to return immediately to Springfield. "We will go abroad among strangers where I can rest," he said. "We will visit the Holy Land. We will visit the Holy Land and see those places hallowed by the footsteps of the Savior. There is no place I so much desire to see as Jerusalem."[7]

"And with that word half spoken on his tongue, the bullet of the assassin entered his brain."[8]

Dr. Gurley rushed to the stricken president's side and was there the next morning when he died. Four days later, Gurley conducted Lincoln's funeral in the East Room of the White House. Perhaps calling to mind how Lincoln had told him he had lost confidence in everything but God, Gurley told the mourners:

> We admired his childlike simplicity, his freedom from guile and deceit, his staunch and sterling integrity, his kind and forgiving temper. . . . But more sublime than any of all these, more holy and influential, more beautiful, and strong, and sustaining, was his abiding confidence in God. . . . This was his noblest virtue, his grandest principle—the secret alike of his strength, his patience, and his success; and this, it seems to me, after being near him steadily and with him often for more than four years, is the principle by which, more than by any other, "He being dead, yet speaketh." By this he speaks to his successor in office, and charges him to "have faith in God." But this he speaks to the members of his cabinet, the men with whom he counseled so often and was associated so long, and he charges them to "have faith in God." By this he speaks to the officers and men of our noble army and navy, and, as they stand at their posts of duty and peril, he charges them to "have faith in God." By this he speaks to all who occupy positions of influence and authority in these sad and troublous times, and he charges them all to "have faith in God." By this he speaks to this great people as they sit in sackcloth today and weep for him with a bitter wailing, and refuse to be comforted, and he charges them to "have faith in God." And by this he will speak through the ages and to all rulers and peoples in every land . . . have confidence in God.[9]

November 20, 1866

The Christian General

The blood of Jesus Christ His Son cleanses us from all sin.

—1 JOHN 1:7

West Point graduate Oliver Otis Howard of Maine was stationed in Tampa, Florida, a town of about six hundred souls. One day he received a letter from his brother, Rowland, who had become a "pronounced Christian." Rowland wrote about his conversion and sent along a biography of a British military hero, Hedley Vicars, who had been converted to Christ while reading 1 John 1:7. As Howard sweltered in the Tampa heat, he read his brother's letter and plunged into Vicars's biography. When Howard came to the quotation of 1 John 1:7, it came alive to him. In this verse, John was reminding his readers of the great truth of the gospel. Jesus died for us, shedding His blood like that of a perfect sacrifice, taking our guilt upon Himself. By the power of His shed blood, we are forgiven, pronounced guiltless in God's sight, and cleansed from the stain of our sins. This message changed Howard's life.

He later recalled:

I had a small office building. . . . In that little office, with my Bible and Vicars' life in my hands, I found my way into a very vivid awakening and change, which were so remarkable that I have always set down this period as that of my conversion. It was the night of the last day of May 1857, when I had the feeling of sudden relief from the depression that had been long upon me. The joy of that night was so great that it would be difficult to attempt in any way to describe it. The next morning everything appeared to me to be changed—the sky was brighter, the trees more beautiful, and the songs of the birds were never before so sweet. . . . Captain Vicars . . . under the influence of a single verse of the First Epistle of John, "The blood of Christ cleanseth us from all sin," had experienced a wonderful change. . . . My own mind took a turn like that on reading the account of it. . . . The influence of the same Scripture produced that strong effect on me and caused me ever after to be a different man, with different hopes and different purposes in life.[1]

Oliver Howard was wonderfully converted to Christ, and his faith permeated every area of his life, including his military service. When the Civil War started, Howard was among the first Union officers to face combat, and he was wounded during the Battle of Fair Oaks when two bullets struck his arm. His brigade surgeon, a Dr. Palmer, came to his bedside and gently informed him that his arm should come off.

"All right," said Howard, "go ahead. Happy to lose only my arm."

He was carried to the amputating room, which was a gruesome place littered with severed arms, legs, and hands not yet carried off. Soldiers waited in line, their faces warped with anxiety, waiting their turn with the saw.

"On the long table I was nicely bolstered," recalled Howard. "A mixture of chloroform and gas was administered, and I slept quietly. Dr. Palmer amputated the arm above the elbow. When I awoke I was surprised to find the heavy burden was gone but was content and thankful."[2]

As soon as he had sufficiently recovered, Howard resumed leading his troops and became known as the Christian General because he promoted the cause of Christ at every opportunity. When no chaplain was available, he preached the gospel himself. He prayed alone and with others, studied God's Word, promoted revival, and sought to represent Christ to every man he commanded.

Near the end of the war, President Lincoln, knowing of Howard's Christian charity, requested he become commissioner of the Bureau of Refugees, Freedmen, and Abandoned Lands, "the first big federal social welfare agency in American history."[3] Its aim was to provide humanitarian help to the South and integrate the nearly four million former slaves into society. Howard pursued his mission with fervor, but he ran into a buzz saw of opposition from the new president, Andrew Johnson, and from white Southerners and Northern politicians unwilling to grant voting rights to blacks.

Though he was stymied in his efforts at genuine reconstruction, Howard would not be denied. He poured himself into feeding the indigent, building hospitals, establishing schools, and encouraging evangelism. On November 20, 1866, he spearheaded plans to establish a college in the nation's capital to train African-American students for the ministry. The school opened in 1867, admitting students, both men and women, both white and black, and he served the school as its president from 1869 to 1874.

Today in Washington thousands of students still attend that school, which is named for the one-armed Christian General—Howard University. All his work, all his energy, and all the results of his life came about for one reason: he was changed by the power of the cleansing blood of Christ.

March 4, 1881

The Prayer That Saved a President

> *Oh, turn to me, and have mercy on me!*
> *Give Your strength to Your servant,*
> *And save the son of Your maidservant.*
>
> —PSALM 86:16

When Abraham and Eliza Garfield married, they built a log cabin in Mentor, Ohio, and that's where James Abram was born in 1831. Two years later, Abraham, thirty-three, died while fighting a fire that threatened their farm. Eliza, a devout follower of Christ, determined to raise her children with prayer as her secret weapon.

When James was a teenager, he left home to work on the Ohio and Pennsylvania Canal. It was a dangerous job, and he could barely swim. One dark night, he woke for his shift and made his way to the deck. While struggling with a coil of rope, he fell headfirst over the railing and sank in the cold waters. As he thrashed about, his hand felt a loose rope. It was taut enough to support him, and he hauled himself to the railing and collapsed onto the deck.

I felt I was coming to drowning. At length, however, [the rope] held and I was able to draw myself up until I could get a breath of air above the stagnant, stifling water. . . . My feeble calls for help [received] no response from the sleeping people in the boat. I was curious to know what had caused the rope to stop unwinding and carefully examining it, I found that just where it came over the edge of the boat it had been drawn into a crack and there knotted itself. I sat down in the cold of the night and in my wet clothes and [thought about] the matter. I thought [God] had saved me . . . for something greater and better than canaling.[1]

James had swallowed a large quantity of water and was chilled to the bone. He developed a high fever as he trudged toward home. Reaching the little house, he saw a light, and through the window there was his mother on her knees, an open Bible before her, praying, "Oh, turn to me, and have mercy upon me; give strength to Thy servant, and save the son of Thy handmaid." James knew this was the prayer his mother offered for him daily.[2]

In Psalm 86, King David was in a crisis, and he begged the Lord to have mercy on him, to help him, to show him strength, to help him for he was the son of a godly mother. The New International Version says, "Turn to me and have mercy on me; show your strength in behalf of your servant; save me, because I serve you just as my mother did." It is one of the very few biblical references to David's mother. In the older translations, the verse simply said, "Save the son of your maidservant," and Eliza made that her prayer.

Hearing those words, James opened the door and fell into her arms.

Eliza nursed her son to health, and shortly afterward, he attended a revival meeting. Listening carefully to the sermons, he told the preacher, "If I could be satisfied that what you have taught tonight is simple truth and would secure happiness, I would embrace the faith."[3] The next night, James gave his life to Christ and soon began preaching the gospel.[4]

His friends were impacted by his faith. One evening as he and his buddies were celebrating the Fourth of July around a campfire, he pulled a copy of the New Testament from his pocket and said, "Boys, I am accustomed to read a chapter with my absent mother every night. Shall I read it aloud?" They agreed, and he read the chapter his mother was reading in her cabin at the same time.[5]

In one of his letters, Garfield described a revival in which he preached the gospel nineteen times, with thirty-four people coming to Christ and thirty-one of them being baptized.[6]

Later while at Williams College, Garfield summarized his philosophy of history for the school magazine: "No man can understand the history of any nation or of the world who does not recognize in it the power of God and behold His stately goings forth as He walks among the nations. It is His hand that is moving the vast superstructure of human history."[7]

At age twenty-six, Garfield was appointed president of Hiram College. He began making political speeches denouncing the evils of slavery, and in 1860, he was elected state senator. When the Civil War broke out, Garfield joined the Union Army and rose to the rank of major-general, but he resigned his commission to run for a seat in the US House of Representatives. His political career was meteoric, and in 1880, he was elected president of the United States.

His aged mother, Eliza, traveled with him to Washington where, on March 4, 1881, she became the first mother of a president to see her son sworn into office and the first mother of a president to live in the White House.

And if you visit the bedroom she occupied at the Garfield home in Mentor, Ohio, you'll see on the wall an old framed embroidery bearing the words "Watch and Pray."

December 6, 1884

A Virtual Bible Engraved in Stone

Praise be to God!

—Psalm 68:35 NIV

On December 6, 1884, Lieutenant Colonel Thomas Casey of the US Army Corps of Engineers, wearing a derby hat and perched on scaffolding 555 feet above the ground, supervised the placing of the capstone atop the Washington Moment, which he then crowned with an aluminum tip bearing the Latin phrase *Laus Deo*—"Praise be to God." When the sun rises every day over the nation's capital, its first rays strike those words.

That wonderful phrase is an exclamation. It is our duty to praise God. All the nation should praise Him. All the world should praise Him. All creation should praise Him.

> Sing to God, you kingdoms of the earth,
> sing praise to the Lord,

228

to him who rides across the highest heavens, the ancient heavens,
who thunders with mighty voice.
Proclaim the power of God. . . .
Praise be to God! (Psalm 68:32–35 NIV)

This is the powerful exclamation chosen to tower above all the other words in Washington, over all the other voices, over all the debates and debacles that rage in our nation's capital. At the pinnacle of national power—above the White House and Congress and the Supreme Court—higher than anything are the words of Psalm 68: *Laus Deo*—"Praise be to God."

At the bottom of the Washington Monument is a 24,500-pound cornerstone with space hollowed out for a zinc case containing a copy of the Holy Bible. Up and down the giant obelisk, a host of Bible verses and prayers are etched into its walls.

Washington is so filled with references to God and scriptural quotations that the city is virtually a Bible engraved in stone. When visiting the Lincoln Memorial, for example, notice the inscription of Lincoln's second inaugural address. It contains fourteen references to God and four Bible verses.[1]

At the National Archives, check out the bronze emblem of the Ten Commandments in the floor. Then go over to the most hallowed spot in Washington—the display of the original Declaration of Independence. Notice its four references to God:

- When in the Course of human events, it becomes necessary for one people . . . to assume among the powers of the earth, the separate and equal station to which the Laws of . . . *Nature's God* entitle them . . . .
- We hold these truths to be self-evident, that all men are created equal, that they are endowed by their *Creator* with certain unalienable Rights . . . .

229

- . . . appealing to *the Supreme Judge* of the world . . . .
- . . . with a firm reliance on the protection of *divine Providence*, we mutually pledge to each other our Lives, our Fortunes, and our sacred Honor.[2]

Moses and the Ten Commandments are all over the Supreme Court Building, where every session opens with the words: "God save the United States and this honorable court."

Across the street, the US Capitol is a treasure trove of spiritual truth. The Rotunda contains eight massive oil paintings. Two portray prayer meetings and a third shows a baptism. One of the paintings has a large open Bible at the center of it; you can read the words "God with us." Two of the paintings feature the cross being held aloft.

Around the walls of the US House of Representatives, ancient law-givers are depicted, but only Moses is shown full-faced, gazing down on the legislators. Above the speaker's rostrum are the words: "In God We Trust." Over at the US Senate you'll see "In God We Trust" over the south entrance, and over the east entrance the phrase *Annuit Coeptis*—"God has favored our undertakings."

In Statuary Hall, you'll find a bronze statue of missionary Marcus Whitman holding a Bible; another of missionary Junipero Serra, holding a cross; and, as of this writing, plans are underway to add evangelist Billy Graham to the Hall.

Along the ornate Cox Corridor of the Capitol are the words "America! God shed His grace on thee." In the private congressional chapel, a stained-glass window depicts Washington kneeling in prayer. Over him are the words "THIS NATION UNDER GOD," and around him in beau-tiful golden letters is Psalm 16:1: "Preserve me, O God, for in Thee do I put my trust."

Walking to the Library of Congress, check out two items there on permanent display—the Giant Bible of Mainz and the Gutenberg Bible.[3] On the ceilings and walls of the Great Hall are inscribed Bible verses like

John 1:5 and Proverbs 4:7. A bronze statue of Moses stands in the Main Reading Room, and nearby are more verses—Micah 6:8, Leviticus 19:18, and Psalm 19:1. The apostle Paul gazes down from the balustrade.

The Martin Luther King Jr. Memorial displays a quotation from the book of Amos. At the National Law Enforcement Officers Memorial, you'll find Proverbs 28:1: "The wicked flee when no man pursueth but the righteous are bold as a lion." The US Holocaust Memorial Museum highlights these words: "You are my witnesses—Isaiah 43:10."

Time doesn't permit a complete biblical tour of the nation's capital, so let's end with this statement etched into the wall of the Jefferson Memorial:

GOD WHO GAVE US LIFE GAVE US LIBERTY. CAN THE LIBERTIES
OF A NATION BE SECURE WHEN WE HAVE REMOVED A
CONVICTION THAT THESE LIBERTIES ARE THE GIFT OF GOD?

December 24, 1898

Christmas Eve in the War Zone

I will never leave you nor forsake you.

—JOSHUA 1:5

Many people know about the famous Christmas Eve truce during World War I, when German and Allied soldiers paused on the Western Front to sing carols and exchange greetings in 1914. But military historians also know that Scripture, hymns, and holidays like Christmas have always stirred the hearts of American service members, especially those deployed overseas, far from family and friends.

When the United States declared war on Spain in 1898, Theodore Roosevelt resigned his position as assistant secretary of the navy to enlist in the war effort. He organized a unit of unusual characters—cowboys and athletes—and led them in a charge up San Juan Hill in Cuba on July 1, 1898. The war only lasted about four months, but the US Army kept a number of soldiers in Cuba to support the peace. Some of these were African-American members of the 9th Cavalry Regiment, and others were members of the Seventh Army Corps.

On Christmas Eve 1898, many of these soldiers were encamped in the hills above Havana. It was a tropical, balmy night, and the thoughts of the men were of home. Some were from the North and others from the South, and the tensions of slavery, segregation, and the Civil War were still raw.

One middle-aged man was sitting in front of his tent—Lieutenant Colonel Curtis Guild Jr., the former governor of Massachusetts. He was a close friend of Roosevelt and had been appointed inspector-general of Havana during the occupation. As he sat talking to a fellow officer their thoughts were mellow, and they spoke of what their families were doing back home. When the midnight hour came, a sentinel cried out, "Twelve o'clock, and all's well."

At that moment a beautiful voice arose from a nearby tent—a clear, booming baritone—singing the hymn "How Firm a Foundation." In those days this hymn was often sung to the tune *Adeste Fideles*, the melody for the Christmas carol "O Come, All Ye Faithful."

This is a hymn of seven verses, and it was well-known and very popular, especially since it was Theodore Roosevelt's favorite hymn. More and more voices joined in with every verse—the Forty-ninth regiment of Iowa, the Sixth of Missouri, the Fourth of Virginia, soldiers from both north and south of the Mason-Dixon line—an entire army, united far from home in the first moments of Christmas 1898.[1]

"How Firm a Foundation" is an unusual hymn because each of its seven stanzas takes a divine promise from Scripture and puts it into the rhyme and rhythm of a verse. The original title of "How Firm a Foundation" was "Exceedingly Great and Precious Promises." The opening stanza says:

> How firm a foundation, ye saints of the Lord,
> Is laid for your faith in His excellent Word!
> What more can He say than to you He hath said,
> You, who unto Jesus, for refuge have fled?

The stanzas go on to remind us of the promises that our strength shall equal our days (Deuteronomy 33:25); that God is with us to strengthen, help, and cause us to stand (Isaiah 41:10); that He will be present when we go through deep waters or encounter fiery trials (Isaiah 43:2); and that He will bless and care for us even down to old age (Isaiah 46:4).

Imagine the comfort felt when this spontaneous, a cappella choir of masculine voices, rising into the heavens from moonlit tents—an entire army, came to the final verse:

> The soul that on Jesus has leaned for repose,
> I will not, I will not desert to its foes;
> That soul, though all hell should endeavor to shake,
> I'll never, no never, no never forsake.

Throughout the history of America, there have been those who have clasped the Bible to their chests and gone to war, entered politics, bettered society, built the nation, reformed its laws, and endured its crises—all because they knew, as these soldiers near Havana knew, that God has promised His people that He will never leave them or forsake them.

And even now, whatever you're going through, it's as true as ever. That soul who on Jesus has leaned for repose, He will not, He cannot desert to its foes. Your soul, though all hell should endeavor to shake, He will never—no never!—no never forsake.

P.S. Years later, on Wednesday, January 8, 1919, Rev. George Talmadge stood before the casket of Theodore Roosevelt and recited "Colonel Roosevelt's favorite hymn, No. 636 in the Episcopal Hymnal, 'How Firm a Foundation Ye Saints of the Lord.'"[2]

75

November 21, 1899

A President Like That

The kingdom of heaven is like a merchant looking for
fine pearls. When he found one of great value, he went
away and sold everything he had and bought it.

—MATTHEW 13:45–46 NIV

William McKinley's most amazing hour was the moment of his greatest danger: July 24, 1864, during the Civil War. He was a twenty-one-year-old first lieutenant wearing blue, and he was ordered to ride through a hail of bullets on a suicide mission. He and his "little brown horse" sprinted, leaped, and dove over the battlefield amid bullet sprays and exploding shells, emerging to everyone's shock through the smoke, having completed the task. His commanding officer, Colonel Rutherford B. Hayes, told him, "I never expected to see you in life again." Neither man could have imagined they were both speaking to a future president of the United States.[1]

McKinley's courage was fueled by his faith in Christ and in God's Word. William grew up in a Methodist family, and his dad was forthright about his commitment to Christ. William's mother was active in the local church in Niles, Ohio, taking care of the building as if it were her own and doing "everything except the preaching."[2] She wanted her son, William, to enter the ministry, and it wasn't a far-fetched idea. He was naturally drawn to the Bible.

In 1856, when William was a teenager, Rev. A. D. Morton, a Methodist preacher, came to town. He preached night after night, aiming his remarks especially at young people. William attended every service, and one evening quietly arose and announced his intention of beginning a Christian life. Morton later recalled the boy said: "I have not done my duty; I have sinned; I want to be a Christian, for I believe that religion is the best thing for our world. I give myself to my Savior, who has done so much for me." A few evenings later, he gave his testimony saying, "I have found the pearl of great price and am happy. I love God!"[3]

This scriptural reference is from Matthew 13, when Jesus told a series of stories, or parables, to explain aspects of His kingdom. He said that those who received Him as Savior and became part of His kingdom were like a merchant who found a priceless pearl, one of great value. The merchant sold all he had and bought the pearl.

In finding Jesus as his Savior, McKinley had found the "pearl of great price."

McKinley went on to become an ardent, lifelong Bible student and a man of prayer. One friend said, "I have been with him many times during all his campaigns. We have frequently attended political meetings, and banquets, and have often retired at a late hour, but I have never known him to go to his bed until he had read from his Bible and had knelt in prayer."[4]

When McKinley became president, he maintained his Christian testimony. One Sunday a political opponent attended McKinley's church to spy on him during worship.

I watched the President. I watched his face while he sang; I gave close attention to his countenance and attitude during all the opening service and his interest in the earnest words which were spoken before the sacrament of the Lord's Supper was administered. And after a while, when I saw William McKinley get up from his place and go and kneel down at the altar, humbly, with the rest, and reverently take the Communion, and then, when he arose, quietly wipe away the traces of emotion from his eyes, his whole attitude showing the deepest religious emotion, I confess to you that I felt a great change coming over myself, and I said to myself, "A country which has a man like that at the head of its efforts is not so badly off, after all."[5]

McKinley's faith also helped guide his policies. On November 21, 1899, five Methodist ministers called on the president at the White House, and when they turned to leave, McKinley called after them: "Hold a minute longer! Not quite yet, gentlemen. Before you go, I would like to say just a word about the Philippine business."

They knew what he meant. During McKinley's presidency, the American Congress had declared war on Spain, which controlled the Philippines. When Spain was defeated, the future of the Philippines became a major international issue with no easy solution. Some wanted America to annex the Philippines, and others demanded he maintain an American military base there. McKinley decided to negotiate with Spain for an acceptable resolution.

He told the Methodists:

I have been criticized a good deal about the Philippines, but I don't deserve it. The truth is I didn't want the Philippines, and then they came to us. . . . I confess that I did not know what to do with them. I sought counsel from all sides—Democrats as well as Republicans—but I got little help. . . . I walked the floor of the White House night after night until midnight; and I am not ashamed to tell you, gentlemen, that I went down on my knees and prayed Almighty God for light and guidance.

The answer came to him, he said, "And then I went to bed and went to sleep and slept soundly."[6]

McKinley's enemy was right. A country that has a person "like that at the head of its efforts is not so badly off, after all."

76

September 14, 1901

The Assassination of William McKinley

Nevertheless not My will, but Yours, be done.

—LUKE 22:42

First Lady Ida McKinley suffered nervous disorders brought on by the deaths of her mother, her two daughters, and her brother, who was murdered. Her migraines, weak immune system, and epilepsy disabled her, and she spent much of her time in a chair crocheting thousands of pairs of slippers for charities across the nation. Her husband's caregiving was the talk of Washington, and he went to great lengths to see she could travel with him.

After McKinley's second inauguration in 1901, he and Ida planned a six-week tour of the nation by presidential train. They swung through the South and Southwest, then up the Pacific coast to San Francisco, where Ida fell ill and hovered between life and death, her temperature at 104 degrees. The president stayed by her bedside as crowds gathered outside, praying for her. At one point flags were lowered to half-staff on the rumor of her death. But Ida recovered enough to return to Washington, and a few months later she was strong enough to accompany her husband to the Pan-American Exposition in Buffalo.

They arrived on the afternoon of September 6, 1901, amid fanfare. Ida went to rest while the president was escorted to the vast Temple of Music, where twenty thousand people hoped to shake his hand. About a hundred did so before tragedy struck. A young man with reddish hair approached the president, offering his left hand instead of his right, which was wrapped in a handkerchief. The stranger gripped McKinley's hand in a vice, drew him forward, and the handkerchief fell away to reveal a derringer that pumped two bullets into the president's chest and abdomen.

McKinley staggered back, exclaiming, "May God forgive him!" As guards tackled the assassin, the stunned president turned to a body-guard near him and asked, "Am I shot?" Seeing the blood spreading over McKinley's shirt, the man replied, "I fear you are, Mr. President." The president's secretary bent over to hear him whisper, "My wife, be careful about her; don't let her know."[1]

The Temple of Music erupted in a cacophony of screams. As news spread, the crowds wept in unrestrained grief. At a nearby hospital, doctors examining the president felt he would survive his wounds, and for several days the world waited in hushed prayer.

McKinley, too, prayed. After the doctors and nurses tended his wounds, he would tell them, "Let us have prayer," and they would kneel around his bed to offer the Lord's Prayer in unison. Every time the president would regain consciousness, he would repeat the Lord's Prayer over and over.[2] For a few days the nation was optimistic about his recovery. But on September 13 the president's condition rapidly deteriorated.

At eight o'clock on the evening of September 14, Mrs. McKinley was brought again to see her husband. He was too weak to speak to her, but later that evening he revived enough to whisper some words into her ear, which were never disclosed. She rose and looked at the doctor, saying through tears, "I know that you will save him. I cannot let him go. The country cannot spare him."

But they could not save him.

"Goodbye, all, goodbye," he said. "It is God's way. His will, not ours, be done." As he sank into unconsciousness, he uttered his final words: "Nearer, my God, to Thee."[3]

At his funeral in Canton, Ohio, Dr. C. E. Manchester, who had known the president for years, gave the sermon, saying,

He was a Christian. . . . His confidence in God was strong and unwavering. It held him steady in many a storm where others were driven before the wind and tossed. He believed in the fatherhood of God and in His sovereignty. His faith in the gospel was deep and abiding. He had no patience with any other theme of pulpit discourse. "Christ and Him crucified," was in his mind the only panacea for the world's disorders. He believed it to be the supreme duty of the Christian minister to preach the Word . . . .

He said at one time, while bearing heavy burdens, that he could not discharge the daily duties of life but for the fact that he had faith in God. William McKinley believed in prayer. Its language was not unfamiliar to him, and his public addresses not infrequently evidenced the fact. It was perfectly consistent with his life-long convictions and his personal experiences that he should say at the first critical moment after the assassination approached: "Thy Kingdom come; Thy will be done," and that he should declare at the last: "It is God's way; His will be done."[4]

March 26, 1905

The Queen of American Hymn Writers

And you shall remember that the LORD your God led you
all the way.

—DEUTERONOMY 8:2

America has been shaped by her singing of hymns. The first book printed in British North America was the *Bay Psalm Book*, a collection from the Psalms translated for singing. It was printed in Cambridge, Massachusetts, in 1640, just twenty years after the Pilgrims landed. Many of the colonial pastors wrote hymns for their congregations, including Samuel Davies and Mather Byles. Samuel Occom, the Native American preacher, wrote hymns, as did one of our early presidents—John Quincy Adams. The First Great Awakening (along with the Wesley Revival in England) produced some of the greatest hymns in history—sturdy, theological, uplifting, objective hymns, many of which we still sing today, or should.

The Second Great Awakening produced a different kind of hymn, more subjective, more personal. The growth of the Sunday School movement in

America sparked the writing of Sunday School songs. "Jesus Loves Me," for example, came from sisters Anna and Susan Warner who lived on Constitution Island across from the US Military Academy at West Point and taught cadets the Bible.

During the evangelistic campaigns of D. L. Moody, these Sunday School songs evolved into gospel songs, which were popularized by Moody's associate, musician Ira Sankey. Sankey's most popular lyricist was Fanny Crosby, whose long career established congregational music in America for a hundred years.

Crosby came from strong Puritan roots. Her great-grandfather had fought in America's War of Independence, and she grew up hearing stories about it. As she once said, "When General Warren was killed at Bunker Hill, it was a Crosby who caught up the flag as it fell from his hands."[1]

Fanny was blinded in childhood, but she memorized vast amounts of Scripture—entire chapters—and when she came to Christ as Savior, these scriptures became the wellspring of her songs. My favorite Crosby hymn is "All the Way My Savior Leads Me," based on Deuteronomy 8:2, which is a verse that expressed her testimony.

This is one of many Bible verses that speaks of God's guidance over the lives of His children. The book of Deuteronomy is essentially a series of messages Moses gave very late in his life to the younger generation, who were getting ready to cross the Jordan River to enter the land of Israel. Moses told them to remember how God had led them out of Egypt, how He had led them through the Red Sea, through the wilderness, and to the very edges of the promised land. He had led them "all the way."

In the same way, God leads us all the way and directs the paths of those who acknowledge Him. We don't meander meaninglessly through life with no God-given purpose or plan for life, trying to figure out what to do. The Lord has appointed His will for us in advance, and He delights in guiding His people. It was this truth that inspired Fanny Crosby's great hymn—one that comforts me every time I sing it or recall its words.

Crosby's most popular song is "Blessed Assurance, Jesus Is Mine."[2] In my three-volume set recounting the stories behind beloved hymns, *Then Sings My Soul*, I tell how "Blessed Assurance" came into being.

> Another of Fanny's dearest friends was Phoebe Knapp. While Fanny lived in the Manhattan slums and worked in rescue missions, Phoebe lived in the Knapp Mansion, a palatial residence in Brooklyn, where she entertained lavishly. She was an extravagant dresser with a wardrobe full of elaborate gowns and diamond tiaras. Her music room contained one of the finest collections of instruments in the country, and Fanny was a frequent house guest.
>
> One day in 1873, while Fanny was staying at the Knapp Mansion, Phoebe said she had a tune she wanted to play. Going to the music room, she sat at the piano and played a new composition of her own while the blind hymnist listened. Fanny immediately clapped her hands and exclaimed, "Why, that says, 'Blessed Assurance!'" She quickly composed the words, and a great hymn was born.[3]

Every generation of Christians has written psalms, hymns, and spiritual songs for their times, adding to the richness of our hymnody year by year. One of my abiding passions is encouraging and enjoying the newest music without losing the 3,400-year-old heritage handed down to us, beginning with the Song of Moses in Exodus 15. Every worship service should lean into the future while staying anchored, in some way, to the past; for if we forget the songs of yesterday, we'll be less equipped to sing tomorrow. America's rich history of hymnody shouldn't be shunned but celebrated.

On Sunday, March 26, 1905, churches throughout New York and around America observed Fanny Crosby Day in appreciation of the blind singer's contributions to worship, and on that day multitudes of churches rang out with Crosby hymns. She was arguably the best-known Christian in America at the time, though she continued living in the

slums to minister to the poverty-stricken and the down-and-outers of
New York, telling them:

> This is my story, this is my song,
> Praising my Savior, all the day long.[4]

78

December 3, 1911

The Biblical Secret of America's Retailer

*But seek first the kingdom of God and His righteousness,
and all these things shall be added to you.*

—MATTHEW 6:33

As an adolescent, John Wanamaker took a large sheet of brown paper and wrote down all the things he wanted to be—a minister of the gospel, an architect, a merchant, a journalist, and a doctor. It finally came down to merchant or minister; in a sense, Wanamaker became both. For many years, Wanamaker ran the largest department store in the world and the biggest Sunday School in America.

Born in 1838 in Philadelphia, Wanamaker grew up working in his father's brickyard and was converted solidly to Christ at age eighteen. At twenty, he took a job with the Young Men's Christian Association for $1,000 a year, and within twelve months had increased the membership from fifty-seven to two thousand. He also started a Sunday School in a downtrodden part of Philadelphia. On the first Sunday he was run out of the building by a local gang. The next week Wanamaker tried again, with volunteer firefighters standing guard. On April 8, 1861, Wanamaker, twenty-two, resigned from the YMCA and opened his own store. Four days later the Civil War began, but Wanamaker persevered and managed to keep his business going during the conflict.

In 1865, Wanamaker reorganized his Sunday School into a Presbyterian church, which, within five years, would accommodate three thousand people, making it one of the largest churches in the nation. Its wide range of ministries included a soup kitchen, an employment service, a savings bank, a library, and a clothing dispensary for the needy.

In 1875, Wanamaker purchased Philadelphia's freight depot and turned it into an arena for evangelist D. L. Moody's campaign, which lasted from November 21, 1875, to January 21, 1876. The platform alone held a thousand people, with nearly nine thousand in the audience. Over a million people attended during the campaign, with thousands coming to Christ as Savior.

After the revival Wanamaker converted the freight depot into the largest store in the world: the Grand Depot. No one had ever seen anything like it—eleven acres of retail space; three thousand employees; electric lights; a ventilating system; elevators; the largest bookstore and piano dealership in America—and prayer services every day at noon. He was very outspoken for Christ and sought to share the gospel at every opportunity. As if he weren't busy enough, he was appointed postmaster general of the United States in 1889.

In 1901, Wanamaker opened a stunning new department store in Philadelphia, which was considered the most remarkable store on earth; it featured a marble atrium with the largest pipe organ in the world and a crystal tea room seating fourteen hundred diners. The store, dedicated by President William Howard Taft on December 3, 1911, boasted forty-six acres of retail space.

Ever indefatigable, Wanamaker worked from seven in the morning until past midnight without showing signs of flagging, even into his seventies. He was an advertising genius, and he had a knack for reaching the masses. He exuded cheer. During the bleak Christmas season of 1917, when America was engaged in the First World War, Wanamaker told his employees, "Try to keep the sunshine all around you, that the people may catch some of it and carry it home, and that the children there and the old people may have a better Christmas, because they have drawn some of the spirit of it from yourself."[1]

When he passed away in 1922, at age eighty-four, he left $40 million to his heirs. Over fifteen thousand people showed up for his funeral, with most of them standing in the snow—a testament to his lifelong impact.

Someone once asked Wanamaker, "How do you get time to run a Sunday School with your four thousand scholars, in addition to the business of your stores, your work as Postmaster-General, and other obligations?"

Instantly Wanamaker replied, "Why, the Sunday School is my business! All other things are just things. Forty-five years ago I decided that God's promise was sure: 'Seek ye first the kingdom of God and His righteousness, and all these things shall be added to you.'"[2]

79

July 16, 1914

The Concoction

For our gospel did not come to you in word only, but also in power.

—1 Thessalonians 1:5

Atlanta businessman Asa Candler once wrote his son a letter express-ing his philosophy of life and paraphrasing 1 Thessalonians 1:5: "My boy, you cannot know how anxious I am about you. I do so greatly desire your success.... Don't be religious in word only, but in your life.... Let your life constantly exhibit Christ. We live for Him."[1]

Here Candler was quoting a favorite verse about the practicality of a biblical faith. The apostle Paul was telling the disciples in Thessalonica that the gospel isn't simply a matter of words. It must show up in our life and affect all our deeds through the power of the Holy Spirit.

Candler knew what he was talking about. He had always been a person of deeds. Born in the hills of northwest Georgia, he had trapped animals and sold furs to make money as a child. He badly wanted a good education, but with ten brothers and sisters, only one would have the funds for college—Candler's brother Warren, who was studying for the ministry.

While Candler had aspired to be a physician, with little education he did the next best thing. He moved to Atlanta, which was rising from the ruins of the Civil War, and he opened a drugstore. In those days, drugstores featured their own concoctions of roots, herbs, elixirs, and tonics. Another nearby druggist, John Pemberton, had developed a medicinal drink to help relieve the pain he suffered from wounds incurred in the Civil War. Knowing he was dying, Pemberton sold the formula and it ended up in the hands of Candler, who began manufacturing and selling it from his drugstore.

He was a natural business leader. His stores and enterprises flourished, and he viewed his wealth as a stewardship from God to be used for the kingdom. With his brother's advice, Candler supported many evangelical Methodist causes. He started a college in Havana to provide a biblical education for Cuban students. He served as vice president of the American Bible Society. He provided the funds to establish Wesley Memorial Hospital (today Emory University Hospital) in Atlanta.

Until Candler's time, the leading Methodist university in the South was Vanderbilt, but the school had strayed from its evangelical beliefs and no longer wanted church oversight. On July 16, 1914, Candler wrote what is now called the "million-dollar letter" to his brother Warren, offering a million dollars to establish a Methodist school in Atlanta—Emory University.

Candler believed that "education without a strong Christian influence would lead to a population of an educated elite with no moral foundation. A person unable to distinguish between right and wrong has as little value to their community as those who could neither read nor write."[2]

In my opinion, the education which sharpens and strengthens the mental faculties without at the same time invigorating the moral powers and inspiring the religious life is a curse rather than a blessing. . . . I am profoundly imprest that what our country needs is not more secularized education, but more of the education that is fundamentally and intentionally religious. . . .

The Church of God is an enduring institution; it will live when individuals and secular corporations have perished. It is not easily carried about by the shifting winds of doctrine. . . .

I rejoice in the work of all the denominations who love our Lord Jesus Christ in sincerity and seek to do good to men. . . . I see no reason to hesitate to trust money to that church to which I look for spiritual guidance. To that church at whose altars I receive the Christian Gospel. . . . The work of higher education is not going to be surrendered to secularism.[3]

In 1916, Candler retired from his business to serve as mayor of Atlanta, where he balanced the city's budget and coordinated the reconstruction efforts following the Atlanta fire of 1917. But his wife of forty years, Lucy, was ill, dying of breast cancer. Candler left office to care for her, and after she died, he was bereft, and his final years were lonely.

Asa Candler has gone down in history primarily for the drugstore concoction he purchased and popularized, which produced millions of dollars for the expansion of the work of the Methodists and the ministry—a drink called Coca-Cola.

80

July 12, 1917

The Book in the Trenches

Holding fast the word of life, so that I may rejoice in the day of Christ.

—PHILIPPIANS 2:16

It's impossible to image the horrors of World War I, which left approximately ten million soldiers and eight million civilians dead.[1] The conflict marked the beginning of modern chemical warfare, as one of every four shells fired on the western front contained mustard gas.[2]

Throughout the War there's no question about the book soldiers kept with them in the trenches. The Bible Society of England and Wales distributed more than nine million copies of God's Word in eighty languages to members of the armed forces and prisoners of war on all sides. The New York Bible Society, the American Bible Society, the Pocket Testament League, and other organizations also distributed millions of Bibles and Testaments in what was surely the largest mass distribution of Scripture thus far in Christian history.

American soldiers headed to France and Belgium—including my uncle, Walter T. Morgan—were given pocket Bibles (I still have his). They included this foreword, dated July 12, 1917, by President Woodrow Wilson, who began by giving the Bible a title derived from Philippians 2:16—the Word of Life. Wilson, the son of a preacher and an ardent Presbyterian, understood that the Bible is a living Book that imparts eternal life to those who embrace its message. Even in the midst of death, the Bible can give life. Wilson wrote:

> The Bible is the word of life. I beg that you will read it and find this out for yourselves—read, not little snatches here and there, but long passages that will really be the road to the heart of it. You will find it full of real men and women not only, but also of the things you have wondered about and been troubled about all your life, as men have been always; and the more you read it the more it will become plain to you what things are worthwhile and what are not, what things make men happy,—loyalty, right dealing, speaking the truth, readiness to give everything for what they think their duty, and, most of all, the wish that they may have the approval of the Christ, who gave everything for them,—and the things that are guaranteed to make men unhappy,— selfishness, cowardice, greed, and everything that is low and mean. When you have read the Bible you will know it is the Word of God, because you will have found in it the key to your own heart, your own happiness, and your own duty.
>
> [SIGNED] WOODROW WILSON

"There is no other book that was as widely owned or read in the trenches," said Dr. Michael Snape of the University of Birmingham (UK).[3]

Soldiers, when they were very badly wounded, had a tendency to produce the New Testament from their breast pocket and read it as they died. This is a phenomenon that was recorded when soldiers were killed on 1 July 1916—the first day of the Battle of Somme—[when they] were recovered and buried, many of them were found dead with the Bible, or New Testament in their hands.[4]

One of the strangest aspects of the War—I heard my uncle speak of this—were the soldiers whose lives were saved when a bullet struck their Testaments.[5] With all the bullets flying and every Allied soldier with a Bible in his shirt or hip pocket, it's not surprising that hundreds of them stopped bullets. Soldiers often wrote home about what verse the bullet had reached.

George Vinall sent his Bible home with the bullet still embedded, saying, "The verse where the bullet stopped contains these words . . . 'I will preserve thee.' (Isaiah 49:8). May this be true of future days until I see you again." After the War, Vinall became a Bible translator in Japan.[6]

Private Leslie Friston, twenty-one, was injured in a gas attack and taken to a makeshift hospital. As he lay in bed, a German aircraft flew over the building and pelted bullets through the roof. Two of them hit Friston's bedside table and would have ricocheted off except they were absorbed by his Bible. He said nothing for decades until his daughter discovered the Bible and asked him about it.[7]

Rev. John Stuart Holden, speaking at an American conference in 1916, told how one of his parishioners was saved when a bullet lodged in the Bible in his hip pocket. A jagged piece of shell cut the pages as clean as a razor and blackened the book. The man was taken to the hospital where the surgeon told the soldier's commanding officer, "It was the book which saved him from instant death."

The general said to the soldier, "It must be very precious to you if it saved your life."

"Oh, sir," replied the man, "it saved my soul long ago."[8]

March 4, 1933

May He Guide Me

Where there is no vision, the people perish.

—PROVERBS 29:18 KJV

The American stock market crashed on Black Tuesday, October 29, 1929, and the ensuing Great Depression left 37 percent of all non-farm workers unemployed. Many people starved, many lost their homes and farms, and millions were uprooted as they sought work. I recall my mother talking about it at length, for it devastated the mountain people of western North Carolina where she grew up—along with every other corner of the nation.

On March 4, 1933, Franklin Roosevelt was sworn into office as the nation's thirty-second president, and his inaugural address sounded like a sermon: "This great Nation will endure as it has endured, will revive and will prosper. So, first of all, let me assert my firm belief that the only thing we have to fear is fear itself—nameless, unreasoning, unjustified terror which paralyzes needed efforts to convert retreat into advance."

FDR went on to say that the nation's difficulties concerned, "thank God, only material things." Referring to the plagues in the book of Exodus, he said we had no such problems and much to be thankful for. Borrowing from the Gospels, he compared unscrupulous businessmen to money changers in the temple. And then he quoted Proverbs 29:18: "Where there is no vision the people perish." Drawing from the words of Jesus, he said, "These dark days will be worth all they cost us if they teach us that our true destiny is not to be ministered unto but to minister to ourselves and to our fellow men."

Roosevelt sought to embody the principle of Proverbs 29:18, for he knew that people cannot survive without a practical plan for a better future—a vision for progress for themselves and their children. Leaders who know how to cast vision keep hope alive and spirits strong.

Roosevelt went on to lay out elements of his plan "to put people to work. This is no unsolvable problem if we face it wisely and courageously." Quoting again from Jesus, he advocated "the policy of the good neighbor." He ended his address saying, "In this dedication of a Nation we humbly ask the blessing of God. May He protect each and every one of us. May He guide me in the days to come."[1]

Beginning with that speech, Franklin Roosevelt offered America a New Deal.

Several years ago I attended a political briefing in Washington, and among the speakers was Senator Jennings Randolph from West Virginia, who had been first elected to Congress in 1933. He was the last surviving member of the New Deal Congress.

Senator Randolph told us that just after inauguration day in 1933, he was called to the White House. There in the president's private quarters sat FDR. The lights were low and a fire was roaring in the fireplace. About a dozen congressional leaders had come at Roosevelt's request. Randolph couldn't believe he'd been included, but Roosevelt had his eye on him for future leadership. The young congressman didn't say much that night. He sat there in awe as Franklin Roosevelt began to speak. He told the men what he had in mind and how quickly he wanted to move during the first one hundred days of his administration.

He had a vision for the country, and he wanted to send Congress a record number of bills quickly and furiously, including the creation of the Civilian Conservation Corps, the Tennessee Valley Authority, and the Federal Emergency Relief Administration. He went on, speaking confidently but in such low tones that Randolph strained to hear him. When FDR finished, Randolph said, the group was speechless until one of the senators said, "Mr. President, if we move that quickly aren't you afraid we'll make mistakes?"

Roosevelt replied, "Senator, if we *don't* move that quickly, we'll soon find that we no longer have the opportunity even of making mistakes."

Roosevelt was not a perfect man, and he did make a lot of mistakes, but he was driven by a firm belief in the biblical principle that without a vision, the people perish. His optimism reassured the nation that even in dark hours he had a plan that included everyone. He reverenced the Bible and maintained confidence in God. Biographer Kenneth Davis wrote, "[Roosevelt's] religious belief, indeed, was the simplest. He believed in a loving God who had created and now ruled the world . . . in Jesus Christ as the Son of God. . . . [His] faith was fused with the music and ritual and formal doctrine of the Episcopal Church. . . . He derived from worship an inner peace."[2]

October 8, 1934

A Letter to Almighty God

*God demonstrates His own love toward us, in that while
we were still sinners, Christ died for us.*

—Romans 5:8

The circuit-riding evangelists of the 1800s gave way to the itinerate evangelists of the 1900s, who crisscrossed America holding evangelistic campaigns in churches, tents, and tabernacles in every corner of the nation. Most were absolutely sincere; a few were shysters; and some were, well, like Mordecai Ham—unique individuals who didn't mind meddling in local affairs and calling out sinners. Hundreds of thousands were converted to Christ under Ham's ministry but not without controversy.

When Ham and his director of music, William Ramsey, came to Charlotte, North Carolina, in the fall of 1934, he tore into the sinfulness of the city and was heavily criticized by pastors, newspapers, and local politicians. His meetings didn't start well. On October 8, discouraged,

Ham sat down and wrote a prayer to almighty God on the stationery in his hotel room. He prayed as bluntly as he preached.

Dear Father: Thou knowest the conduct of all in this town: how the antichrist has made his power felt; how the ministers have opposed. Father, please, for Thy Name sake and Thy Son's sake, begin to deal with these: the scoffers and the enemies. Father, only a miracle will crush them. Deal with the Baptists, my own Brotherhood . . . the Methodists and their leaders. Dear Father, may this week be a series of warnings and crushing blows. Deal with the newspapers. O Lord, You know how the testimony of Jesus has been opposed in this city. Deal with the city councilmen and with all that would try to drive us out of the city. . . .

O Dear Lord, come on Thy servant and make his messages a burning fire. Lord, give us a Pentecost here and deal a blow to that infidel Saunders.[1] O Lord, please make this the greatest meeting we have ever witnessed. Pour out Thy Spirit tomorrow. Dear Lord, may this city be made to tremble . . . Dear Lord, give me wisdom to plan a work and enlist 10,000 souls. . . .

Send Angels now and make this city a stronghold of holy angels and begin to make examples of some from hell. . . . Bring the enemies to where they will publicly confess and apologize to You. O Father, in Jesus' Name and for His Glory do wonders. I am in Thy hands, ready for Thy glorious rebuke to the City Conference.

O Lord, I need Your endorsement, and show this city that You are with me. . . . In His Name . . .

[SIGNED] M. F. HAM[2]

The meetings were held in a temporary tabernacle built on Pecan Avenue, and one local teenager decided not to attend—Billy Graham. But the sensational nature of meetings, coupled with an appeal from his neighbor, Albert McMakin (who offered to let Graham drive his truck to the campaign), persuaded him to attend.

During the sermon that night, the Holy Spirit spoke to Graham, and he began attending the meetings night after night. He became so convicted he joined the choir to sit behind the evangelist and away from his pointing finger. But one night, Ham ended his sermon by stressing Romans 5:8—how God demonstrated His love for us, and how Christ died for us. When the invitation was given, Graham responded, coming forward to receive Christ as his Savior.

Mordecai Ham lived long enough to see Graham become the best-known evangelist in the world. Graham became America's Pastor, the friend of presidents from Truman to Trump, and a powerful preacher who spoke with authority, punctuating his sermons with, "The Bible says . . . !"

Billy Graham preached the gospel to more people in live audiences than anyone else in history—nearly 215 million people in more than 185 countries and territories, and his autobiography, *Just As I Am*, is a gripping and grace-filled account of his remarkable life and ministry.[3]

The Lord read Mordecai Ham's letter and answered his prayer as He so often does—exceedingly, abundantly above all we can ask or imagine (Ephesians 3:20).

January 17, 1941

The Verse That Made Churchill Weep

> *For wherever you go, I will go;*
> *And wherever you lodge, I will lodge;*
> *Your people shall be my people,*
> *and your God my God.*
>
> —RUTH 1:16

President Franklin Roosevelt was deeply concerned about the rise of Hitler and the conflict in Europe; but in 1940, the American public was divided about the war, and FDR didn't have the political support needed to assist the British. The crisis deepened that summer when the German Luftwaffe bore down on London night after night during the Battle of Britain.

The ailing Harry Hopkins was one of Roosevelt's dearest and closest advisors. He drew no salary and had no title, but everyone knew he wielded great influence. He lived in the White House—in the Lincoln Bedroom—and was someone with whom FDR felt totally relaxed. On January 3, 1941, the president told reporters he was sending Hopkins to London, saying, "He's just going over to say, 'How do you do?' to a lot of my friends."[1]

It was much more than that, of course, and it was a rigorous trip—five days aboard a Pan American Clipper flying a circuitous route. Hopkins arrived so tired he couldn't even unbuckle his seatbelt.[2] But at once Churchill was dragging him all over London and the UK, lobbying for American support. The two men developed a deep admiration for each other, and Hopkins was convinced America must commit itself to defeating Hitler. Yet he was in no position to make promises or broker commitments.

On January 17, Churchill took the weary American to Glasgow to show him the peril and strategic defenses of the Scottish coastline. At the end of the day, local officials planned a private state dinner at the North British Hotel. After the meal Churchill rose and gave a speech and then reportedly turned and said, "And now Mr. Hopkins will say a few words."

Hopkins rose without preparation, his suit crumpled, a cigarette dangling between his fingers. What could or should he say? Somehow, he found the perfect words tucked away in his memory from his knowledge of the Old Testament book of Ruth.[3]

"I suppose you wish to know what I am going to say to President Roosevelt on my return," he said. "Well, I'm going to quote you one verse from that Book of Books: 'Wither thou goest, I will go and where thou lodgest, I will lodge, thy people shall be my people, and thy God my God." Then Hopkins added his own words in a whisper, "even to the end."

Churchill began to weep. "He knew what it meant," said a man sitting near the prime minister. "Even to us the words seemed like a rope thrown to a drowning man."[4]

In its original context, Ruth was expressing her commitment to her mother-in-law, Naomi, and to Naomi's God. The two women had decided to leave Moab for Bethlehem, and Ruth's dedication to Naomi and to the God of Israel represented an unbreakable bond.

Hopkins's quoting of Ruth 1:16 reverberated around the world.

Returning to Washington, he told Roosevelt all he had seen and heard, paving the way for Roosevelt and Churchill to meet later that year aboard the battleship HMS *Prince of Wales* in Newfoundland. When the two leaders appeared under the massive guns on the quarterdeck, the Royal Navy Band played both national anthems. The crowd sang the hymn "O God Our Help in Ages Past," and the head chaplain offered this prayer:

> *Let us pray for the invaded countries in the grief and havoc of oppression; for the upholding of their courage; and the hope for the speedy restoration of their freedom. O Lord God, whose compassions fail not, support, we entreat Thee, the peoples on whom the terrors of invasion have fallen; and if their liberty be lost to the oppressor, let not this spirit and hope be broken, but stayed upon Thy strength till the day of deliverance. Through Jesus Christ our Lord. Amen.*[5]

Still, not until December 7 would America enter what we now refer to as World War II—not until Pearl Harbor.

December 7, 1941

From Pearl Harbor to Calvary

Father, forgive them, for they do not know what they are doing.

—LUKE 23:34 NIV

My friend George Westover was aboard the USS *Tennessee* at Pearl Harbor on December 7, 1941. His battle station was so high on the ship that, as he told me, he could see the faces of the Japanese bombers. The first of those faces belonged to Commander Mitsuo Fuchida, who coordinated the attack and led the first wave of 183 planes from Japanese aircraft carriers 250 miles away. At 7:53 a.m., Fuchida ordered his radio operator to send the message, "Tora! Tora! Tora!"—the final go-ahead for the attack.[1]

That day, the US Pacific fleet lost 2,403 lives, 21 ships, and 188 aircraft.[2] The next day, America declared war on Japan and entered World War II.

Fuchida served with Japanese forces throughout the conflict, but after the war he bitterly returned to his farm, saying, "Life had no taste or meaning."[3] Then one day in 1948, as he walked past a Tokyo train station, someone handed him a pamphlet titled *I Was a Prisoner of Japan*.

———

On December 7, 1941, Sergeant Jacob DeShazer was peeling potatoes at a stateside army base when news of Pearl Harbor blared over a loudspeaker. Jake, seized with rage toward the Japanese, flung a potato into the wall. Shortly afterward, he volunteered as one of Jimmy Doolittle's raiders.[4] This was an elite group of Army Air corpsmen commissioned to prepare for offensive action against targets in Asia during World War II.

On April 19, 1942, Doolittle's crews embarked on their dangerous mission—the first American effort to bomb Japan. DeShazer dropped two thousand pounds of incendiary bombs onto an oil installation in Nagoya, three hundred miles south of Tokyo. The plane ran out of fuel over Japanese-occupied China, and the crew bailed out in the darkness. DeShazer landed "with an awful jolt" on top of a grave in a cemetery, breaking some of his ribs.[5]

The next day he was captured.

Jake spent forty months as a prisoner of war, enduring starvation, beatings, torture, and solitary confinement. His hatred for his captors grew by the day, but so did his desire for a Bible. Finally he acquired a copy, and he found Christ as Savior while reading Romans 10:9: "If you declare with your mouth, 'Jesus is Lord,' and believe in your heart that God raised Him from the dead, you will be saved" (NIV).[6]

The hatred Jake felt for his captors melted away. He later wrote, "I read in my Bible that . . . on the cross [Jesus] tenderly prayed in His moment of excruciating suffering, 'Father, forgive them for they know not what they do.' And now, from the depths of my heart, I too prayed for God to forgive my torturers."[7]

When American paratroopers liberated DeShazer, he returned home and enrolled in Seattle Pacific University, where he met his wife, Florence. In December 1948, the couple sailed as missionaries to Japan, where a million copies of his evangelistic pamphlet, *I Was a Prisoner of Japan*, were being distributed.

———

When a passerby gave Fuchida a copy of *I Was a Prisoner of Japan*, he read it with such conviction that it prompted him to purchase a Bible in a shop near the train station. While reading the Gospels, he came across the words of Jesus from the cross: "Father, forgive them, for they do not know what they do" (Luke 23:34).

By the time Fuchida had finished reading the gospel of Luke, he had become a Christian. "It was like having the sun rise," he said.[8]

Both men began preaching Christ across Japan, and the world took notice. Fuchida's book, *From Pearl Harbor to Calvary*, was widely read. The two men met, and their stories showed up in magazines, TV programs, movies, and books. Millions of people felt a sense of healing after the war, and only heaven knows how many souls came to Christ as Fuchida and DeShazer spent the rest of their lives preaching the gospel of Him who said, "Father, forgive them, for they do not know what they do."

"I saw him just before he died," DeShazer said in 2001. "We shared in that good, wonderful thing that Christ has done."[9]

85

February 3, 1942

The Four Chaplains

Greater love has no one than this, than to lay down one's life for his friends.

—JOHN 15:13

After the attack on American naval forces at Pearl Harbor, four American clergymen left family and friends to enlist as chaplains during World War II: George Lansing Fox, a Methodist; Alexander Goode, a Jewish rabbi; Clark Poling, from the Dutch Reformed faith; and John Washington, a Catholic. The four men were assigned to accompany soldiers heading to Europe via Greenland aboard the transport ship *Dorchester*. From the beginning, these four men worked in harmony and love, doing their best to boost the morale and calm the nerves of the sailors, who knew that their ship was a likely target of German U-boats.

At 12:55 a.m. on February 3, 1943, the *Dorchester* was sailing among icebergs when an explosion occurred. A torpedo from a German submarine ripped into the starboard side of the ship near the engine room. The lights went out, steam pipes broke, and the ship was filled with screams and panic. The four chaplains raced to the deck and began handing out life jackets to panicked men who were jumping through blackness into the freezing water.

When one soldier kept screaming, "I can't find my life jacket," Chaplain Fox said, "Here's one, soldier." He took off his own life jacket and handed it to the terrified man.

Navy lieutenant John Mahoney, running into the main deck, realized he had forgotten his gloves. "Don't bother, Mahoney," said Chaplain Goode. "I have another pair. You can have these." Pulling off his gloves, he handed them to the lieutenant. First Sergeant Michael Warish, who had been injured in the explosion, hobbled toward the railing in time to see Chaplain Goode unlace his boots and use the string to secure the jacket of a wounded man who was about to plunge into the frigid waters.

One by one, all four chaplains comforted the fleeing men, giving them their life jackets and whatever else they could and praying with them as the *Dorchester* listed and sank.

Survivor Grady Clark later recounted, "As I swam away from the ship, I looked back. The flares had lighted everything. The bow came up high and she slid under. The last thing I saw, the Four Chaplains were up there praying for the safety of the men. They had done everything they could. I did not see them again. They themselves did not have a chance without their life jackets."[1]

Another survivor, James Eardley, was the last man known to have seen the chaplains alive. He later testified, "I was on a life raft and . . . when [the ship] rolled over . . . that's when I saw the four chaplains, [who] had climbed up on the keel, and they were standing arm in arm. . . . And then . . . she nosed down [and] they slid off . . . into the water."[2]

The courage and oneness of these four men—all from different backgrounds and faiths—gripped the world, and today memorials to the Four Immortal Chaplains are found across the nation. On February 3, 1951, exactly eight years after the sinking of the *Dorchester*, President Harry Truman dedicated the Chapel of the Four Chaplains in Philadelphia:

This chapel commemorates something more than an act of bravery or courage. It commemorates a great act of faith in God. The four chaplains whose memory this shrine was built to commemorate were not required to give their lives as they did. They gave their lives without being asked. When their ship was sinking, they handed out all the life preservers that were available and then took off their own and gave them away in order that four other men might be saved. . . . They really lived up to the moral standard that declares "Greater love hath no man than this, that a man lay down his life for his friends." They were not afraid of death because they knew the Word of God is stronger than death. Their belief, their faith, in His Word enabled them to conquer death.[3]

86

June 6, 1944

FDR's Prayer on D-Day

Your will be done.

—MATTHEW 6:10

As word spread of the Allied invasion of Europe on D-Day, Americans were overcome with thoughts of their boys storming the beaches of Normandy, of their men taking the cliffs. Franklin Roosevelt announced he would address the nation by radio; but on that evening, he didn't give a speech. He offered a prayer. In one of the most moving addresses to pass over the lips of an American president, FDR simply prayed. He prayed earnestly and eloquently. He prayed like a pastor leading his flock through stress and sacrifice. He prayed boldly, ending his prayer by emphasizing the words: "Thy will be done, Almighty God." Never before or since have so many tears dripped from so many eyes as that evening when a nation joined its president in prayer.

Roosevelt began by explaining that on the previous evening, when he had spoken to the nation on the radio about the fall of Italy, he knew at that moment Allied Forces were crossing the English Channel for the long-anticipated offensive drive to liberate Europe from the Nazis. While the invasion had just begun, there had been signs of initial success. But, said FDR, much now depended on prayer. He took it upon himself to lead that prayer.

"Almighty God," he said, "Our sons, pride of our Nation, this day have set upon a mighty endeavor, a struggle to preserve our Republic, our religion, and our civilization, and to set free a suffering humanity."

He asked God to lead them straight and true, to give "strength to their arms, stoutness to their hearts, steadfastness in their faith." Roosevelt acknowledged the difficulties of coming days, for the road is long and the enemy is strong. He told the Lord he didn't expect rushing success, but he prayed for resiliency and determination and eventual victory.

He prayed for Allied Forces who would have little rest by night or by day until the victory was won. Their souls may be shaken by violence, he said, especially because they were flung into battle from lives of peace. "They fight not for the lust of conquest. They fight to end conquest. They fight to liberate. They fight to let justice arise, and tolerance and good will among all Thy people. They yearn but for the end of battle, for their return to the haven of home."

Then Roosevelt prayed realistically, poignantly, "Some will never return. Embrace these, Father, and receive them, Thy heroic servants, into Thy kingdom."

Nor did he forget those listening by radio across the hearths of America. "And for us at home—fathers, mothers, children, wives, sisters, and brothers of these brave men overseas—whose thoughts and prayers are ever with them—help us, Almighty God, to rededicate ourselves in renewed faith in Thee in this hour of great sacrifice."

He said many people had encouraged him to call for a single day of national prayer, but the conflict was such a long one that constant prayer was needed. "As we rise to each new day, and again when each day is spent," he said, "let words of prayer be on our lips, invoking Thy help to our efforts." The president prayed for daily strength for all Americans, for the courage to go about their daily tasks and to redouble their efforts in the physical and material support of the Armed Forces. "And let our hearts be stout, to wait out the long travail, to bear sorrow that may come, to impart our courage unto our sons wheresoever they may be. And, O Lord, give us Faith. Give us Faith in Thee; Faith in our sons; Faith in each other; Faith in our united crusade. Let not the keenness of our spirit ever be dulled. Let not the impacts of temporary events, of temporal matters of but fleeting moment, let not these deter us in our unconquerable purpose."

Roosevelt brought his prayer to a conclusion by asking God to bring peace to the world and a unity among nations that would sustain that peace and allow people everywhere to live in freedom. He ended his prayer with the words of Jesus. "Thy will be done, Almighty God. Amen."[1]

The prayer "Your will be done" has frequently been on the lips of presidents and the leaders of America through the ages. It's frequently been on my lips too. When circumstances are out of our control, when conditions are dire, and fear threatens our peace of mind, there's wonderful comfort in remembering the words of our Lord's prayer: "Your kingdom come. Your will be done on earth as it is in heaven."

87

December 14, 1944

Patton's Prayer for Clear Skies

The LORD is with you, you mighty man of valor!

—JUDGES 6:12

James O'Neill, chief chaplain of the Third Army, answered the phone on Friday, December 8, 1944, at the Third Army headquarters in the Lorraine region of France. "This is General Patton," said the voice. "Do you have a good prayer for weather? We must do something about those rains if we are to win the war." O'Neill, looking out his window at the rain that had bogged down the army, promised to find an appropriate prayer. Presently he typed these words on a 3 x 5 card:

Almighty and most merciful Father, we humbly beseech Thee, of Thy great goodness, to restrain these immoderate rains with which we have had to contend. Grant us fair weather for Battle. Graciously hearken to us as soldiers who call upon Thee that, armed with Thy power, we may advance from victory to victory, and crush the oppression and wickedness of our enemies and establish Thy justice among men and nations.

O'Neill was curious as to how Patton would use the prayer. Was he wanting it for his own private devotions, or did he intend to distribute it among the chaplains? Donning his trench coat, the chaplain crossed the quadrangle toward the general's office. Patton read the prayer and said, "Have 250,000 copies printed and see to it that every man in the Third Army gets one."

O'Neill, shocked, simply said, "Very well, sir."

"Chaplain," said Patton, "sit down for a moment; I want to talk to you about this business of prayer."

I am a strong believer in prayer. There are three ways that men get what they want; by planning, by working, and by praying. Any great military operation takes careful planning, or thinking. Then you must have well-trained troops to carry it out; that's working. But between the plan and the operation there is always an unknown. That unknown spells defeat or victory, success or failure. It is the reaction of the actors to the ordeal when it actually comes. Some people call that getting the breaks; I call it God. . . . That's where prayer comes in. Up to now, in the Third Army, God has been very good to us. We have never retreated; we have suffered no defeats, no famine, no epidemics. This is because a lot of people back home are praying for us. . . . But we have to pray for ourselves too.

Then Patton brought up the biblical character of Gideon and asked O'Neill to put out a training letter on prayer to all the chaplains. "Write about nothing else," he said, "just the importance of prayer. . . . We must ask God to stop these rains."

O'Neill returned to his office and prepared Training Letter No. 5, which Patton approved. It was published December 14, 1944, calling the Third Army to prayer.

As chaplains it is our business to pray. We preach its importance. We urge its practice. But the time is now to intensify our faith in prayer, not alone with ourselves, but with every believing man. . . . Those who pray do more for the world than those who fight; and if the world goes from bad to worse, it is because there are more battles than prayers. . . . Gideon of Bible fame was least in his father's house. He came from Israel's smallest tribe. But he was a mighty man of valor. His strength lay not in his military might, but in his recognition of God's proper claims upon his life. . . . Urge all your men to pray. . . . Pray when driving. Pray when fighting. Pray alone. Pray with others. Pray by night and pray by day. Pray for the cessation of immoderate rains. . . . This army needs the assurance and the faith that God is with us. With prayer, we cannot fail.

O'Neill's training letter harkened back to Judges 6 and the story of Gideon. This was the same biblical passage that Samuel Doak referred to at Sycamore Shoals before the Overmountain Men marched off to the Battle at King's Mountain. Gideon is one of the Bible's greatest military strategists, but his prowess came from the God who empowered him in battle. He thought himself ill-equipped for leadership, but the angel of the Lord said to him, "The LORD is with you, you mighty man of valor!" That has become the motto of many soldiers.

Soon 250,000 soldiers had Patton's prayer in their hands, and thousands of copies of Training Letter No. 5 were distributed to chaplains and organization commanders down to the regimental level.

O'Neill later wrote, "On December 20, to the consternation of the Germans and the delight of American forecasters who were equally surprised at the turnabout—the rains and the fogs ceased. For the better part of a week came bright clear skies and perfect flying weather. . . . General Patton prayed for fair weather for Battle. He got it."[1]

88

April 12, 1945

You Are the One in Trouble Now

Therefore give to Your servant an understanding heart to judge Your people, that I may discern between good and evil. For who is able to judge this great people of Yours?

—1 KINGS 3:9

Franklin D. Roosevelt and Harry Truman won the election of 1944, but there was little contact between the two men before or after their inauguration on January 20, 1945. FDR was preoccupied with the final phases of victory in Europe and with the prolonged struggle in the Pacific. Truman kept his vice president's office in the Senate Office Building, where many of his old buddies dropped by for a chat.

About 5:00 p.m. on April 12, Truman left his office and ducked into the private hideaway office of Speaker of the House Sam Rayburn for an afternoon drink. Rayburn told him, "Steve Early wants you to call him right away." Truman picked up the phone and dialed National 1414, saying, "This is the V.P."

Early, the White House press secretary, speaking tensely, instructed Truman to come to the White House immediately. Truman darted from Rayburn's office and literally ran through the Capitol, jumping into his Mercury without any Secret Service protection, fighting traffic, and entering the White House's main entrance on Pennsylvania Avenue. Two ushers were waiting at the North Portico, and they escorted him to a small elevator that served the family quarters. The doors opened, and First Lady Eleanor Roosevelt met him, saying, "Harry, the president is dead."

Truman stood speechless, then said, "Is there anything I can do for you?"

"Is there anything we can do for *you*?" she replied. "For you are the one in trouble now."

Truman called his wife, Bess, and a car fetched her to the White House. The cabinet assembled in shocked silence, along with the leaders of Congress. As the group was assembled in the Cabinet Room, the White House staff frantically searched the building for a Bible. Finally, someone located a Gideon Bible with red edging in the desk drawer of the head usher. It was dusted off and placed on the table.

Harlan Stone, chief justice of the Supreme Court, took his place before the fireplace beneath a painting of Woodrow Wilson, and Truman picked up the Bible, took the oath of office, and then, like George Washington, lifted the Bible to his lips and kissed it.

As the dignitaries filed out, Secretary of State Edward Stettinius remained behind to inform Truman of a matter of utmost urgency. American scientists had created a new explosive device of unimagined power. It was Truman's first knowledge of the atomic bomb.

Returning to his apartment at 4701 Connecticut Avenue, Truman had a turkey sandwich and glass of milk. He called his mother with the news and went to bed while much of America stayed awake, worried about the little man from Missouri who was taking over for the bigger-than-life Roosevelt. But those who best knew him didn't underestimate the fiber of his character and the tenacity of his mind. His mother simply told reporters, "Harry will get along all right."[1]

The next morning Truman arrived at the White House at nine o'clock and worked until noon before traveling to the Capitol to see his buddies. "Boys," he said, "if you ever pray, pray for me now. I don't know whether you fellows ever had a load of hay fall on you, but when they told me yesterday what had happened, I felt like the moon, the stars, and all the planets had fallen on me."[2]

After Roosevelt's funeral, Truman again traveled to Capitol Hill, this time to address a joint session of Congress and the American people. Much of the speech had been composed by his staff and concerned America's determined continuation of World War II, but Truman himself wrote the words he wanted to say in conclusion:

At this moment, I have in my heart a prayer. As I have assumed my heavy duties, I humbly pray Almighty God, in the words of King Solomon: "Give therefore Thy servant an understanding heart to judge Thy people, that I may discern between good and bad; for who is able to judge this Thy so great a people." I ask only to be a good and faithful servant of my Lord and my people.[3]

89

May 14, 1948

The Rebirth of the State of Israel

I have set the land before you; go in and possess the land which the LORD *swore to your fathers—to Abraham, Isaac, and Jacob—to give to them and their descendants after them.*

—DEUTERONOMY 1:8

Clark Clifford, legendary Washington powerbroker and advisor to multiple presidents, opened his gripping memoir, *Counsel to the President*, with an event he called "Showdown in the Oval Office." He said, "Of all the meetings I ever had with Presidents, this one remains the most vivid."[1]

The subject: the recognition of the modern state of Israel.

Clifford, the young naval aide to Truman, had become the president's close friend and primary advisor. One of the biggest decisions facing Truman was whether to recognize a new nation getting ready to announce its statehood—Israel. Truman's staff and cabinet were almost universally against recognition. Secretary of State George C. Marshall, one of the most renowned men in America, was adamant in his opposition. The State Department did everything in its power to prevent recognition, but the clock was ticking. At midnight on May 14, the British would relinquish control of Palestine, and David Ben-Gurion was prepared to proclaim the new state after nearly two thousand years of nonexistence.

In his heart Truman badly wanted to recognize the Jewish state. "He was a student and believer in the Bible since his youth," wrote Clifford. "From his reading of the Old Testament he felt the Jews derived a legitimate historical right to Palestine, and sometimes he cited such biblical lines as Deuteronomy 1:8."[2]

This is the passage in which Moses recalled how God had given the land of Israel to the Jewish people as a homeland where they could grow into a great nation and produce a Messiah—the Lord Jesus Christ. The Lord had told the Israelites, "See, I have set the land before you; go in and possess the land which the LORD swore to your fathers—to Abraham, Isaac, and Jacob—to give to them and their descendants after them." That promise of four thousand years ago was on the verge of being reaffirmed again through the miracle of the rebirth of Israel.

Furthermore, Truman's old friend and former business partner, Eddie Jacobson, a Jew, passionately pleaded with Truman to be sympathetic to the plight of the Jewish people and to support their right to statehood. Truman found himself pressed by all sides.[3]

At the Oval Office showdown on Wednesday, May 12, Marshall argued fervently against recognition, as did Secretary of Defense James Forrestal and Undersecretary of State Robert Lovett. Truman turned to Clifford, whom he had previously asked to prepare a countering argument. Clifford contended for the recognition of Israel, and the discussion became heated. General Marshall's face grew noticeably red, and he finally exploded, "Mr. President, I thought this meeting was called to consider an important and complicated problem in foreign policy. I don't even know why Clifford is here. He is a domestic advisor."

"Well, General," said Truman curtly, "he's here because I asked him to be here." The arguments escalated, with Clifford reminding the men of the murder of six million Jews by the Nazis and quoting the pertinent lines of Deuteronomy 1:8.[4]

Marshall glowered at Truman and declared, "If you follow Clifford's advice and if I were to vote in the election, I would vote against you." The room was stunned into silence, and the meeting quickly came to an end.

"Well, that was rough as a cob," Truman told Clifford as the men left. "That was about as tough as it gets, but you did your best."

"Boss," said Clifford, "this isn't the first case I've lost. . . . Maybe it's not over yet."

"You might be right. . . . But be careful," said Truman, "I can't afford to lose General Marshall."[5]

Over the next two days, Clifford engaged in tense negotiations, finally eliciting a promise from Marshall that if he would not support Truman's decision, at least he would not oppose it.

On midnight Jerusalem time, Friday, May 14, 1948, standing in the Tel Aviv Museum, David Ben-Gurion declared. "We hereby proclaim the establishment of the Jewish state in Palestine, to be called Israel." Eleven minutes later, at 6:11 p.m. Washington time, Charlie Ross, the White House press secretary, read a simple but world-changing dispatch:

STATEMENT BY THE PRESIDENT. THE GOVERNMENT HAS BEEN INFORMED THAT A JEWISH STATE HAS BEEN PROCLAIMED IN PALESTINE. . . . THE UNITED STATES RECOGNIZES THE PROVISIONAL GOVERNMENT AS THE DE FACTO AUTHORITY OF THE NEW STATE OF ISRAEL.[6]

America had decided to stand with the Jewish people who, after centuries of dispersion and persecution, were, miraculously, back in their biblical homeland.

Sometime later when the chief rabbi of Israel, Isaac HaLevi Herzog, visited Truman in the White House, he said to the president, "God put you in your mother's womb so you would be the instrument to bring the rebirth of Israel after two thousand years."

Some thought the rabbi was overdoing it until they looked at Truman and saw tears running down his cheeks.[7]

90

January 20, 1953

Eisenhower and His Preacher

If My people who are called by My name will humble themselves, and pray and seek My face, and turn from their wicked ways, then I will hear from heaven, and will forgive their sin and heal their land.

—2 CHRONICLES 7:14

In his autobiography, *Just As I Am*, Billy Graham pulled back the curtains to give us a behind-the-scenes glimpse into American political life in the 1950s, and to describe some of his fascinating encounters with Dwight D. Eisenhower.

In 1951, Graham's friend Sid Richardson asked him to contact General Eisenhower and encourage him to run for president. Graham didn't know Eisenhower, but he did write, "The American people have come to the point where they want a man with honesty, integrity, and spiritual power. I believe the General has it. I hope you can persuade him to put his hat in the ring."[1]

Richardson sent the letter to Eisenhower in France, where he was serving as commander at the Supreme Headquarters of the Allied Powers in Europe. Eisenhower wrote to Graham, and when the evangelist was in Europe sometime later, he met the General.

In July 1952, Eisenhower was nominated by the Republicans. He asked for Graham's help in knowing how to add a religious note to some of his campaign speeches. Graham shared some scriptures with him, and their relationship developed. One day Graham asked, "General, do you still respect the religious teaching of your father and mother?"

"Yes," Eisenhower said, adding softly, "but I've gotten a long way from them." Graham felt free to share the gospel with him and to give him a red leather Bible.[2]

After the election the president-elect asked to meet Graham in a New York hotel, wanting to receive Bible verses to use at the inauguration. As Graham recalled,

> The General stepped to a window in the Commodore Hotel and looked out across the city as we talked. "I think one of the reasons I was elected was to help lead this country spiritually," he said. "We *need* a spiritual renewal."
>
> I told him I could not agree more and suggested that he make one of his first official acts the proclamation of a national day of prayer. He said he would. Eisenhower's own spiritual pilgrimage had moved rapidly. Prior to the inaugural ceremony at the Capitol, he arranged a worship service for his incoming administration. I was as astounded as anyone else, though, when at the conclusion of the inaugural address he read a prayer he had written himself for the occasion.[3]

When Eisenhower took the oath of office, his hand rested on one of the Bible verses Graham had suggested—2 Chronicles 7:14. Many people view this as the Bible's key verse for unlocking the secrets of national spiritual revival. An awakening only begins when God's people who are called by His name humble themselves and pray and seek His face, turning from their wicked ways. As a result, God will hear from heaven, forgive their sin, and heal their land.

Three years later Graham was awakened on a Sunday night in Washington. Sid Richardson was on the line. "Billy, I've had a hard time tracking you down. The President wants to see you, and the White House couldn't locate you. I'll let them know where you are." The next morning, a car whisked Graham to the president's farm in Gettysburg. Not knowing what to expect, Graham prayed the whole way for wisdom.

In his little den, [Eisenhower] paced in front of the fireplace. I sensed that the real reason for my visit would soon be made clear.

"Billy, do you believe in Heaven?" he asked.

"Yes, sir, I do."

"Give me your reasons."

With my New Testament open, I gave the President a guided tour through the Scriptures that spoke of the future life.

"How can a person know he's going to Heaven?" he asked.

I explained the Gospel to him all over again, as I had on previous occasions. I sensed he was reassured by that most misunderstood message: salvation is by grace through faith in Christ alone, and not by anything we can do for ourselves.[4]

After two terms in office, Eisenhower retired to his farm in Gettysburg. In 1968, he was admitted to Walter Reed Army Hospital, battling congestive heart failure. Once again he called for his preacher.

The details of our conversation were so intimate and sacred that I never hinted of them until after his death; then I asked Mamie's permission to reveal them, which she gave willingly.

As my scheduled twenty minutes with him extended to thirty, he asked the doctor and nurses to leave us. Propped up on pillows amid intravenous tubes, he took my hand and looked into my eyes. "Billy, you've told me how to be sure my sins are forgiven and that I'm going to Heaven. Would you tell me again?"

I took out my New Testament and read to him again the familiar Gospel verses, the precious promises of God about eternal life. Then, my hand still in his, I prayed briefly.

"Thank you," he said. "I'm ready."[5]

91

August 28, 1963

Let Freedom Ring!

But let justice run down like water, and righteousness like a mighty stream.

—AMOS 5:24

One summer's day in 1963, my friend Tom Tipton was a young musician working on his mother's gospel music radio program at the all-black radio station WUST when Dr. Martin Luther King Jr. arrived for an interview. "My mom introduced me to Dr. King," Tom said, "and he invited me to join him and others at the Dunbar Hotel that evening."

Tom went to the meeting and listened as civil rights leaders planned the March on Washington for August 28 and discussed what Dr. King should say in his speech. Tom told me he didn't have any input as to the speech, but he was assigned an important duty. He was put in charge of all the portable public toilets along the route.

"There was something spiritual about the preparation for the march," Tom said.

I felt calm and assured that with Dr. King as the leader, there would not be any trouble. Also keeping things calm was the participation of so many white churches. It was like the time had come at this specific time for a peaceful march of grievance. Many things could have gone wrong, but they didn't. If you ask me what the most amazing thing [was] that happened in the March on Washington, I would say that there was peace. . . . We prayed a lot and hugged a lot.[1]

As Dr. King began his speech at the Lincoln Memorial, Tom, who was standing four rows back, said he felt disappointed for a moment. "[Dr. King] started out slow. But then as he approached the 'I have a dream' segment, the spirit of the Baptist preacher came out. . . . The whole place just vibrated. It hit me and went all the way back to the Washington Monument."

Woven into Dr. King's famous "I Have a Dream" speech were four scriptures he knew and loved and often quoted. Midway through, King recited one of his favorite verses, one now inscribed on his own memorial in Washington—Amos 5:24: "But let justice run down like water, and righteousness like a mighty stream."

Amos was a farmer from the land of Judah. God sent him to the northern kingdom of Israel to preach for social reform, human justice, a respect for the rights of others, and compassion toward the needy. Amos spoke with striking metaphors, and his words have historically been used by civil rights advocates. They were among King's most quoted words. The righteousness of God needed to become a great river flooding the United States of America and sweeping away injustice, segregation, and prejudice.

Dr. King went on to quote Isaiah 40:4–5: "Every valley shall be exalted and every mountain and hill brought low; the crooked places shall be made straight and the rough places smooth; the glory of the LORD shall be revealed, and all flesh shall see it together; for the mouth of the LORD has spoken."

He referred to Psalm 30:5: "Weeping may endure for a night, but joy comes in the morning." And near the end of his speech he also quoted Galatians 3:28: "There is neither Jew nor Greek, there is neither slave nor free, there is neither male nor female; for you are all one in Christ Jesus." Finally he concluded with the rousing, unforgettable quotation from the old African-American spiritual: "Free at last, Free at last, Great God a-mighty, we are free at last."

As Andy Rau said, "King is remembered primarily as a civil-rights figure who fought for social and political change, but he was also a pastor—and he considered his ideas about civil rights to be firmly rooted not just in common sense or political theory, but in Scripture itself."[2]

Dr. King's speech at the Lincoln Memorial is one of the most powerful speeches in American history, and many of us know at least parts of it by heart. Hearing it in person that day must have been the experience of a lifetime.

Tom Tipton, who went on to become a beloved gospel singer, said in wonderment,

> I was a part of it. I brought the chicken—my mother had concessions of fried chicken, potato salad, and bread for $1.50. I drove a bus, I held the babies in the nursery, I helped an elderly woman up off the ground where she had fainted. We became proud! There was no looting or stealing or fights. And it drifted across the nation from the Lincoln Memorial—across the North and the South and into the White House. . . . The world was changed after Dr. King spoke at the Lincoln Memorial.[3]

92

March 15, 1965

Bloody Sunday

For what profit is it to a man if he gains the whole world, and loses his own soul?

—MATTHEW 16:26

Congressman John Lewis was a young Baptist preacher. On March 7, 1965, Lewis and fellow minister Hosea Williams led a group of six hundred people, mostly African-Americans, across the Edmund Pettis Bridge toward Selma, Alabama, in a peaceful march to combat segregation and to register black voters in the South. They were motivated by faith in God and in the unalienable rights He had endowed on all people. As Lewis later told historian Jon Meacham, "Without religion—without the example of Christ, who sacrificed for others—as the foundation of the movement, it would have been impossible for us to endure the setbacks, and to hope, and to go on. . . . [W]e were in Selma that day because of our faith."[1]

As Lewis and Williams led the procession down Water Street and began crossing the bridge, they saw trouble on the other side: a sea of blue-uniformed Alabama state troopers wielding guns, bully clubs, and gas canisters. At the top of the bridge, Williams realized he could not go forward and he couldn't go backward, so he did the only thing left to do— he knelt down and prayed. What followed stunned the nation as peaceful protestors were gassed, beaten, kicked, attacked, and injured—all in full view of cameras that brought the images to every home in America and became known as Bloody Sunday.

Eight days later, President Lyndon Johnson convened a joint session of Congress to demand passage of the Voting Rights Act of 1965. As he began speaking, his expression was grim, and he seemed tired. He said, "At times history and fate meet at a single time in a single place to shape a turning point in man's unending search for freedom. So it was at Lexington and Concord. So it was a century ago at Appomattox. So it was last week in Selma, Alabama."

His speechwriters had infused his words with eloquence, but Johnson was not an eloquent man. He spoke slowly, lumbering out the words in his Texas drawl. The room was stone silent.

There is no cause for pride in what happened in Selma. There is no cause for self-satisfaction in the long denial of equal rights of millions of Americans. But there is cause for hope and for faith in our democracy in what is happening here tonight.

No applause. Behind him, Vice President Hubert Humphrey and Speaker of the House John McCormack sat awkwardly. Johnson pressed on.

In our time we have come to live with moments of great crisis. Our lives have been marked with debate about great issues; issues of war and peace, issues of prosperity and depression. But rarely in any time does an issue lay bare the secret heart of America itself. Rarely are we met with a challenge, not to our growth or abundance, our welfare or

291

our security, but rather to the values and the purposes and the meaning of our beloved Nation.

Johnson's eyes narrowed, and he seemed to latch on to his syllables.

The issue of equal rights for American Negroes is such an issue. And should we defeat every enemy, should we double our wealth and conquer the stars, and still be unequal to this issue, then we will have failed as a people and as a nation.

And then Johnson capped his opening argument with the words of Jesus Christ, quoting from Matthew 16:26:

For with a country as with a person, "What is a man profited, if he shall gain the whole world, and lose his own soul?"

Someone began clapping, and with those words Congress broke into applause, and the ice was broken. Johnson went on to deliver one of the greatest speeches of his life, punctuated with applause and drawing emotions from everyone in the room. He ended with these words:

Above the pyramid on the great seal of the United States it says—in Latin—"God has favored our undertaking." God will not favor everything that we do. It is rather our duty to divine His will. But I cannot help believing that He truly understands and that He really favors the undertaking that we begin here today.[2]

The Voting Rights Act of 1965 was passed by the Senate 77-19 and by the House of Representatives 333-85. Johnson signed it into law on August 6, 1965.

93

December 24, 1968

For All the People Back on Earth

In the beginning God created the heavens and the earth.

—GENESIS 1:1

I remember Christmas Eve 1968. I was a high school student preparing for college in troubled times. The Vietnam War was ripping America to pieces. Campuses were battle zones, cities were burning from race riots, and the land was violent. I registered with the local draft board and wondered about my future. Martin Luther King Jr. and Robert F. Kennedy had been slain, Lyndon Johnson abandoned hopes for reelection, and the Democratic National Convention in Chicago was engulfed in tear gas. In November Richard Nixon won the presidency, but the Soviet Union was threatening America on earth and in space.

In the middle of the chaos, in August, NASA made a sudden and precarious decision to refit the Apollo 8 mission to go to the moon. On December 21, the Saturn V rocket lifted off with Frank Borman, Jim Lovell, and Bill Anders strapped into a small capsule. Many within the

NASA community wondered if they would ever return—experts gave the mission a fifty-fifty chance of success—and Frank Borman's wife, Susan, prepared his eulogy.[1] Some officials worried openly that if the astronauts perished in lunar orbit, no one would ever again look at the moon—or at Christmas—in the same way. But John F. Kennedy had set a deadline to take men to the moon by the end of the decade, and NASA was determined to keep it.

The astronauts traveled faster and farther than anyone before in history and effectively won the space race. As Frank Borman gazed out the window at the receding marble of earth, he thought to himself, "This must be what God sees."[2]

Robert Kurson wrote in his gripping book *Rocket Men*:

To Anders, Earth appeared as a Christmas tree ornament, hung radiant blue and swirling while in an endless black night. From here, it was no longer possible to pick out countries or even continents; all a person could see was Earth, and it occurred to Anders, in this last week of 1968, this terrible year for America and the world, that once you couldn't see boundaries, you started to see something different. You saw how small the planet is, how close all of us are to one another, how the only thing any of us have, in an otherwise empty universe, is each other.[3]

On Christmas Eve we all stopped our suppers and celebrations and gathered around our television sets for one of the most extraordinary moments in television—a worldwide broadcast from lunar orbit. No one knew what the astronauts would say, not even Mission Control.[4]

At 8:30 p.m. Central, networks interrupted their programming as a grainy black-and-white image appeared on the screen. Through the static of space, Borman said, "This is Apollo 8 coming to you live from the moon." The men aimed their camera at the moon, at the Earth, and at the stars as they described their sights and sensations.

Then Anders said, "We are now approaching lunar sunrise and for all the people back on earth, the crew of Apollo 8 has a message we would like to send to you." There was a pause, and then he began reading from Genesis 1: "In the beginning God created the heavens and the earth. The earth was without form, and void; and darkness was upon the face of the deep."

One by one the astronauts passed around a fireproof copy of Genesis 1 taken from a Gideon Bible and read the creation account.[5] After Borman finished verse 10, he ended the broadcast saying, "And from the crew of Apollo 8, we close with good night, good luck, a Merry Christmas, and God bless all of you—all of you on the good Earth."

In Mission Control, scientists and engineers wept openly. We all wept. An estimated one billion people in sixty-four countries had heard the message. And all around the world, men and women and children went outside and gazed into the sky, wondering at the words and sights we had just witnessed from 240,000 miles away.

January 22, 1973

The Conscience of an Honest Woman

Sir, give me this water, that I may not thirst.

—JOHN 4:15

I f slavery is not wrong," said Abraham Lincoln, "then nothing is wrong."[1]
In our world today we can say the same for the slaying of preborn and newborn children. The right to life is the civil rights issue of our time, and future generations will look back on our killing of the innocents with the same horror with which we now view slavery.

Just ask Norma McCorvey.

When she was twenty-two, unmarried and pregnant, two pro-abortion lawyers confronted her at a Dallas pizza joint and persuaded her to let them represent her as Jane Roe in a case that landed in the Supreme Court. The Court's decision on January 22, 1973, legalized abortion nationwide. But later Pastor "Flip" Benham led Norma to faith in Jesus Christ. Norma explained how Benham "passed along a cup of refreshing spiritual water, confident that I was thirsty and that I would take a drink."[2]

That image is drawn from John 4, when Jesus stopped at the well of Samaria and engaged in a conversation with a troubled woman. Jesus told her, "If you knew the gift of God, and who it is who says to you, 'Give me a drink,' you would have asked Him, and He would have given you living water" (John 4:10). When the woman questioned Him, Jesus explained that He alone could meet her spiritual needs and give her everlasting life.

Like the woman by Jacob's well, McCorvey was suffering from an intense spiritual thirst, which could only be quenched by Him who said, "Whoever drinks of the water that I shall give him will never thirst. . . . [It] will become in him a fountain of water springing up into everlasting life" (John 4:14).

McCorvey came to see the horrors she had unleashed, and she spent the rest of her life fighting them. On June 23, 2005, she appeared before a Senate subcommittee and gave this gripping testimony:

> I am the woman once known as the Jane Roe of *Roe v. Wade*. But I dislike the name Jane Roe and all that it stands for. I am a real person named Norma McCorvey, and I want you to know the horrible and evil things that *Roe v. Wade* did to me and others. . . . Instead of helping women in *Roe v. Wade*, I brought destruction to me and millions of women throughout the nation.

She explained to the senators that in 1970, she was pregnant for the third time, unmarried, confused, and at her wit's end. She had already put one child up for adoption, but the pain of breaking the natural bond between mother and child had been hard to bear.

"My lawyers were looking for a young, white woman to be a guinea pig for a great new social experiment, somewhat like Adolf Hitler did," said McCorvey with characteristic bluntness. "I wanted an abortion at the time, but my lawyers did not tell me that I would be killing a human being. My lawyers did not inform me about the life-changing consequences of this decision."[3]

Looking back, she felt only almighty God could forgive America for unleashing so much destruction on so many tiny lives. "We must repent of our action as a nation in allowing this holocaust to come to our shores. We have to turn from our wicked ways. Senators, I urge you to examine your own conscience before Almighty God. God is willing and able to forgive you. He sent His own son Jesus Christ to die on the cross for my sins as Roe of *Roe v. Wade*, and for our sins in failing to act to end abortion and to truly help women in crisis pregnancies. I finally asked the Lord Jesus to forgive me in 1995 and immediately dedicated my life to saving children's and women's lives."

McCorvey drew the natural parallel between the enslaving of life and the destruction of life—between racial inequality and the right of life. "The Rev. Martin Luther King and the Southern Christian Leadership Conference helped lead America non-violently to end the scourge of segregation," she said. "When slavery was constitutional, we treated one class of humans as property. We are treating the humans in the mother's womb as property and less than human when we say it is OK to kill them. How can we have life, liberty, and the pursuit of happiness, when we have death by abortion?"

She ended her testimony with her honest opinion of the infamous ruling she had been a part of, one that bore her name, as it were: "The Supreme Court of the United States should be ashamed of itself."[4]

Millions of men, women, boys, and girls have a spiritual thirst for God, and when we find everlasting life in Christ, all of life becomes precious.

95

January 19, 1979

The Holy Spirit Was Present

For all have sinned and fall short of the glory of God.

—ROMANS 3:23

I n his book *A Full Life: Reflections at Ninety,* Jimmy Carter described losing his 1966 bid for the governorship of Georgia. He ran against Lester Maddox, and the loss was exceptionally hard because Carter had given up a virtually assured seat in the US House of Representatives to make the race. Furthermore, Maddox was an avowed segregationist.

Carter, disappointed and disillusioned, turned to his sister, evangelist Ruth Carter Stapleton, who encouraged him with Bible verses. She told him to get into his Bible and strengthen his Christian faith. Her advice prompted him to sign up for a trip to share Christ with others. He joined a mission to Lock Haven, Pennsylvania, where he teamed up with a zealous Texas farmer named Milo Pennington.[1]

With the names and addresses on a handful of three-by-five cards, we went from one home to another, always pausing to pray before knocking on the door. With some exceptions, we were invited in to meet with the family members. . . . Milo was a simple, relatively uneducated man blessed with supreme self-assurance. I agreed that he should be the primary witness, and he would explain, in basic words, the plan of salvation: All of us fall short of the glory or perfection of God and deserve punishment; but God loves us, and through his grace and our faith in Christ, not because we have earned it, we are offered complete forgiveness. Jesus had taken on himself our punishment, and through repentance and accepting this forgiveness, we are reconciled to God and, with the Holy Spirit dwelling within us, we can have a full life now and forever.[2]

Carter was astonished at the reception he found in many homes. There was true spiritual hunger and lives were transformed. "I knew the Holy Spirit was present," he said.

This experience and others like it had a profound effect on energizing Carter for a life of deeper service and for seizing opportunities to share his faith. When he ran for president, he had no hesitation telling reporters he was a "born again Christian," and as president he became the best-known Sunday School teacher in the nation, proclaiming "a belief in the Trinity; Christ being both human and God; Jesus' virgin birth, death, and resurrection; and the second coming."[3]

Behind closed doors, Carter also took advantages of opportunities to share Christ. When the president visited Soviet-dominated Warsaw, Poland, First Secretary Edward Gierek asked to speak with him privately. As Carter later recalled,

He said that he espoused atheism as a Communist, but that his mother was a Christian and had recently visited the Vatican. Then, somewhat ill at ease, he asked me if I could explain the foundations of my Christian faith. He listened as I responded, and then I asked him if he would consider accepting Jesus as his personal savior. I had done this hundreds of times as a deacon and in my lay mission work. He replied that he would like to remove the distance from his mother, but he was prohibited from making any public profession of faith. . . . I never knew what his decision was about becoming a Christian before his death in 2001.[4]

On another occasion, President Carter traveled to South Korea where he engaged in contentious negotiations with General Park Chung-hee. After the official meetings, the general asked to see the president privately to ask him about his Christian faith and, as they talked, the general asked Carter to send one of his Baptist friends for further spiritual counseling. "I did this before leaving South Korea," Carter wrote, "and I was later informed that the requested meeting occurred. General Park was assassinated the following year."[5]

In another series of meetings that began in Washington on January 29, 1979, President Carter told Chinese Vice Premier Deng Xiaoping, "When I was a little boy my supreme heroes were Baptist missionaries who served in China, and I used to give five cents a week to help build hospitals and schools for Chinese children. Since 1949, missionaries, Bibles, and worship have been prohibited in your country, and my request is that these three things be permitted."[6]

As a result of his request, some of the prohibitions against Christians were relaxed.

Jimmy Carter's open Bible and deep faith have fueled his work as our longest-living former president, and his life shows us how our temporary defeats can lead to a deeper faith and to a life of greater service.

September 19, 1979

The National Day of Prayer

"Not by might nor by power, but by My Spirit," says the
LORD *of hosts.*

—ZECHARIAH 4:6

Long before America became a nation, our leaders frequently proclaimed national days of fasting, repentance, humility, prayer, and thanksgiving. For example, the Continental Congress, apprehensive of tensions with England and mindful of "the present critical, alarming, and calamitous state of these Colonies," declared July 20, 1775,

> as a Day of Public Humiliation, Fasting and Prayer, that we may with
> united hearts and voices, unfeignedly confess and deplore our many
> sins and offer up our joint supplications to the all-wise, omnipotent,
> and merciful Disposer of all events. . . . And it is recommended to
> Christians of all denominations to assemble for public worship and to
> abstain from servile labor and recreations on the said day.[1]

Such proclamations have frequently punctuated the pages of American history. In his book *One Nation Under God*, James P. Moore Jr. wrote, "To dismiss prayer in the life of America is to embark on a fool's errand. Prayer has been and always will be an integral part of the national character."[2]

During the Korean War and amid the rising threat of global Communism, Americans felt a growing need for united prayer. On April 17, 1952, at the urging of Billy Graham and hotel giant Conrad Hilton, the United States Senate passed a bill, proposed by Senator Frank Carson and championed by Tennessee Congressman Percy Priest, calling on the president to set aside an appropriate day each year as a National Day of Prayer. President Truman signed the bill and issued a proclamation:

> Whereas from the earliest days of our history our people have been accustomed to turn to Almighty God for help and guidance . . . now therefore, I, Harry S. Truman, President of the United States, do hereby proclaim Friday, July 4, 1952, as a National Day of Prayer, on which all of us, in our churches, in our homes, and in our hearts, may beseech God to grant us wisdom to know the course which we should follow, and strength and patience to pursue that course steadfastly.[3]

The presidents' annual proclamations provide insight into their own views of prayer. On September 19, 1979, President Jimmy Carter, a diligent student of the Bible and most famous Sunday School teacher in the nation, called America to prayer with one of his favorite texts, saying, "We accept our responsibilities and make our choices with all the will and determination at our command, but always in the full knowledge that we are finally in the hands of God. In the words of the prophet Zechariah, 'Not by might, not by power but by my Spirit saith the Lord of Hosts.'"[4]

Carter's reference from Zechariah 4:6 comes from one of my favorite Old Testament stories. After Israel's defeat by Babylon and their deportation as refugees, a series of delegations returned to Jerusalem to rebuild the city. The task seemed too great for them politically, monetarily, and emotionally. But God told them it could be done—not by their might or power, but by the presence of His Holy Spirit. And the Spirit's power is gained through prayer.

In his proclamation on April 12, 1994, President Bill Clinton wrote, "From patriots and presidents to advocates for justice, our history reflects the strong presence of prayer in American life. Presidents, above all, need the power of prayer, their own and that of all Americans."[5]

Two years later, Clinton said,

> Prayer remains at the heart of the American spirit. We face many of the same challenges as our forebears—ensuring the survival of freedom and sustaining faith in an often hostile world—and we continue to pray, as they did, for the blessings of a just and benevolent God to guide our Nation's course. This occasion calls us to affirm our country's spiritual roots and to humbly express our gratitude to the source of our abundant good fortune.[6]

In 1988, the law was amended to establish the National Day of Prayer on the first Thursday of each May, stating that it should be a hallowed day. Our nation has never more needed earnest, prevailing prayer for a reversal of evil and for a revival of faith, for wise and godly leaders, and for peace and goodwill in the world.

On the next first Thursday of May, join millions of Americans in beseeching God to bless America. Our problems are not primarily political; they are moral and spiritual—and the answers are spiritual. They will come to us, not by might nor by power, but only by the Spirit of God.

97

August 7, 1982

Ronald Reagan's Remarkable Letter

For God so loved the world that He gave His only begotten Son, that whoever believes in Him should not perish but have everlasting life.

—JOHN 3:16

One Saturday in 1982, Ronald Reagan reached for his White House stationery and wrote a remarkable four-page letter in his distinctive scrawl. It was addressed to his father-in-law, Loyal Davis, a neurosurgeon and an atheist who was dying of cancer. By reading this letter you'll better understand Reagan's cheerful "Morning in America" attitude about life. He also knew, loved, and quoted the most famous verse in the Bible— John 3:16, which is sometimes called the gospel in a nutshell. I'm grateful to the Ronald Reagan Presidential Foundation and Institute for allowing me to publish the letter here exactly as Reagan wrote it, spelling, abbreviation, punctuation, and all:

Aug. 7 [1982]

Dear Loyal,

I hope you'll forgive me for this, but I've been wanting to write you ever since we talked on the phone. I am aware of the strain you are under and believe with all my heart there is help for that.

First I want to tell you of a personal experience I've kept to myself for a long time. During my first year as Governor you'll recall the situation I found in Calif. was almost as bad as the one in Wash. today. It seemed as if the problems were endless and insolvable.

Then I found myself with an ulcer. In all those years at Warner Bros., no one had been able to give me an ulcer and I felt ashamed as if it were a sign of weakness on my part. John Sharpe had me on Malox and I lived with a constant pain that ranged from discomfort to extremely sharp attacks.

This went on for months. I had a bottle of Maalox in my desk, my briefcase and of course at home. Then one morning I got up, went into the bathroom, reached for the bottle as always and some thing happened. I knew I didn't need it. I had gone to bed with the usual pain the night before but I knew that morning I was healed. The Malox went back on the shelf.

That morning when I arrived at the office Helene brought me my mail. The first letter I opened was from a lady—a stranger—in the Southern part of the state. She had written to tell me she was one of a group who met every day to pray for me. Believe it or not, the second letter was from a man, again a stranger, in the other end of the state telling me he was part of a group that met weekly to pray for me.

Within the hour a young fellow from the legal staff came into my office on some routine matter. On the way out he paused in the door and said: "Gov. I think maybe you'd like to know—some of us on the staff come in early every morning and get together to pray for you."

Coincidence? I don't think so. A couple of weeks later Nancy and

I went down to L.A. and had our annual checkup. John Sharpe, a little puzzled, told me I no longer had an ulcer but added there was no indication I'd ever had one. Word of honor—I never told him about that particular day in Sacramento.

There is a line in the bible—"Where ever two or more are gathered in my name there will I be also."

Loyal, I know of your feeling—your doubt but could I just impose on you a little longer? Some seven hundred years before the birth of Christ the ancient Jewish prophets predicted the coming of a Messiah. They said he would be born in a lowly place, would proclaim himself the Son of God and would be put to death for saying that.

All in all there were a total of one hundred and twenty three specific prophesys about his life all of which came true. Crucifixion was unknown in those times, yet it was foretold that he would be nailed to a cross of wood. And one of the predictions was that he would be born of a Virgin.

Now I know that is probably the hardest for you as a Dr. to accept. The only answer that can be given is—a miracle. But Loyal I don't find that as great a miracle as the actual history of his life. Either he was who he said he was or he was the greatest faker & charlatan who ever lived. But would a liar & faker suffer the death he did when all he had to do to save himself was admit he'd been lying?

The miracle is that a young man of 30 yrs. without credentials as a scholar or priest began preaching on street corners. He owned nothing but the clothes on his back & he didn't travel beyond a circle less than one hundred miles across. He did this for only 3 years and then was executed as a common criminal.

But for two thousand years he has . . . had more impact on the world than all the teachers, scientists, emperors, generals and admirals who ever lived, all put together.

The apostle John said, "For God so loved the world that he gave his only begotten son that who so ever believed in him would not perish but have everlasting life."

We have been promised that all we have to do is ask God in Jesus name to help when we have done all we can—when we've come to the end of our strength and abilities and we'll have that help. We only have to trust and have faith in his infinite goodness and mercy.

Loyal, you and Edith have known a great love—more than many have been permitted to know. That love will not end with the end of this life. We've been promised this is only a part of life and that a greater life, a greater glory awaits us. It awaits you together one day and all that is required is that you believe and tell God you put yourself in his hands.

Love

Ronnie

According to journalist and biographer Karen Tumulty, Nancy Reagan later said, "Two days before he [my father] died, he asked to see the hospital chaplain. I don't know what the chaplain did or said, but whatever it was, it was the right thing, and it gave my father comfort. When he died the next day, he was at peace, finally. And I was so happy for him. My prayers were answered."[1]

February 22, 1990

Why Did God Spare Me?

The grass withers, the flower fades,
But the word of our God stands forever.

—Isaiah 40:8

I was surprised at the emotions I felt—they seemed to be shared by people around the world—while watching the funeral of President George H. W. Bush, who died in 2018 at age ninety-four. Bush grew up in the home of devout Episcopalians Prescott and Dorothy Bush, who led family worship every morning from the *Book of Common Prayer*. During World War II, Bush volunteered for the US Navy and became the youngest Navy pilot to receive his wings. He flew over fifty combat missions and was shot down in the South Pacific. His crew perished, but Bush was almost miraculously rescued by an American submarine. He earnestly began asking himself, "Why had I been spared and what did God have for me?"[1]

He came to believe God had spared him to be of service to his country, and Bush went on to serve as a Texas congressman, ambassador to the

United Nations, chairman of the Republican Party, US liaison to China, director of the Central Intelligence Agency, vice president, and finally president of the United States.

He was sworn into office on January 20, 1989, with his hand resting on George Washington's Bible, which was opened to the Beatitudes in Matthew 5. He began his inaugural address, saying,

My first act as President is a prayer. I ask you to bow your heads.

Heavenly Father, we bow our heads and thank You for Your love. Accept our thanks for the peace that yields this day and the shared faith that makes its continuance likely. Make us strong to do Your work, willing to heed and hear Your will, and write on our hearts these words: "Use power to help people." For we are given power not to advance our own purposes, nor to make a great show in the world, nor a name. There is but one just use of power, and it is to serve people. Help us remember, Lord. Amen.[2]

On February 22, 1990, Bush issued this proclamation declaring the International Year of the Bible:

The Bible has had a critical impact upon the development of Western civilization. Western literature, art, and music are filled with images and ideas that can be traced to its pages. More important, our moral tradition has been shaped by the laws and teachings it contains. It was a biblical view of man—one affirming the dignity and worth of the human person, made in the image of our Creator—that inspired the principles upon which the United States is founded. . . . On the American frontier, the Bible was often the only book a family owned. For those pioneers living far from any church or school, it served both as a source of religious instruction and as the primary text from which children learned to read. . . . Today the Bible continues to give courage and direction to those who seek truth and righteousness. In recognizing its enduring value, we recall the words of the prophet Isaiah, who declared, "The grass withereth, the flower fadeth; but the word of our God shall stand forever."[3]

Bush referred to prayer in 220 different speeches, proclamations, and remarks. No other chief executive asserted so often as Bush did that the United States was "one nation under God," and few were so revered for their sympathetic love of others.[4] James Baker, a fellow Christian and Bush's closest colleague, credited Bush with rescuing him years before when Baker was lapsing into alcoholism after the death of his wife from cancer, and the two men shared an uncommon loyalty.

Baker stayed near Bush during his final days, tended to his needs, rubbing his feet, and providing comfort. He called the former president *Jefe* (pronounced Hef'-a), a Spanish word meaning "chief."

On November 30, 2018, Baker entered the bedroom and Bush opened his eyes, looked at him, and asked, "Bake, where are we going today?"

"Well, *Jefe*," said Baker, pausing, "we're going to heaven."

"Good, that's where I want to go."[5]

George H. W. Bush made the journey safely about ten o'clock that night.

September 11, 2001

The Day We'll Never Forget

> *Yea, though I walk through the valley of the*
> *shadow of death,*
> *I will fear no evil;*
> *For You are with me.*
>
> —Psalm 23:4

The horrific terrorist attacks on September 11, 2001, united America as no other event in our lifetimes. Two hijacked airliners crashed into the towers of the World Trade Center, a third plane crashed into the Pentagon, and a fourth was headed toward either the White House or the Capitol.[1]

Aboard United Flight 93, Todd Beamer, using the GTE Airfone at his seat, contacted operator Lisa Jefferson. "We're going to do something," he said. "I'm going to have to go out on faith. . . . It's what we have to do." He asked the operator to recite the Lord's Prayer with him, and they did so: *Our Father which art in heaven. . . .* At the conclusion of the prayer, Todd said, "Jesus, help me." He proceeded to recite the Twenty-third Psalm, apparently with some of the men around him. Then with a deep breath, Todd turned from the phone and said, "Are you ready? Okay. Let's roll."[2] At the cost of their lives, those heroes spared further destruction to the nation's capital.

That night, President George W. Bush addressed the nation from the Oval Office, and he, too, quoted Psalm 23.

> Tonight, I ask for your prayers for all those who grieve, for the children whose worlds have been shattered, for all whose sense of safety and security has been threatened. And I pray they will be comforted by a Power greater than any of us, spoken through the ages in Psalm 23: "Even though I walk through the valley of the shadow of death, I fear no evil for you are with me."[3]

Three days later American and world leaders gathered at the National Cathedral for a service of prayer and remembrance. The choir began with the great hymn "O God Our Help in Ages Past." America's aged pastor Billy Graham, who was helped up the steps and into the pulpit, described the horror and heartbreak of the week and went on to say, in part, "The Bible says, 'God is our refuge and strength, an ever-present help in trouble. Therefore we will not fear, though the earth give way and the mountains fall into the heart of the sea.'"

Graham addressed the question on everyone's mind. Why does God allow evil like this to take place? "I've been asked hundreds of times why God allows tragedy and suffering," said Graham.

> I have to confess that I really do not know the answer totally. I have to accept, by faith, that God is sovereign, and that He is a God of love and mercy and compassion in the midst of suffering. The Bible says God is not the Author of evil. In 1 Thessalonians 2:7 the Bible talks about the mystery of iniquity. The Old Testament Prophet Jeremiah

said, "The heart is deceitful above all things and beyond cure. Who can understand it?"

He explained how Jesus' death on the cross and resurrection was at the core of God's answer and also said,

> I've become an old man now, and I've preached all over the world. And the older I get, the more I cling to that hope that I started with many years ago. . . . In that hymn, "How Firm a Foundation," the words say, "Fear not, I am with thee; O be not dismayed, / For I am thy God, and will give thee aid; / I'll strengthen thee, help thee, and cause thee to stand, / Upheld by My righteous, omnipotent hand."[4]

I was serving as senior pastor of a church in Nashville in 2001, and on the Sunday following the disaster, our congregation was packed—as full as a building can be. For a moment everyone's hearts were shaken, tender, needing courage, and looking toward God. People meeting spontaneously on the streets wept, hugged each other, and prayed. For a few weeks I thought the horrendous events of September 11 had awakened the soul of the nation to another great awakening. But as every pastor of that era will tell you, within a few weeks the crowds fell away, and it almost seemed church attendance returned to normal, or even below normal. I've been haunted ever since, wondering if our nation missed an opportunity to truly return to God.

One thing I know. World conditions are not getting better, and the coming days seem more perilous than ever before. My life's greatest burden and drive is to hold up the cross of Jesus Christ, whether we're in green pastures, by still waters, or traveling through the valley of the shadow of death. Even there, He is with us.

February 7, 2019

The National Prayer Breakfast

*For God has not given us a spirit of fear, but of power
and of love and of a sound mind.*

—2 TIMOTHY 1:7

The National Prayer Breakfast has taken place since 1953, and since the 1980s it has been held at the Washington Hilton ballroom, where more than three thousand people gather from over one hundred countries. It began when Billy Graham was in Portland, Oregon, and met Abraham Vereide, who had been active in starting prayer groups among business leaders in the Northwest. Vereide appealed to Graham about launching a prayer ministry in the nation's capital—an annual Presidential Prayer Breakfast. Graham approached President Eisenhower, who was initially cool to the idea but later gave it his support. Hotel magnate Conrad Hilton agreed to underwrite the event.

The highpoint of the breakfast is a united time of prayer that, for a few minutes, unites souls from diverse parties and governments. But the breakfast has also become a fitting place for presidents to discuss their faith more openly.

On February 13, 2015, President Barack Obama said,

On this occasion, I always enjoy reflecting on a piece of scripture that's been meaningful to me and otherwise sustained me throughout the year. And lately, I've been thinking and praying on a verse from Second Timothy: "For God has not given us a spirit of fear but of power and of love and of a sound mind." [He repeated] For God has not given us a spirit of fear, but of power, and of love and of a sound mind. . . .

For me, and I know for so many of you, faith is the great cure for fear. Jesus is a good cure for fear. God gives believers the power, the love, the sound mind required to conquer any fear. And what more important moment for that faith than right now! What better time than these changing, tumultuous times to have Jesus standing beside us, steadying our minds, cleansing our hearts, pointing us towards what matters. . . .

My faith tells me that I need not fear death; that acceptance of Christ promises everlasting life and the washing away of sins. If Scripture instructs me to "put on the full armor of God" so that when trouble comes, I'm able to stand, then surely I can face down these temporal setbacks, surely I can battle back doubts, surely I can rouse myself to action. . . .

And so, yes, like any person, there are times when I'm fearful. But my faith, and, more importantly, the faith that I've seen in so many of you, the God I see in you, that makes me inevitably hopeful about the future. I have seen so many who know that God has not given us a spirit of fear. He has given us power, and love, and a sound mind.[1]

On February 7, 2019, President Donald Trump looked to President Franklin Roosevelt's prayer for the nation on D-Day and drew inspiration for the power of a praying America:

President Franklin Delano Roosevelt led our nation in prayer. . . . Since the founding of our nation, many of our greatest strides—from gaining our independence, to abolition, to civil rights, to extending the vote for women—have been led by people of faith and started in prayer. . . .

As Jesus promises in the Bible, "Ask and you will receive, and your joy will be complete." We are blessed to live in a land of faith where all things are possible. Our only limits are those we place on ourselves. So true. So today, and every day, let us pray for the future of our country. Let us pray for the courage to pursue justice and the wisdom to forge peace. Let us pray for a future where every child has a warm, safe, and loving home. Let us come together for the good of our people, for the strength of our families, for the safety of our citizens, for the fulfillment of our deepest hopes and our highest potential. And let us always give thanks for the miracle of life, the majesty of creation, and the grace of Almighty God.[2]

May God always give us leaders who pray, who seek His face, who keep their Bibles open and their knees bent, and who willingly say—not as a formality but as the sincere desire of their hearts—may God bless the United States of America.

Conclusion

The Miracle of America

When James A. Garfield was shot, Americans trembled at the thought of Vice President Chester Arthur ascending to the presidency. He was the puppet of crooked political bosses, and he anguished over his reputation of corruption and cronyism. When he heard the president was wounded, he said, "I pray to God that the President will recover. God knows I do not want the place I was never elected to."[1]

But there was one person who admired Arthur though they had never met. Julia Sand was a thirty-one-year-old invalid who lived on New York's East Seventy-Fourth Street, and she took it upon herself to write the vice president. She bluntly told him no one believed in him and that millions of people thought him unfit for office, but that he could be a better man than he was. "Making a man President can change him," she wrote. "Great emergencies awaken generous traits which have lain dormant half a life. If there is a spark of true nobility in you, now is the occasion to let it shine."[2]

Arthur was gripped by the letter. After he moved into the White House, Sand continued writing, and the new president pored over each page as it came. His strange correspondent guided him to find better convictions and deeper ethics than he had known. He surprised America by being, while not a great president, a solid and honest president.

No one knew about the secret correspondence for decades until

319

Arthur's grandson, Chester Arthur III, gained access to a lockbox in a Colorado bank containing some of the late president's private papers, including twenty-three handwritten letters from Miss Sand, who is remembered as perhaps the strangest presidential advisor of them all.

Reading that story, I couldn't help but wonder what would have happened if Chester Arthur had also pored over the sixty-six letters God sent him in the Bible. What if he had studied them as intently as he did the letters of Sand? Jesus said, "Therefore whoever hears these sayings of Mine, and does them, I will liken him to a wise man who built his house on the rock: and the rain descended, the floods came, and the winds blew and beat on that house; and it did not fall, for it was founded on the rock" (Matthew 7:24–25).

The Bible is the cornerstone of American history, which is why throughout the centuries this land has withstood the fury of the winds, tides, and storms.

That our shores should become homeland to persecuted believers seeking freedom to practice their faith; that people would follow by the thousands with Bibles under their arms; that a handful of larger-than-life men and women would converge in Philadelphia as they did; that a freezing, fledgling army led by a bulletproof man should somehow defeat the most powerful military machine on earth; that millions of people here would experience spiritual awakenings of biblical proportions; that the United States would produce generations of preachers, missionaries, educators, businessmen, businesswomen, teachers, statesmen, homemakers, and evangelists to take the gospel to the nations and turn the world upside down; that we would have the mettle to send our nation's sons and daughters into wars for the freedom of tyrannized peoples around the globe; and that this nation would be at the forefront of the greatest humanitarian causes of our day—this is no accident of history. It is the miracle of America.

This is a land upon which God has shed His grace, from sea to shining sea. For this nation to now marginalize, minimize, and malign the role of the Bible in our culture leads to the second half of Christ's analogy: "But everyone who hears these sayings of Mine, and does not do them, will be like a foolish man who built his house on the sand: and the rain descended, the floods came, and the winds blew and beat on that house; and it fell. And great was its fall" (Matthew 7:26–27).

President Harry Truman said,

> The fundamental basis of this Nation's law was given to Moses on the Mount. The fundamental basis of our Bill of Rights comes from the teachings which we get from Exodus and St. Matthew, from Isaiah and St. Paul. . . . If we don't have the proper fundamental moral background, we will finally wind up with a totalitarian government which does not believe in rights for anybody except the state.[3]

To find its future, the United States must recall its past and reform its present. The Bible is the world's only moral compass that points true north, as our founders knew. The hands of the compass have never changed, but somehow we seem headed in different directions today: downward into confusion, division, corruption, and a murky Darwinian morality forged by fickle societal consensus that is shifting by the hour. How strange that a nation would reject its finest founding document and exhibit a tolerance for everyone except those who still affirm the Book that resides at the heart of our history.

Not since the early 1800s have we so needed a great awakening!

But I am truly encouraged now, seeing a new generation emerge with fortitude on their faces, Bibles in their hands, and hope in their hearts. Our nation is not beyond the redemption point. Millions of people are discovering the passion of living counter-culturally, walking with God, and truly becoming, as Jesus said, a shining city upon a hill.

If you look around, you'll see a multiplying army of young adults assertively shining their lights. They—we—cannot be intimidated by secularists, daunted by pundits, corrupted by immorality, or silenced by mockers. We have a God to glorify, a Savior to magnify, and a message to amplify to the world and to generations unborn.

God is not finished with us, nor is the Bible obsolete. It is absolute—absolutely needed and absolutely true. It can be the founding document for your own personal revolution as you turn toward Christ and His kingdom.

Recently I attended a question-and-answer event with former president George W. Bush. The interviewer asked him about his regular daily routine now that he was out of the White House. What does a former president do all day?

I jotted down Bush's reply on a scrap of paper. He said, "There is no regular routine. Every day is different. Today I'm here in Jackson, and tonight I'm flying back to Houston and getting Laura, and we'll be in New York tomorrow. No two days are alike."

Then he paused and said, "Well, there is one part of my routine that doesn't change. Every morning I spend time reading my Bible. I started when I was forty years old. I read the Bible every morning during my presidency, and I do the same now. In fact, I find I need it now more than ever."[4]

So do I!

I hope that, as you lay down this book, you will pick up His Book, which is better by far. Read it daily. Learn its truths. Memorize its verses. Put it into practice and build your life on its teachings and on the Savior whose story is on every page—our Lord Jesus Christ. Put your life on the solid rock, not on the shifting sands.

May God bless you as you do so.

And may He bless the United States of America.

Acknowledgments

O ne of my greatest joys is working with the kind and competent people at HarperCollins Christian Publishing / Thomas Nelson Publishers. My first Thomas Nelson book came out in 1996. Now a quarter-century later, I'm more thrilled than ever to continue partnering with this great company.

100 Bible Verses That Made America has been especially challenging because it's packed with facts, names, dates, quotations, and sources that had to be triple-checked in an earnest attempt at accuracy. It took all of us to produce a book that is factual, historical, readable, and relevant. We've tried our best to do that.

I don't know how to adequately express my thanks to Daisy Hutton, Megan Jayne Dobson, Paula Major, Sam O'Neal, Natalie Nyquist, Kristi Smith, Kristen Andrews, and the entire team of editors, designers, and marketers at W Publishing who have brought this book to you.

Sealy Yates and Matt Yates, my literary agents, guided me through the entire project. It wouldn't have happened without them. I'm especially grateful to Sealy for acquiring permission to use Ronald Reagan's letter. He can pull rabbits out of hats.

My assistant, Sherry Anderson, is a lifesaver, as is Casey Pontious, who tracked down the attributions.

My deepest gratitude goes to my wife, Katrina, who encouraged me, endured the pressures of this project with me, and served as my in-house proofreader and cheerleader.

It's our unwavering conviction that we don't need to apologize for the Bible's role in American history. We don't need to neglect it or minimize it. We need to know about it, celebrate it, and get back to it.

Our combined prayer for this book is that it will reach and teach many people regarding the biblical heritage of America and help steer our nation back to the Bible and back to Christ, who alone is the hope of the world.

Notes

Prologue

1. For additional historical support of Washington's kissing the Bible, see Frederick B. Jonassen, "Kiss the Book . . . You're President . . .: 'So Help Me God' and Kissing the Book in the Presidential Oath of Office," *William and Mary Bill of Rights Journal* 20, no. 3, article 5 (2012): 885–92. My account is also drawn from numerous other sources including "George Washington Inaugural Bible," St. John's Lodge No. 1, http://www.stjohns1 .org/portal/gwib; "George Washington Inaugural Bible," Wikipedia, updated November 22, 2018, https://en.wikipedia.org/wiki/George _Washington_Inaugural_Bible. The visual details of the inauguration are found in Ron Chernow, "George Washington: The Reluctant President," *Smithsonian Magazine* (February 2011), https://www.smithsonianmag.com /history/george-washington-the-reluctant-president-49492/. The fatigue on Washington's face was also observed: "Congressman Fisher Ames of Massachusetts noted that 'time has made havoc' on Washington's face, which already looked haggard and careworn." Quoted in Ron Chernow, *Washington: A Life* (New York: Penguin Books, 2010), 567.

2. George Washington, "Washington's Inaugural Address of 1789," National Archives, https://www.archives.gov/exhibits/american_originals/inaugtxt .html.

3. Quoted in Alexander Biddle, *Old Family Letters* (Philadelphia: J. B. Lippincott Company, 1892), 127–28.

4. John Jay to Peter Augustus Jay, April 8, 1784, in *John Jay: The Winning of the Peace; Unpublished Papers 1780–1784*, vol. 2, ed. Richard B. Morris (New York: Harper & Row Publishers, 1980), 709. My gratitude to WallBuilders .com for this quote.

5. Abraham Lincoln, "To the Coloured Men of Baltimore for a Present of a

Bible," in *Abraham Lincoln's Speeches,* comp L. E. Chittenden (New York: Dodd, Mead & Company, 1896), 346.

6. Ronald C. White, *American Ulysses: A Life of Ulysses S. Grant* (New York: Random House, 2016), 574.

7. Newt Gingrich, *Rediscovering God in America* (Nashville: Thomas Nelson, 2009), 50.

8. Christian F. Reisner, *Roosevelt's Religion* (New York: Abingdon Press, 1922), 306. Also "Vice President Roosevelt on the Bible," *New York Times,* June 12, 1901, 5; Theodore Roosevelt, "On Reading the Bible," speech delivered on June 6, 1901, quoted in Thomas B. Reed, ed., *Modern Eloquence, Vol. 15: Political Oratory ROO–W* (Philadelphia: John D. Morris & Company, 1900), 1770–76, http://www.theodore-roosevelt.com/images/research/txtspeeches/764.pdf.

9. Franklin D. Roosevelt, "Statement on the Four Hundredth Anniversary of the Printing of the English Bible," *American Presidency Project,* October 6, 1935, https://www.presidency.ucsb.edu/documents/statement-the-four-hundredth-anniversary-the-printing-the-english-bible.

10. From various sources, including Jonassen, "Kiss the Book . . . You're President," 854–55.

11. George Washington, "Address to the Delaware Nation, 12 May 1799," National Archives, https://founders.archives.gov/documents/Washington/03-20-02-0388.

1: December 21, 1511: Antonio de Montesinos

1. Francis Augustus MacNutt, *Bartholomew de Las Casas* (New York: G. P. Putnam's Sons, 1909), 54.

2. Lewis Hanke, *The Spanish Struggle for Justice in the Conquest of America* (Philadelphia: University of Pennsylvania Press, 1949), 17.

3. Hanke, *Spanish Struggle,* 22.

4. "Statue of Antonio de Montesinos," Wikimedia Commons, updated April 3, 2018, https://commons.wikimedia.org/wiki/File:Statue_of_Antonio_de_Montesinos,_Santo_Domingo_D.R.jpg.

2: April 20, 1534: Jacques Cartier

1. Joseph Pope, *Jacques Cartier: This Life and Voyages* (Ottawa, ON: A. S. Woodburn, 1891), 35.

2. Pope, *Jacques Cartier,* 36.

3. Sydney Gould, *Inasmuch: Sketches of the Beginnings of the Church of England in Canada in Relation to the Indian and Eskimo Tribes* (Toronto: Missionary Society of the Church of England in Canada, 1917), 70.

4. Pope, *Jacques Cartier*, 86.

5. Pope, *Jacques Cartier*, 87.

3: September 10, 1608: Jamestown

1. Peter Marshall and David Manuel, *The Light and the Glory* (Grand Rapids: Revell, 2009), 112.

2. Lambert Lilly, *The Adventures of Captain John Smith* (New York: D. Appleton & Company, 1842), 155.

4: July 20, 1620: The Pilgrims

1. Nathaniel Philbrick, *Mayflower* (New York: Penguin Books, 2007), 5.

2. Philbrick, *Mayflower*, 5.

3. Philbrick, *Mayflower*, 7.

4. Ozora Stearns Davis, *John Robinson, the Pilgrim Pastor* (Boston: Pilgrim Press, 1903), 238.

5: September 22, 1620: The Mayflower Compact

1. "Mayflower Compact," Wikipedia, updated June 4, 2019, https://en.wikipedia .org/wiki/Mayflower_Compact.

2. Peter Marshall and David Manuel, *The Light and the Glory* (Grand Rapids: Revell, 2009), 153.

6: April 8, 1630: The City on a Hill

1. *Some Old Puritan Love-Letters—John and Margaret Winthrop–1618-1638*, edited by Joseph Hopkins Twichell (New York: Dodd, Mead, and Company, 1894), 152.

2. Edmund Clarence Stedman and Ellen Mackey Hutchinson, eds., *A Library of American Literature from the Earliest Settlement to the Present Time*, vol. 1 (New York: Charles L. Webster & Company, 1891), 306. Punctuation slightly updated.

7: September 8, 1636: The Founding of Harvard

1. *New England's First Fruits* (London: R. O. and J. D. for Henry Overton, 1643), 23, https://archive.org/details/NewEnglandsFirstFruitsInRespect

FirstOfTheCounversionOfSome. Spelling slightly updated. These words still appear on a plaque at Harvard.

2. Harvard University, founded in 1636, claims to be the oldest institution of higher learning in the United States, but the University of Pennsylvania, established in 1740, claims to be America's first university; the College of William and Mary claims to be the first college to become a university.

3. Josiah Quincy, *The History of Harvard University*, vol. 1 (Cambridge, MA: John Owen, 1840), 8.

4. Quincy, *History of Harvard University*, 1, 8–10.

5. Kelly Monroe Kullberg, *Finding God Beyond Harvard* (Downers Grove, IL: IVP Books, 2006), 53.

6. Andrew DelBanco, ed., *Writing New England: An Anthology from the Past to the Present* (Cambridge, MA: Harvard University Press, 2001), 204–5.

7. Kullberg, *Finding God Beyond Harvard*, 57.

8: May 31, 1638: Thomas Hooker

1. Michael Besso, "Thomas Hooker and His May 1638 Sermon," *Early American Studies* (Winter 2012), http://pulpitandpen.org/wp-content/uploads/2015/05/hooker.pdf.

2. Besso, "Thomas Hooker."

3. George L. Walker, *History of the First Church in Hartford: 1633–1883* (Boston: Brown & Gross, 1884), 105–6, quoted in Baird Tipson, *Hartford Puritanism: Thomas Hooker, Samuel Stone, and Their Terrifying God* (New York: Oxford University Press, 2015), 7.

4. United States Congress, *Index to Miscellaneous Documents of the House of Representatives for the Second Session of the Forty-First Congress* (Washington, DC: Government Printing Office, 1870), 267.

5. Deryck Collingwood, *Father of American Democracy: Thomas Hooker* (Interlaken, NY: Heart of the Lakes Pub., 1996). A biographical sketch of Thomas Hooker.

9: December 29, 1649: "God Stept In and Helped"

1. Martin Moore, *Memoirs of the Life and Character of Rev. John Eliot* (Boston: T. Bedlington, 1822), 14.

2. J. Traviss Lockwood, *John Eliot: A Sketch* (Hertford, UK: Stephen Austin & Sons, 1894), 14.

3. Moore, *Memoirs of the Life and Character of Rev. John Eliot*, 23.

4. J. H. Temple, *History of North Brookfield, Massachusetts* (Boston: Rand Avery Company, 1887), 40.

5. Moore, *Memoirs of the Life and Character of Rev. John Eliot*, 87, 163.

6. "Headmaster's Welcome," Roxbury Latin School, https://www.roxburylatin.org/page/about/headmasters-welcome.

7. Lockwood, *John Eliot*, 14.

8. Lockwood, *John Eliot*, 15.

9. Moore, *Memoirs of the Life and Character of Rev. John Eliot*, 148.

10. Joseph Belcher, *The Clergy of America* (Philadelphia: J. B. Lippincott & Company, 1869), 254.

11. *Missionary Book for the Young* (London: Religious Tract Society, 1842), 25.

10: November 22, 1739: William Tennent's Log Cabin Seminary

1. Thomas Murphey, *The Presbytery of the Log College* (Philadelphia: Presbyterian Board of Publication and Sabbath School Work, 1889), 508.

2. Murphey, *Presbytery*, 119–20.

3. George Whitefield, *A Continuation of the Rev. Mr. Whitefield's Journal* (London, 1740), 44.

4. George Whitefield, *George Whitefield's Journals* (London: Banner of Truth Trust, 1965), 354–55.

5. Murphey, *Presbytery*, 78, 120.

6. Murphey, *Presbytery*, 126.

11: May 5, 1740: Citizens of Heaven

1. George Whitefield, *George Whitefield's Journals* (London: Banner of Truth Trust, 1965), 418.

2. Frank R. Symmes, *History of the Old Tennent Church* (Freehold, NJ: James S. Yard & Son, 1897), 39.

3. David T. Myers, "The Remarkable Trance of William Tennent (1705–1777)," *Theology Today* 34, no. 2 (July 1977): 188–91, https://doi.org/10.1177/004057367703400207.

4. Symmes, *Old Tennent Church*, 39–40.

12: October 23, 1740: The News from Heaven

1. Elesha Coffman, "Before Billy Graham There Was . . . ," *Christianity Today*, November 12, 2014, https://www.christianitytoday.com/ct/2014/november-web-only/before-there-was-billy-graham-there-was.html.

2. Quoted in Sinclair Ferguson, *In Christ Alone: Living the Gospel Centered Life* (Orlando: Reformation Trust, 2007), 127.

3. George Whitefield, *George Whitefield's Journals* (London: Banner of Truth Trust, 1965), 479.

4. George Leon Walker, *Some Aspects of the Religious Life of New England* (New York: Silver, Burdett & Company, 1897), 89–92, slightly edited to smooth out archaic language and spellings, https://archive.org/details /someaspectsofrel00walk/page/90.

13: July 8, 1741: America's Most Famous Sermon

1. Jonathan Edwards, *The Works of President Edwards,* vol. 1 (New York: Leavitt, Trow & Company, 1844), 19.

2. Jonathan Edwards, *The Works of President Edwards,* vol. 4 (New York: Leavitt & Allen, 1852), 313–21.

14: October 16, 1746: The Prayer That Sunk a Navy

1. Everett Watson Burdett, *History of the Old South Meeting-House in Boston* (Boston: B. B. Russell, 1877), 26.

2. Catherine Drinker Bowen, *John Adams and the American Revolution* (New York: Grosset & Dunlap, 1950), 10–11.

3. Joseph Cook, *Boston Monday Lectures: Fifth Series* (London: R. D. Dickinson, 1880), 36.

4. William J. Federer, *American Minute* (Louisville: Amerisearch, Inc., 2004), 298.

5. Bowen, *John Adams and the American Revolution*, 10–11.

6. James Pritchard, *Anatomy of a Naval Disaster: The 1746 French Expedition to North America* (Montreal: McGill-Queen's University Press, 1995), 4–5.

7. Bowen, *John Adams and the American Revolution*, 12.

8. Bowen, *John Adams*, 10–12.

9. Burdett, *History of the Old South Meeting-House in Boston*, 105.

15: October 9, 1747: "I Dared to Rejoice in God"

1. Jonathan Edwards, *An Account of the Life of the Late Reverend Mr. David Brainerd* (Edinburgh: Gray & Alston, 1765), vi.

2. Edwards, *David Brainerd*, 71.

3. Edwards, *David Brainerd*, 338.

4. Edwards, *David Brainerd*, 253 (emphasis original).
5. David B. Calhoun, "David Brainerd: 'A Constant Stream,'" *Knowing and Doing* (Summer 2011), http://www.cslewisinstitute.org/David%20Brainerd _A_Constant_Stream_SinglePage.
6. Calhoun, "David Brainerd."
7. Henry Martyn, *Journals and Letters of the Rev. Henry Martyn*, vol. 1 (London: R. B. Seeley & W. Burnside, 1837), 162.
8. John Piper, *The Hidden Smile of God* (Wheaton, IL: Crossway Books, 2001), 13.

16: January 30, 1750: The Catechism of the Revolution

1. Larry Witham, *A City on a Hill: How Sermons Changed the Course of American History* (New York: HarperOne, 2007), 22.
2. Bernard Bailyn, ed., *Pamphlets of the American Revolution, 1750–1776* (Cambridge, MA: Harvard University Press, 1965), 204.
3. John Adams to Thomas Jefferson, July 18, 1818, in *The Papers of Thomas Jefferson*, vol. 13, *22 April 1818 to 31 January 1819*, Retirement Series (Princeton: Princeton University Press, 2004) quoted in Daniel L. Dreisbach, *Reading the Bible with the Founding Fathers* (New York: Oxford University Press, 2017), 128–29.
4. Witham, *A City on a Hill*, 61.
5. Benjamin Hart, *Faith & Freedom: The Christian Roots of American Liberty* (San Bernardino, CA: Here's Life Publishers, 1988), quoted in Pat Robertson, *Courting Disaster: How the Supreme Court Is Usurping the Power of Congress* (Nashville: Thomas Nelson, 2008), chap. 2.
6. Jonathan Mayhew, *A Discourse Concerning Unlimited Submission and Non-Resistance to the Higher Powers* (sermon, Boston, MA, January 30, 1749), 24, 28, 25, https://archive.org/details/discourseconcern1818xmayh /page/24 (emphasis original).

17: June 7, 1753: The Liberty Bell Cracks the Case

1. Gary Nash, *The Liberty Bell* (New Haven, CT: Yale University Press, 2010), 2.
2. "Liberty Bell," *Encyclopedia Britannica*, updated October 26, 2018, https://www.britannica.com/topic/Liberty-Bell.
3. Nash, *The Liberty Bell*, 11.
4. Ben Carson, "What You Don't Know About the Liberty Bell," *Time*, August 24, 2016, https://time.com/4464934/ben-carson-liberty-bell-history/.

18: August 17, 1755: Divine Body Armor

1. "Robert Dinwiddie," *Encyclopedia Brittanica*, updated January 1, 2019, https://www.britannica.com/biography/Robert-Dinwiddie.

2. John Frederick Schroeder, *The Life and Times of Washington*, vol. 1 (New York: Johnson, Fry & Company, 1857), 92.

3. Schroeder, *Life and Times*, 94.

4. Schroeder, *Life and Times*, 94.

5. George Washington Parke Custis, *Recollections and Private Memoirs of Washington* (New York: Derby & Jackson, 1860), 304.

6. Samuel Davies, "Religion and Patriotism: The Constituents of a Good Soldier," (sermon, Captain Overton's Independent Company of Volunteers, Hanover County, VA, August 17, 1755), https://quod.lib.umich .edu/cgi/t/text/text-idx?c=evans;idno=N05830.0001.001;rgn=div1;view =text;cc=evans;node=N05830.0001.001%3A2.

7. Schroeder, *The Life and Times of Washington*, 96; Custis, *Recollections and Private Memoirs of Washington*, 304.

19: December 7, 1771: Sermon at an Execution

1. *The Missionary Review of the World*, 33, no. 12 (December 1910), 915.

2. *Missionary Review of the World*, 915–16.

3. Samson Occom, *The Collected Writings of Samson Occom, Mohegan*, ed. Joanna Brooks (New York: Oxford University Press, 2006), 177–90.

20: March 5, 1774: Parson Parsons

1. Charles Samuel Hall, *Hall Ancestry* (New York: G. P. Putnam's Sons, 1896), 281.

2. Arnold A. Dallimore, *George Whitefield,* vol. 2 (Westchester, IL: Cornerstone Books, 1980), 503–4.

3. Daniel L. Dreisbach, *Reading the Bible with the Founding Fathers* (New York: Oxford University Press, 2017), 195–96.

4. Dreisbach, *Reading the Bible*, 195–96.

5. Dreisbach, *Reading the Bible*, 196.

6. Jim Lampos and Michaelle Pearson, *Revolution in the Lymes* (Charleston, SC: The History Press, 2016), 85.

7. Hall, *Hall Ancestry*, 284.

21: September 7, 1774: The First Prayer of the Continental Congress

1. *Journal of the Proceedings of the Congress Held in Philadelphia, September 5, 1774* (Washington, DC: Government Printing Office, 1904), 26.
2. Kevin J. Dellape, *America's First Chaplain: The Life and Times of the Reverend Jacob Duché* (Bethlehem, PA: Lehigh University Press, 2013), xiii.
3. Office of the Chaplain, "First Prayer of the Continental Congress, 1774," United States House of Representatives, https://chaplain.house.gov/archive/continental.html.
4. John Ward, *The Continental Congress Before the Declaration of Independence with Memoirs of Gov. Samuel Ward and Leut.-Col. Samuel Ward* (New York: 1878), 11.
5. Dellape, *America's First Chaplain*, 2.

22: March 23, 1775: America's Orator Gives the Speech of His Life

1. William Wirt, *Sketches of the Life and Character of Patrick Henry* (Philadelphia: Claxton, Remsen & Haffelfinger, 1878), 43–44.
2. Wirt, *Sketches*, 124–25.
3. In a letter to his daughter on August 20, 1796, Henry wrote, "The view which the rising greatness of our country presents to my eyes is greatly tarnished by the general prevalence of deism; which, with me, is but another name for vice and depravity. I am, however, much consoled by reflecting that the religion of Christ has, from its first appearance in the world, been attacked in vain. . . . I find much to reproach myself that I have lived long and have given no decided and public proofs of my being a Christian. But, indeed, my dear child, this is a character which I prize far above all this world has." Wirt, *Sketches*, 402–3.
4. Condensed and slightly adapted from Wirt, *Sketches*, 138–42.

23: April 19, 1775: The Shot Heard Round the World

1. William Buell Sprague, *Annals of the American Pulpit*, vol. 1 (New York: Robert Carter & Brothers, 1866), 515, https://archive.org/details/annalsofamerican01spra/page/515.
2. Sprague, *Annals*, 516.
3. J. T. Headley, *The Chaplains and Clergy of the Revolution* (New York: Charles Scribner, 1864), 75.

4. Headley, *Chaplains and Clergy*, 75.

5. Sprague, *Annals of the American Pulpit*, 517–18.

6. Eleanor Lexington, "Clark," *The Spirit of '76*, vol. 11, no. 4 (December 1904), 41.

7. Headley, *The Chaplains and Clergy of the Revolution*, 82.

8. Jonas Clark, "The Fate of Blood-Thirsty Oppressors and God's Tender Care of His Distressed People" (sermon, Lexington, KY, April 19, 1776) (Boston: Powars and Willis, 1786), 3–4, http://ota.ox.ac.uk/tcp/headers/N11/N11617 .html.

24: April 23, 1775: The Origin of America's Military Chaplains

1. J. T. Headley, *The Chaplains and Clergy of the Revolution* (New York: Charles Scribner, 1864), 291.

2. William Emerson is often considered the first clergyman to serve solely in the capacity of chaplain in the Revolutionary Army. He was the pastor in Concord when the war began and was the first to arrive when the alarm was sounded. He died of camp fever in 1776. He is the grandfather of Ralph Waldo Emerson. See "Ralph Waldo Emerson," Encyclopedia Britannica, updated May 21, 2019, https://www.britannica.com/biography /Ralph-Waldo-Emerson; https://en.wikipedia.org/wiki/William_Emerson _(minister)#cite_note-2, citing Henry S. Nourse, *History of the Town of Harvard Massachusetts: 1732–1893* (Harvard: Printed for Warren Hapgood, 1894), 212.

3. Headley, *The Chaplains and Clergy of the Revolution*, 292.

4. Headley, *Chaplains and Clergy*, 295.

5. Thomas S. Kidd, *God of Liberty* (Philadelphia: Basic Books, 2010), 3.

25: June 17, 1775: The Boy Who Saw the Battle of Bunker Hill

1. Abigail Adams, *Letters of Mrs. Adams,* vol. 1 (Boston: Charles C. Little & James Brown, 1840), 36–37.

2. Harlow Giles Unger, *John Quincy Adams* (Boston: De Capo Press, 2012), 12.

3. Adams, *Letters of Mrs. Adams*, 39–40.

4. Nathaniel Philbrick, *Bunker Hill* (New York: Viking, 2013), 293.

5. Edward Everett Hale, ed., *Old and New,* vol. 10 (Boston: Roberts Brothers, 1875), 508, quoting John Quincy Adams, *Memoirs of John Quincy Adams, Comprising Portions of His Diary from 1795 to 1848*, vols. 1–2, Charles Frances Adams, ed. (Philadelphia: Lippincott & Company, 1874).

6. Unger, *John Quincy Adams*, 17.

7. Unger, *John Quincy Adams*, 17.

26: January 21, 1776: The Fighting Parson of the Revolution

1. Henry Augustus Muhlenberg, *The Life of Major-General Peter Muhlenberg* (Philadelphia: Carey & Hart, 1849), 53.

2. J. T. Headley, *The Chaplains and Clergy of the Revolution* (New York: Charles Scribner, 1864), 124.

3. Headley, *Chaplains and Clergy*, 126.

27: March 5, 1776: Dorchester Heights

1. John Fiske, *The American Revolution*, vol. 1 (Boston: Houghton, Mifflin & Company, 1899), 170.

2. Hugh Howard, *The Painter's Chair: George Washington and the Making of American Art* (New York: Bloomsbury Press, 2009), 52.

3. Washington Irving, *Life of George Washington*, vol. 1 (New York: G. P. Putnam's Sons, 1876), 222.

4. Michael Medved, *The American Miracle* (New York: Crown Forum, 2016), 52.

5. Elizabeth Bryant Johnston, ed., *George Washington Day by Day* (New York: Baker & Taylor Company, 1895), 41.

6. William Jackson Johnstone, *George Washington the Christian* (New York: Abingdon Press, 1919), 80.

28: May 17, 1776: When Politics Got into the Pulpit

1. Jeffry H. Morrison, *John Witherspoon and the Founding of the American Republic* (Notre Dame, IN: University of Notre Dame, 2005), 4.

2. John Witherspoon, *The Dominion of Providence over the Passions of Men* (Glasgow: Booksellers in Town and Country, 1777), passim.

29: August 29, 1776: The Fog of War

1. Thomas Balch, *Papers Relating Chiefly to the Maryland Line During the Revolution* (Philadelphia: Seventy-Six Society, 1857), 40.

2. David McCullough, *1776* (New York: Simon & Schuster, 2005), 148.

3. J. T. Headley, *The Chaplains and Clergy of the Revolution* (New York: Charles Scribner, 1864), 169.

4. Henry Phelps Johnston, *The Campaign of 1776 Around New York and Brooklyn*, vol. 3 (Brooklyn, NY: Long Island Historical Society, 1878), 78–79.

5. McCullough, *1776*, 191.

30: May 28, 1777: The Prayers That Turned the Tide

1. *The West Parish Church* (Boston: Gunn Curtis Company, 1885), 14.
2. J. T. Headley, *The Chaplains and Clergy of the Revolution* (New York: Charles Scribner, 1864), 13–14.
3. Headley, *Chaplains and Clergy*, 50–51.

31: September 30, 1777: A Speech to Bewildered Men

1. William Wells, *The Life and Public Services of Samuel Adams,* vol. 2 (Boston: Little, Brown & Company, 1865), 490.
2. Wells, *Life and Public Services*, 490.
3. Ira Stoll, *Samuel Adams: A Life* (New York: Free Press, 2008), 9.
4. *Proceedings of the Massachusetts Historical Society,* vol. 20, *1882–1883* (Boston: Massachusetts Historical Society, 1884), 225.
5. Stoll, *Samuel Adams: A Life*, 254.
6. Samuel Adams, *The Writings of Samuel Adams,* vol. 3, *1773–1777,* ed. Harry Alonzo Cushing (New York: G. P. Putnam's Sons, 1907), 334.
7. Wells, *The Life and Public Services of Samuel Adams*, 492–93.

32: October 26, 1777: Watchman, What of the Night?

1. J. T. Headley, *The Chaplains and Clergy of the Revolution* (New York: Charles Scribner, 1864), 311.
2. Headley, *Chaplains and Clergy*, 312.
3. Headley, *Chaplains and Clergy*, 312–13.
4. Headley, *Chaplains and Clergy*, 314–15. This story is also told in Gerald Stanley Lee, *About An Old New England Church* (Sharon, CT: W. W. Knight & Company, 1891), 23–24.
5. Headley, *Chaplains and Clergy*, 315.

33: December 31, 1777: How Prayer Funded the Army at Valley Forge

1. Henry Woodman, *The History of Valley Forge* (Oaks, PA: J. U. Francis, 1920), 30.
2. Kenneth Cain Kinghorn, *The Heritage of American Methodism* (New York: Abingdon Press, 1999), 74.
3. Kinghorn, *Heritage of American Methodism*, 74.
4. James P. Moore Jr., *One Nation Under God: The History of Prayer in America* (New York: Doubleday, 2005), 63.
5. Ryan K. Smith, *Robert Morris's Folly: The Architectural and Financial Failures of an American Founder* (New Haven, CT: Yale University Press, 2014), 5.

34: September 26, 1780: The Sword of the Lord and of Gideon

1. Earle W. Crawford, *Samuel Doak: Pioneer Missionary in East Tennessee* (Washington College, TN: Pioneer Printers, 1980), 25.

2. Pat Alderman, *The Overmountain Men* (Johnson City, TN: Overmountain Press, 1970), 83. The notation at the bottom of the page says, "The sermon and prayer of Samuel Doak are used through the courtesy of Mrs. Rollo H. Henley, Washington College, Tennessee. It was taken from the scrapbook of her father, J. Fain Anderson."

3. Alderman, *The Overmountain Men*, 83.

35: October 19, 1781: The Victory Sermon at Yorktown

1. Israel Evans, "A Discourse Delivered Near York in Virginia on the Memorable Occasion of the Surrender of the British Army to the Allied Forces of America and France" (sermon, York, VA, October 20, 1781), https://quod.lib.umich.edu/cgi/t/text/text-idx?c=evans;cc=evans;view=text;idno=N13869.0001.001;rgn=div1;node=N13869.0001.001:3.

2. Evans, "A Discourse Delivered Near York."

3. John Calvin Thorne, *A Monograph of the Rev. Israel Evans* (monograph, Sixtieth Annual Meeting of the Concord Congregational Union, October 20, 1902), 12.

36: December 11, 1783: God's Instructions to a New Nation

1. Daniel L. Dreisbach, *Reading the Bible with the Founding Fathers* (New York: Oxford University Press, 2017), 98.

2. "February 2: Rev. George Duffield [1732–1790]," This Day in Presbyterian History, February 2, 2012, http://www.thisday.pcahistory.org/2012/02/february-2/.

3. George Duffield, "A Sermon Preached on a Day of Thanksgiving" (sermon, Philadelphia, PA, December 11, 1783), https://www.consource.org/document/a-sermon-preached-on-a-day-of-thanksgiving-by-george-duffield-1783-12-11/.

37: June 28, 1787: The Prayer That Saved the Constitution

1. Quotes in Timothy Pitkin, *A Political and Civil History of the United States of America*, vol. 2 (New Haven, CT: Hezekiah Howe and Durrie & Peck, 1828), 246.

2. Quotes in Timothy Pitkin, *A Political and Civil History*, 246.

3. *The American Museum, or Repository of Ancient and Modern Fugitive*

Pieces, Prose and Poetry, for January 1788, vol. 3, no. 1 (Philadelphia: Mathew Carey, 1788), 17–18.

4. *The Federalist on the New Constitution*, no. 37 (Hallowell, ME: Masters, Smith & Company, 1857), 166.

38: October 26, 1788: Kindling the Second Great Awakening

1. J. Edwin Orr, *Campus Aflame* (Glendale, CA: Regal Books, 1971), 20.
2. Orr, *Campus Aflame*, 25.
3. William Henry Foote, *Sketches of Virginia Historical and Biographical* (Philadelphia: William S. Martien, 1850), 417–18.
4. Foote, *Sketches of Virginia*, 422.

39: September 26, 1789: The Founder Who Walked with God

1. *Calendar of Historical Manuscripts Relating to the War of the Revolution*, vol. 1 (Albany, NY: Weed, Parsons & Company, 1868), 571. Also, William Jay, *The Life of John Jay*, vol. 1 (New York: J. & J. Harper, 1833), 54.
2. Jay, *Life of John Jay*, 262.
3. Quoted in Ellis Washington, *The Progressive Revolution*, vol. 5 (Lanham, MD: Hamilton Books, 2017), 27.
4. Jay, *The Life of John Jay*, 430–31.
5. Jay, *Life of John Jay*, 443.
6. Jay, *Life of John Jay*, 458.
7. G. C. Verplanck, quoted in Jay, *Life of John Jay*, 463.
8. John Jay to Peter Augustus Jay, April 8, 1784, Jay Papers (online edition), Columbia University Library, https://dlc.library.columbia.edu/jay/ldpd:40390.

40: November 26, 1789: An American Holiday Is Born

1. Benjamin Franklin Morris, *Christian Life and Character of the Civil Institutions of the United States* (G. W. Childs, 1874), 274.
2. "George Washington, October 3, 1789, Thanksgiving," Library of Congress, https://www.loc.gov/resource/mgw8a.124/?q=1789+Thanksgiving&sp =132&st=text.
3. T. K. Byron, "Thanksgiving," George Washington's Mount Vernon, www .mountvernon.org/library/digitalhistory/digital-encyclopedia/article /thanksgiving/.
4. William Spohn Baker, *Washington After the Revolution: 1784–1799* (Philadelphia: 1897), 149.

5. "Thanksgiving Proclamation," George Washington Papers, June 21, 2013, http://gwpapers.virginia.edu/documents/thanksgiving-proclamation/.

6. Mary G. Woodhull, "The Early History of Thanksgiving Day," *The Church Standard* 82 (November 23, 1901), 142.

41: December 10, 1795: Invaluable Treasure

1. David Holmes, *The Faiths of the Founding Fathers* (New York: Oxford University Press, 2006), 150.

2. "Personalities George Washington," Central Intelligence Agency, https://www.cia.gov/library/publications/intelligence-history/intelligence/pers.html.

3. William Wallace Atterbury, *Elias Boudinot: Reminiscences of the American Revolution* (Princeton University, 1894), passim.

4. Elias Boudinot, *The Age of Revelation* (Philadelphia: Asbury Dickins, 1801), iv.

5. Boudinot, *Age of Revelation*, xv–xvi.

6. Atterbury, *Elias Boudinot*.

7. *The National Portrait Gallery of Distinguished Americans*, vol. 3 (Philadelphia: Henry Perkins, 1836), s.v. "Elias Boudinot."

42: April 25, 1799: The Father of American Geography

1. William Buell Sprague, *The Life of Jedidiah Morse* (New York: Anson D. F. Randolph, 1874), xv.

2. Sprague, *Life of Jedidiah Morse*, xviii.

3. Sprague, *Life of Jedidiah Morse*, xxxii.

4. Jedidiah Morse, "A Sermon, Exhibiting the Present Dangers, and Consequent Duties of the Citizens of the United States of America" (sermon, Charlestown, MA, April 25, 1799), https://archive.org/details/sermonexhibiting00morsrich/page/n15.

5. Sprague, *Life of Jedidiah Morse*, i.

6. Sprague, *Life of Jedidiah Morse*, 192.

7. Sprague, *Life of Jedidiah Morse*, 194.

8. Sprague, *Life of Jedidiah Morse*, passim.

43: June 6, 1799: Patrick Henry's Sealed Envelope

1. Samuel Adams to Richard Henry Lee, December 23, 1784, in *Memoirs of the Life of Richard Henry Lee and His Correspondence,* 2 vols. (Philadelphia: William Brown, 1825), 129, quoted in Daniel L. Dreisbach, *Reading the Bible with the Founding Fathers* (New York: Oxford University Press, 2017), 146–47.

2. Samuel Cooper, *A Sermon Preached Before His Excellency John Hancock* (Boston: T. and J. Fleet and J. Gill, 1780), quoted in Dreisbach, *Reading the Bible*, 146.

3. "Thanksgiving, Fasting and Prayer Proclamations of the Founders," Utah Society Sons of the American Revolution, http://utahsocietysar.org/wordpress /home/resources/educational-resources/thanksgiving-fasting-and-prayer -proclamations-of-the-founders.

4. Moses Coit Tyler, *Patrick Henry* (Boston: Houghton Mifflin & Company, 1899), 422.

5. Quoted in J. N. Larned, *History for Ready Reference*, vol. 5 (Springfield, MA, 1895), 3187–88.

44: June 4, 1800: Noah Webster and His Dictionary

1. "Noah Webster," Wikipedia, updated June 4, 2019, https://en.wikipedia.org /wiki/Noah_Webster.

2. Joshua Kendall, *The Forgotten Founding Father: Noah Webster's Obsession and the Creation of an American Culture* (New York: Berkley Books, 2012), 6.

3. Kendall, *Forgotten Founding Father*, 87.

4. Kendall, *Forgotten Founding Father*, for this and preceding paragraphs, passim.

5. Noah Webster, *Letter from Noah Webster, Esq of New Haven, Connecticut to a Friend* (New York: J. Seymour, Printer, 1809), 10–11.

45: August 6, 1801: America's Pentecost

1. Richard J. Hooker, *The Carolina Backcountry on the Eve of the Revolution* (Chapel Hill, NC: University of North Carolina Press, 1953), 77.

2. William Francis Noble, *A Century of Gospel Work* (Philadelphia: H. C. Watts & Company, 1876), 30.

3. James R. Rodgers, *The Cane Ridge Meeting-House* (Cincinnati: Standard Publishing Company, 1910), 155.

4. Rodgers, *Cane Ridge Meeting-House*, 157–58. Barton's estimate of the attendance is thought to have been too generous. Most scholars suggest that between ten thousand and twenty-five thousand people attended at some point during the meetings.

5. Paul K. Conkin, *Cane Ridge: America's Pentecost* (Madison, WI: University of Wisconsin Press, 1990), 3.

46: July 11, 1804: The Death of Alexander Hamilton

1. Samuel M. Smucker, *The Life and Times of Alexander Hamilton* (Boston: L. P. Crown & Company, 1857), 366–76.

47: June 27, 1810: The Haystack Prayer Meeting

1. Thomas C. Richards, *Samuel J. Mills* (Boston: Pilgrim Press, 1906), 25.
2. Gardiner Spring, *Memoirs of the Rev. Samuel J. Mills* (London: Francis Westley, 1820), 9.
3. Spring, *Memoirs*, 15.
4. Today a monument at Williams College commemorates the Haystack Prayer Meeting, but there are ongoing discussions about removing it because critics consider it offensive.
5. Richards, *Samuel J. Mills*, 30.
6. *The One Hundredth Anniversary of the Haystack Prayer Meeting* (Boston: American Board of Commissioners for Foreign Missions, 1907), 4.
7. Spring, *Memoirs of the Rev. Samuel J. Mills*, 23–24.
8. Spring, *Memoirs*, 27.
9. Richards, *Samuel J. Mills*, 212.

48: April 19, 1813: The Father of American Medicine

1. Benjamin Rush, *Letters of Benjamin Rush*, vol. 1, ed. L. H. Butterfield (Princeton: The American Philosophical Society, 1952), 414.
2. Benjamin Rush, "To the Citizens of Philadelphia: A Plan for Free Schools," March 28, 1787. Also see David Barton, *Benjamin Rush* (Aledo, TX: WallBuilders, 1999), 50.
3. Benjamin Rush, *Six Introductory Lectures, to Courses of Lectures, Upon the Institutes and Practice of Medicine, Delivered in the University of Pennsylvania* (Philadelphia: John Conrad & Co.; E. Maxwell, Printer, 1801), 121–42. Also see Barton, *Benjamin Rush*, 73.
4. Barton, *Benjamin Rush*, 83–84.

49: August 24, 1814: The Tornado That Saved Washington

1. Dolley Madison, *Memoirs and Letters of Dolley Madison* (Boston: Houghton, Mifflin & Company, 1886), 110–11, https://archive.org/details/memoirslettersof00madi/page/110.
2. Madison, *Memoirs and Letters*, 113–14.

3. Joel Richard Paul, *Without Precedent: Chief Justice John Marshall and His Times* (New York: Riverhead Books, 2018), 323–24.

4. Sarah Zielinski, "The Tornado That Saved Washington," *Smithsonian Magazine*, August 25, 2010, www.smithsonianmag.com/science-nature /the-tornado-that-saved-washington-33901211/.

5. NCC Staff, "The Tornado That Stopped the Burning of Washington," Constitution Center, August 25, 2015, constitutioncenter.org/blog /the-tornado-that-stopped-the-burning-of-washington/.

6. Kevin Ambrose, "The Thunderstorm That Saved Washington," *Washington Post*, July 15, 2010, voices.washingtonpost.com/capital weathergang/2010/07/the_thunderstorm_that_saved_wa.html.

7. James Madison, "Presidential Proclamation, 4 March 1815," National Archives, https://founders.archives.gov/documents/Madison/99-01-02 -4146, from an Early Access documents of The James Madison Papers, https://rotunda.upress.virginia.edu/founders/default.xqy?keys=FOEA -print-02&mode=TOC.

8. Dolley Madison, *Memoirs and Letters of Dolley Madison*, 113–209.

50: March 31, 1816: Circuit Riders Who Tamed the Frontier

1. *Christian History Magazine*, 14, no. 1, issue 45 (1995): 29.

2. Francis Asbury, *Journal of Francis Asbury*, vol. 2 (New York: Lane & Scott, 1852), 23.

3. *Christian History Magazine*, 3 and 22.

4. Peter Cartwright, *The Autobiography of Peter Cartwright* (New York: Abingdon Press, 1956), 143.

51: May 11, 1816: "Give Me That Book!"

1. William Peter Strickland, *History of the American Bible Society* (New York: Harper & Brothers, 1849), 17.

2. *Journals of the American Congress: From 1774 to 1788,* vol. 4 (Washington, DC: Way and Gideon, 1823), 76.

3. "The Bible of the American Revolution: The Aitken Bible," Museum of the Bible, https://www.museumofthebible.org/book/minutes/487.

4. Strickland, *History of the American Bible Society*, 59.

5. Strickland, *American Bible Society*, 83.

6. Strickland, *American Bible Society*, 84.

7. Strickland, *American Bible Society*, 415.

52: December 30, 1823: Preaching in Sodom

1. Charles G. Finney, *Memoirs of Rev. Charles G. Finney* (New York: Fleming H. Revell Company, 1876), 98–105.

53: July 4, 1826: Benjamin Rush's Amazing Dream

1. Thomas Jefferson, "Editorial Note," *Founders Online*, National Archives, accessed April 11, 2019, https://founders.archives.gov/documents /Jefferson/03-04-02-0296-0001, from *The Papers of Thomas Jefferson*, Retirement Series, vol. 4, *18 June 1811 to 30 April 1812*, ed. J. Jefferson Looney (Princeton: Princeton University Press, 2007), 389.
2. "To John Adams from Benjamin Rush, 17 February 1812," National Archives, https://founders.archives.gov/documents/Adams/99-02-02 -5758, from an Early Access document from The Adams Papers, https://founders.archives.gov/about/Adams.
3. David Barton, *Benjamin Rush: Signer of the Declaration of Independence* (Aledo, TX: WallBuilder Press, 1999), 200.

54: April 23, 1833: The Nation's Schoolmaster

1. John H. Westerholf III, *McGuffey and His Readers* (Milford, MI: Mott Media, 1982), 52.
2. Westerholf, *McGuffey and His Readers*, 61.
3. Westerholf, *McGuffey and His Readers*, 77.
4. Charles Bryan, "Books That Changed the Course of U.S. History" (lecture, Alexandria Library Company, Alexandria, VA, 2008), quoted in Quentin R. Skrabec Jr., *William McGuffey: Mentor to American Industry* (New York: Algora Publishing, 2009), 7.
5. Westerholf, *McGuffey and His Readers*, 13.
6. Hugh Fullerton, "That Guy McGuffey," *Saturday Evening Post*, November 26, 1927, https://archive.org/details/ SaturdayEveningPostV200N2219271126/page/n16.
7. Skrabec, *William McGuffey*, 1.
8. W. H. McGuffey, *The Eclectic Second Reader* (Cincinnati: Truman & Smith, 1836), 22–23.

55: December 4, 1833: The Tappan Brothers

1. Lewis Tappan, *The Life of Arthur Tappan* (New York: Hurd & Houghton, 1870), 46–48.

2. Barry Hankins, *The Second Great Awakening and the Transcendentalists* (Westport, CT: Greenwood Press, 2004), 98.

3. Tappan, *The Life of Arthur Tappan*, 112.

4. Tappan, *Life of Arthur Tappan*, 144–45.

5. Tappan, *Life of Arthur Tappan*, 173–75.

6. Tim Stafford, "The Abolitionists," *Christian History*, issue 33, 24, https://christianhistoryinstitute.org/magazine/article/abolitionists.

7. Tappan, *The Life of Arthur Tappan*, 378.

56: June 21, 1834: Better Make It a Hundred

1. Herbert N. Casson, *Cyrus Hall McCormick* (Chicago: A. C. McClurg & Company, 1909), 40.

2. Casson, *Cyrus Hall McCormick*, 53.

3. Casson, *Cyrus Hall McCormick*, 160.

4. Casson, *Cyrus Hall McCormick*, 151.

5. Casson, *Cyrus Hall McCormick*, 97.

6. Casson, *Cyrus Hall McCormick*, 188.

7. Casson, *Cyrus Hall McCormick*, vi, 47.

57: November 7, 1837: Freedom of the Press

1. Joseph and Owen Lovejoy, *Memoir of the Rev. Elijah P. Lovejoy* (New York: John S. Taylor, 1838), passim.

58: March 1, 1841: The Friend of Both Washington and Lincoln

1. Harlow Giles Unger, *John Quincy Adams* (New York: Da Capo Press, 2012), 3.

2. Samuel W. Baily, comp., *Homage of Eminent Persons to the Book* (New York: Rand, Avery & Frye, 1870), 17.

3. Baily, *Homage*, 18.

4. C. Edward Spann and Michael E. Williams, Sr., *Presidential Praise* (Macon, GA: Mercer University Press, 2008), 43.

5. Argument of John Quincy Adams, Before the Supreme Court of the United States [. . .] delivered on the 24th of February and 1st of March 1841 (New York: S. W. Benedict, 1841), quoted in David Barton, *A Spiritual Heritage* (Aledo, TX: WallBuilders, 2012), 92–93.

59: May 24, 1844: The Artist Who Struck Lightning

1. Michael Farris, *American Commencement* (Nashville: B&H Publishing Group), 129.

2. Daniel Walker Howe, *What Hath God Wrought* (New York: Oxford University Press, 2007), 692.
3. Kenneth Silverman, *Lightning Man* (New York: Alfred A. Knopf), chap. 3.
4. Howe, *What Hath God Wrought*, 692.
5. Louis Albert Banks, *The Religious Life of Famous Americans* (New York: American Tract Society, 1904), 31.
6. William Kloss, *Samuel F. B. Morse* (New York: Harry N. Abrams, Inc., 1988), 148.
7. Banks, *The Religious Life of Famous Americans*, 36–37.
8. Banks, *Religious Life*, 37.
9. John Trowbridge, *Samuel Finley Breese Morse* (Boston: Small, Maynard & Company, 1901), vii, 1.

60: June 8, 1845: Old Hickory's Firm Foundation

1. Cyrus Townsend Brady, *The True Andrew Jackson* (Philadelphia: J. B. Lippincott Company, 1906), 377–78.
2. Amos Russell Wells, *A Treasure of Hymns* (Boston: United Society of Christian Endeavor, 1914), 41.
3. Brady, *The True Andrew Jackson*, 372.
4. Samuel G. Heiskell, *Andrew Jackson and Early Tennessee History*, vol. 3 (Nashville: Ambrose Printing Company, 1921), 687.
5. James Parton, *The Life of Andrew Jackson*, vol. 3 (New York: Mason Brothers, 1861), 672.
6. Parton, *Life of Andrew Jackson*, 673.
7. Robert V. Remini, "The Final Days and Hours in the Life of General Andrew Jackson," *Tennessee Historical Quarterly* 39, no. 2 (Summer 1980), 176.
8. Remini, "Final Days and Hours," 175–76.
9. Remini, "Final Days and Hours," 176.
10. Parton, *The Life of Andrew Jackson*, 677.
11. Parton, *The Life of Andrew Jackson*, 677.
12. Parton, *The Life of Andrew Jackson*, 678.
13. Remini, "Final Days and Hours in the Life of General Andrew Jackson," 177.

61: February 23, 1848: Death in the House

1. William H. Seward, *Life and Public Services of John Quincy Adams* (Auburn: Derby, Miller & Company, 1849), 326.
2. This paragraph along with preceding and following paragraphs adapted from Seward, *Life and Public Services*, chap. 15.

3. Seward, *Life and Public Services*, 339.

4. Seward, *Life and Public Services*, 349.

62: September 17, 1849: Go Down, Moses

1. Sarah H. Bradford, *Scenes in the Life of Harriet Tubman* (Auburn, NY: W. J. Moses, 1869), 10.

2. Bradford, *Life of Harriet Tubman*, 14–15, language updated.

3. Bradford, *Life of Harriet Tubman*, 20, language updated.

4. Bradford, *Life of Harriet Tubman*, 25, language updated.

5. Bradford, *Life of Harriet Tubman*, 35, language updated.

63: June 5, 1851: Book of the Century

1. Charles Edward Stowe, *Life of Harriet Beecher Stowe* (London: Sampson Low, Marston, Searle & Rivington, 1889), 9–10.

2. Stowe, *Harriet Beecher Stowe*, 33–34.

3. Stowe, *Harriet Beecher Stowe*, 145.

4. Stowe, *Harriet Beecher Stowe*, 156.

5. Stowe, *Harriet Beecher Stowe*, 159.

6. Stowe, *Harriet Beecher Stowe*, 160.

7. Attributed to Abraham Lincoln.

8. Stowe, *Life of Harriet Beecher Stowe*, 507.

64: July 5, 1852: Frederick Douglass and the Fourth of July

1. Adelle M. Banks, "5 Religious Facts You Might Not Know About Frederick Douglass," *Washington Post*, June 19, 2013, https://www.washingtonpost.com/national/on-faith/5-religious-facts-you-might-not-know-about-frederick-douglass/2013/06/19/25cca02e-d922-11e2-b418-9dfa095e125d_story.html?noredirect=on&utm_term=.2f122a5ee5a1.

2. Timothy Sandefur, *Frederick Douglass* (Washington, DC: Cato Institute, 2018), 17.

3. Frederick Douglass, "Oration, Delivered in Corinthian Hall, Rochester, by Frederick Douglass, July 5th, 1852," at https://rbscp.lib.rochester.edu/2945.

65: September 23, 1857: Revival Sweeps the Country

1. Some of the details of Lanphier's life are taken from his obituary in the *New York Observer*, May 29, 1898.

2. S. Irenaeus Prime, *Prayer and Its Answer: Illustrated in the First*

Twenty-Five Years of the Fulton Street Prayer Meeting (New York: Charles Scribner's Sons, 1882), 24.

3. Henry W. Adams, "God and One Man: The Story of America's Greatest Revival," *The Christian Worker's Magazine*, December 1916, 274.

4. Jay Benson Hamilton, ed., "Noonday Prayer Meetings Throughout the Union," *Bible Champion*, vols. 18–19 (1914–15), 214.

5. Hamilton, "Noonday Prayer Meetings," 216.

6. Wesley Duewel, *Revival Fire* (Grand Rapids: Zondervan, 1995) 133.

7. J. Edwin Orr, *The Second Evangelical Awakening* (London: Marshall, Morgan & Scott, 1955), 16–17. Also J. Edwin Orr, *Campus Aflame* (Glendale, CA: Regal Books, 1971), 54.

66: January 1, 1863: The Day the Nation Felt Clean

1. Frederick Douglass, *The Life and Times of Frederick Douglass* (London: Christian Age Office, 1882), 307–9.

2. John S. Dwight, "The Jubilee Concert," in *Dwight's Journal of Music,* vols. 21–22 (Boston: Oliver Ditson & Company, 1863), 326–28.

3. Dwight, "The Jubilee Concert," 326–28.

67: July 5, 1863: Wrestling in Prayer for Gettysburg

1. James Fowler Rusling, *Men and Things I Saw in the Civil War Days* (New York: Eaton & Mains Press 1899), 12–17.

2. L. P. Brockett, *The Life and Times of Abraham Lincoln* (Philadelphia: Bradley & Company, 1865), 711.

68: September 6, 1863: Revival in the Ranks

1. Rachel Coker, "Historian Revises Estimate of Civil War Dead," Discover-e Binghamton Research, September 21, 2011, https://discovere.binghamton.edu/news/civilwar-3826.html.

2. "Did You Know?," *Christian History Magazine* 11, no. 1, issue 33, 2, 30.

3. "Did You Know?," 3.

4. William R. Moody, *Life of D. L. Moody* (New York: Fleming Revell Company, 1900), 89–90.

5. John William Jones, *Christ in the Camp* (Atlanta: Martin & Hoyt Company, 1887), 246.

6. Jones, *Christ in the Camp*, 259.

69: August 16, 1864: Providence Spring

1. John L. Maile, *Prison Life in Andersonville* (Los Angeles: Grafton Publishing Company, 1912), 56, https://archive.org/details/prisonlifeinande00mail/page/56.
2. Maile, *Prison Life in Andersonville*, 62.
3. Maile, *Prison Life in Andersonville*, 62–63.
4. Maile, *Prison Life in Andersonville*, 65–66.
5. Maile, *Prison Life in Andersonville*, 69.
6. Barry Loudermilk, *And Then They Prayed* (Campbell, CA: FastPencil, 2011), 29.
7. As would be expected with thirty-three thousand prisoners, there are various accounts of this story, but most agree on the basic facts—a devastating scarcity of water, prayer, and a terrible storm that somehow released an underground spring.

70: April 14, 1865: Lincoln's Last Words

1. Ward Hill Lamon and Chauncey F. Black, *The Life of Abraham Lincoln* (Boston: James R. Osgood & Company, 1872), 493.
2. Lamon and Black, *Life of Abraham Lincoln*, 494.
3. James A. Reed, "The Later Life and Religious Sentiments of Abraham Lincoln," in *Scribner's Monthly*, vol. 6 (New York: Scribner & Company, 1873), 338–39.
4. Stephen Mansfield, *Lincoln's Battle with God* (Nashville: Thomas Nelson, 2012), 153.
5. Amos Stevens Billingsley, *Christianity in the War* (Philadelphia: Claxton, Remsen & Haffelfinger, 1872), 336.
6. Reed, "The Later Life and Religious Sentiments of Abraham Lincoln," 339.
7. Mansfield, *Lincoln's Battle With God*, xvii. This account comes from Mary Todd Lincoln's recollections given to Noyes W. Miner, pastor of the First Baptist Church in Springfield, Illinois. Mansfield points out in a footnote that some historians believe this conversation may have occurred the day before the assassination when the Lincolns went for a carriage ride. Also Reed, "The Later Life and Religious Sentiments of Abraham Lincoln," 339.
8. Reed, "Later Life," 343.
9. Billingsley, *Christianity in the War*, 339.

71: November 20, 1866: The Christian General

1. Oliver Otis Howard, *Autobiography of Oliver Otis Howard*, vol. 1 (New York: Baker & Taylor Company, 1907), 81.
2. Howard, *Autobiography*, 249–50.

3. Daniel Sharfstein, "The Namesake of Howard University," *Smithsonian*, May 23, 2017, https://www.smithsonianmag.com/history/namesake-howard -university-spent-years-kicking-native-americans-out-180963409/.

72: March 4, 1881: The Prayer That Saved a President

1. See Stephen G. Yanoff, *The Second Mourning: The Untold Story of America's Most Bizarre Political Murder* (Bloomington, IN: AuthorHouse, 2014), 38. Also William M. Thayer, *From Log Cabin to the White House* (Boston: James H. Earle Publisher, 1881), 208–10; Ruth Tenzer Feldman, *James Garfield* (Minneapolis: Leaner Publications Company, 2005), 8. Also Candice Millard, *Destiny of the Republic* (New York: Doubleday, 2011), 21.
2. William Judson Hampton, *Our Presidents and Their Mothers* (Boston: Cornhill Publishing Company, 1922), 159.
3. Benson John Lossing, *A Biography of James A. Garfield* (New York: Henry S. Goodspeed & Company, 1882), 66.
4. Lossing, *James A. Garfield*, 75.
5. Lossing, *James A. Garfield*, 94.
6. David Barton, *A Spiritual Heritage* (Aledo, TX: WallBuilders, 2000), 36. Barton attributes this to a personal letter from Garfield, which is in his possession.
7. Lossing, *A Biography of James A. Garfield*, 83.

73: December 6, 1884: A Virtual Bible Engraved in Stone

1. Newt Gingrich, *Rediscovering God in America* (Nashville: Thomas Nelson, 2009), 30.
2. "Declaration of Independence: A Transcription," National Archives, https://www.archives.gov/founding-docs/declaration-transcript. The text is a transcription of the Stone Engraving of the parchment Declaration of Independence, and the spelling and punctuation reflect the original.
3. Gingrich, *Rediscovering God in America*, 80.

74: December 24, 1898: Christmas Eve in the War Zone

1. Louis F. Benson, *Studies of Familiar Hymns* (Philadelphia: Westminster Press, 1903), 46–48.
2. Albert Loren Cheney, *Personal Memoirs of the Home Life of the Late Theodore Roosevelt* (Washington, DC: Cheney Publishing Company, 1919), 125.

75: November 21, 1899: A President Like That

1. Karl Rove, *The Triumph of William McKinley* (New York: Simon & Schuster, 2015), 1.
2. Rove, *Triumph of William McKinley*, 4.
3. Elwood Corning, *William McKinley: A Biographical Study* (New York: Broadway Publishing Company, 1907), 172.
4. Corning, *William McKinley*, 172–73.
5. Louis Albert Banks, *The Religious Life of Famous Americans* (Boston: American Tract Society, 1904), 69.
6. George A. Malcolm, *The Government of the Philippine Islands* (Rochester, NY: The Lawyers Co-Operative Publishing Company, 1916), 187.

76: September 14, 1901: The Assassination of William McKinley

1. Marshall Everett, *Complete Life of William McKinley and Story of His Assassination* (n.p., 1901), 35.
2. James P. Moore Jr., *One Nation Under God* (New York: Doubleday, 2005), 240.
3. Samuel Fallows, ed., *Life of William McKinley Our Martyred President* (Chicago: Regan Printing House, 1901), 13–25.
4. Fallows, *Life of William McKinley*, 36–39.

77: March 26, 1905: The Queen of American Hymn Writers

1. Bernard Ruffin, *Fanny Crosby* (Philadelphia: United Church Press, 1976), 19.
2. This hymn appears in over 850 hymnals, making it her most popular work. http://www.hymntime.com/tch/htm/b/l/e/s/s/e/blesseda.htm.
3. Robert J. Morgan, *Then Sings My Soul* (Nashville: Thomas Nelson, 2003), 183.
4. Fanny Crosby, "Blessed Assurance" (1873).

78: December 3, 1911: The Biblical Secret of America's Retailer

1. Herbert Ershkowitz, *John Wanamaker: Philadelphia Merchant* (Conshohocken, PA: Combined Publishing, 1999), 176–77.
2. Paul Lee Tan, *Encyclopedia of 7700 Illustrations* (Rockville, MD: Assurance Publishers, 1980), 736.

79: July 16, 1914: The Concoction

1. Mark Pendergrast, *For God, Country, and Coca-Cola* (New York: Basic Books, 2000), 61.

2. Anna Tyszkiewicz, "Candler, Asa Griggs," Learning to Give, www.learning togive.org/resources/candler-asa-griggs.

3. "Methodism's $1,000,000 Reply to Mr. Carnegie," *Literary Digest* 49, part 1, April 1, 1914, 196.

80: July 12, 1917: The Book in the Trenches

1. "World War I Casualties," Wikipedia, updated June 4, 2019, https://en .wikipedia.org/wiki/World_War_I_casualties.

2. Jay Winter, "How the Great War Shaped the World," *Atlantic*, World War I Commemorative Issue (August 2014), https://www.theatlantic.com /magazine/archive/2014/08/how-the-great-war-shaped-the-world/373468/.

3. "The Most Read Book in the Trenches of World War I," United Bible Societies, July 28, 2014, https://www.unitedbiblesocieties.org/the-most -widely-read-book-in-the-trenches-of-world-war-i/.

4. "BBC Report Highlights Importance of Bible to WW1 Soldiers," Bible Society, November 6, 2018, https://www.biblesociety.org.uk/latest/news /bbc-report-highlights-importance-of-bible-to-ww1-soldiers/.

5. "The Progress of a Bullet," *Bible Society Record*, vol. 62, June 1917, 112, https:// babel.hathitrust.org/cgi/pt?id=nyp.33433089912566&view=1up&seq=372.

6. Hazel Southam, "A Lantern Unto Their Feet," *Church Times*, August 1, 2014, https://www.churchtimes.co.uk/articles/2014/1-august/features /features/a-lantern-unto-their-feet.

7. Chuck Norris, "Bullet-Ridden Bible Saves Soldier," WND, November 11, 2018, https://www.wnd.com/2018/11/bullet-ridden-bible-saves-soldier/.

8. "Notes and Comments," *Bible Society Record*, vol. 61, July 1916, 149, https:// babel.hathitrust.org/cgi/pt?id=nyp.33433089912566&view=1up&seq=157. Owen Davies, *A Supernatural War* (Oxford: Oxford University Press, 2018), 181.

81: March 4, 1933: May He Guide Me

1. The Avalon Project, "First Inaugural Address of Franklin D. Roosevelt," Yale Law School, http://avalon.law.yale.edu/20th_century/froos1.asp.

2. Kenneth S. Davis, *FDR: The Beckoning of Destiny, 1882–1928* (New York: Random House/History Book Club, 1971, 2003 ed.), 83, quoted in C. Edward Spann and Michael E. Williams Sr., *Presidential Praise* (Macon, GA: Mercer University Press, 2008), 215.

82: October 8, 1934: A Letter to Almighty God

1. W. O. Saunders was a North Carolina newspaper editor who constantly attacked Ham and wrote a book, *The Book of Ham*, targeting him.
2. Edward E. Ham, *50 Years on the Battle Front with Christ: A Biography of Mordecai F. Ham* (Louisville: Old Kentucky Home Revivalist, 1950), 231–32. I am indebted to Bob Shuster at the Billy Graham Center Archives for helping me locate this letter.
3. "Billy Graham: Profile," Billy Graham Evangelistic Association, https://billy graham.org/about/biographies/billy-graham/.

83: January 17, 1941: The Verse That Made Churchill Weep

1. David L. Roll, *The Hopkins Touch: Harry Hopkins and the Forging of the Alliance to Defeat Hitler* (New York: Oxford University Press, 2013), 79.
2. Doris Kearns Goodwin, *No Ordinary Time* (New York: Simon & Schuster, 1994), 212.
3. James MacManus, "This Is Winston Churchill in Glasgow," *The Sunday Mail* (Glasgow, Scotland), February 15, 2015.
4. Goodwin, *No Ordinary Time*, 213. Also Alan Chanter, "Harry Hopkins," World War II Database, updated August 2018, https://ww2db.com/person _bio.php?person_id=1075; Roll, *Hopkins Touch*, 90.
5. H. V. Morton, *Atlantic Meeting* (London: Methuen & Company, 1943), 100, quoted in James P. Moore Jr., *One Nation Under God* (New York: Doubleday, 2005), 303.

84: December 7, 1941: From Pearl Harbor to Calvary

1. Paul Newell, "Pearl Harbor Pilot Became Evangelist," *Stars and Stripes*, December 7, 2008, https://www.stripes.com/news/pearl-harbor-pilot -became-evangelist-1.85934.
2. Newell, "Pearl Harbor Pilot."
3. Newell, "Pearl Harbor Pilot."
4. David Seamands, "The Kamikaze of God," *Christianity Today*, December 3, 2001, https://www.christianitytoday.com/ct/2001/december3/7.58.html.
5. Charles Hoyt Watson, *DeShazer, the Doolittle Raider Who Turned Missionary* (Winona Lake, IN: Light and Life Press, 1950), 47.
6. Jacob DeShazer, "*I Was a Prisoner of Japan*," Doolittle Tokyo Raiders, updated March 15, 2008, http://www.doolittleraider.com/raiders/deshazer.htm.
7. DeShazer, "*Prisoner of Japan*."

8. Peter Hammond, "Mitsuo Fuchida: From Pearl Harbor to Calvary," Reformation SA, https://www.reformationsa.org/index.php/history/376 -mitsuo-fuchida-from-pearl-harbour-to-calvary.

9. DeShazer, "*I Was a Prisoner of Japan.*"

85: February 3, 1942: The Four Chaplains

1. "The Four Chaplains," Wikipedia, updated May 10, 2019, https://en .wikipedia.org/wiki/Four_Chaplains#cite_note-sculpture-14.

2. Dan Kurzman, *No Greater Glory: The Four Immortal Chaplains and the Sinking of the Dorchester in World War II* (New York: Random House, 2005), 174.

3. Harry S. Truman, "Address in Philadelphia at the Dedication of the Chapel of the Four Chaplains, February 3, 1951," *Public Papers of the Presidents of the United States: Harry S. Truman*, vol. 7, *1951*, 139, https:// www.trumanlibrary.org/publicpapers/index.php?pid=235&st=&st1=.

86: June 6, 1944: FDR's Prayer on D-Day

1. "A 'Mighty Endeavor': D-Day," Franklin D. Roosevelt Presidential Library and Museum, https://fdrlibrary.org/d-day.

87: December 14, 1944: Patton's Prayer for Clear Skies

1. Chaplain James H. O'Neill, "The True Story of the Patton Prayer," *Military Chaplain* 85, no. 3 (Fall 2012): 8–11.

88: April 12, 1945: You Are the One in Trouble Now

1. Harry S. Truman, *Off the Record: The Private Papers of Harry S. Truman*, ed. Robert H. Ferrell (Columbia, MO: University of Missouri Press, 1980), 21.

2. See David McCollough, *Truman* (New York: Simon & Schuster, 1992), 341–60; Robert J. Donovan, *Conflict and Crisis* (Columbia, MO: University of Missouri Press, 1977), 4–9; John C. Culver and John Hyde, *American Dreamer* (New York: W. W. Norton & Company, 2000), 388; John Toland, *The Last 100 Days* (New York: Modern Library, 2003), 379–80.

3. Harry S. Truman, "Address Before a Joint Session of the Congress," *Public Papers of the Presidents of the United States: Harry S. Truman*, vol. 1, *1945* (Washington, DC: Office of the Federal Register, 1961).

89: May 14, 1948: The Rebirth of the State of Israel

1. Clark Clifford, *Counsel to the President* (New York: Random House, 1991), 3.

2. Clifford, *Counsel to the President*, 8.

3. David McCullough, *Truman* (New York: Simon & Schuster, 1992), 599.

4. McCullough, *Truman*, 615.

5. Clifford, *Counsel to the President*, 15.

6. Clifford, *Counsel to the President*, 22.

7. McCullough, *Truman*, 620.

90: January 20, 1953: Eisenhower and His Preacher

1. Billy Graham, *Just As I Am* (New York: HarperCollins Publishers, 1997), 188–89.

2. Graham, *Just As I Am*, 191–92.

3. Graham, *Just As I Am*, 199.

4. Graham, *Just As I Am*, 204.

5. Graham, *Just As I Am*, 205.

91: August 28, 1963: Let Freedom Ring!

1. James R. Newby, *Shining Out and Shining In: Understanding the Life Journey of Tom Tipton* (Bloomington, IN: AuthorHouse, 2013), 32–36. The quotes in Tom Tipton's biography reflect what he told me in a personal conversation.

2. Andy Rau, "The Bible Passages Behind Martin Luther King, Jr.'s Message," Bible Gateway, January 17, 2011, https://www.biblegateway.com/blog/2011/01/the-bible-passages-behind-martin-luther-king-jr-s-message/.

3. Newby, *Shining Out and Shining In*, 32–36.

92: March 15, 1965: Bloody Sunday

1. Jon Meacham, *American Gospel: God, the Founding Fathers, and the Making of a Nation* (New York: Random House, 2007), 192.

2. Lyndon Baines Johnson, "President Johnson's Special Message to the Congress: The American Promise," *Public Papers of the Presidents of the United States: Lyndon B. Johnson*, vol. 1, *1965* (Washington, DC: Government Printing Office, 1966), entry 107, 281–87, http://www.lbjlibrary.org/lyndon-baines-johnson/speeches-films/president-johnsons-special-message-to-the-congress-the-american-promise. The characterizations of the speech are mine.

93: December 24, 1968: For All the People Back on Earth

1. Robert Kurson, *Rocket Men* (New York: Random House, 2018), 230, 253.

2. Kurson, *Rocket Men*, 184.

3. Kurson, *Rocket Men*, 249.

4. The astronauts themselves struggled for weeks to come up with appropriate words. Frank Borman had turned to his friend Si Bourgin for help. Bourgin had appealed to his buddy, journalist Joe Laitin. It was Laitin's wife, Christine, who had come up with the idea in the middle of the night while reading from the biblical story of creation in a Gideon Bible.

5. Kevin McIntosh, *The Christmas Eve When Gideon Scriptures Circled the Moon*, December 24, 2018. I'm indebted to Trevor Johns for accessing this article for me in the Gideon files.

94: January 22, 1973: The Conscience of an Honest Woman

1. Quoted in Horace Greeley, *Reflections of a Busy Life* (New York: J. B. Ford & Company, 1869), 281.

2. Norma McCorvey, *Won by Love* (Nashville: Thomas Nelson, 1997), 49.

3. Hearing on "The Consequences of *Roe v. Wade* and *Doe v. Bolton*," Before the Subcommittee on the Constitution of the Senate Judiciary Committee, 109th Cong. (2005) (testimony of Norma McCorvey, former Roe of *Roe v. Wade*), https://www.judiciary.senate.gov/meetings/the-consequences-of -roe-v-wade-and-doe-v-bolton; transcript of McCorvey testimony: https://www.judiciary.senate.gov/imo/media/doc/McCorvey%20 Testimony%20062305.pdf.

4. "The Consequences of *Roe v. Wade* and *Doe v. Bolton*," McCorvey.

95: January 19, 1979: The Holy Spirit Was Present

1. Jimmy Carter, *A Full Life: Reflections at Ninety* (New York: Simon & Schuster, 2015), 92.

2. Carter, *A Full Life*, 93.

3. Carter, *A Full Life*, 135.

4. Carter, *A Full Life*, 133.

5. Carter, *A Full Life*, 134.

6. Carter, *A Full Life*, 134–35.

96: September 19, 1979: The National Day of Prayer

1. *Journals of the American Congress from 1774–1788*, vol. 1 (Washington, DC: Way and Gideon, 1823), 82.

2. James P. Moore Jr., *One Nation Under God: The History of Prayer in America* (New York: Doubleday, 2005), xxiii.

3. *"The President: 1949–1953,"* 3 C.F.R., National Day of Prayer, 1952: Proclamation 2978 (Washington, DC: Federal Register Division, National Archives and Records Service, General Services Administration, as a Special Edition of the Federal Register, 1958), 160.

4. Jimmy Carter, "National Day of Prayer, 1979: Proclamation 4689," *Public Papers of the Presidents of the United States: Jimmy Carter*, vol. 6, *June 23 to December 31, 1979* (Washington, DC: Office of the Federal Register, 1977), 1694, https://quod.lib.umich.edu/p/ppotpus/4732197.1979.002/568?rgn=full+text;view=image.

5. 3 C.F.R., *Compilation and Parts 100–102*, April 12, 1994, rev. January 1, 1995, National Day of Prayer, 1994: Proclamation 6668 (Washington, DC: Federal Register Division, National Archives and Records Service, General Services Administration, as a Special Edition of the Federal Register, 1995), 29.

6. 3 C.F.R., *Compilation and Parts 100–102*, April 2, 1996, rev. January 1, 1997, National Day of Prayer, 1996: Proclamation 6877 (Washington, DC: Federal Register Division, National Archives and Records Service, General Services Administration, as a Special Edition of the Federal Register, 1997), 19.

97: August 7, 1982: Ronald Reagan's Remarkable Letter

1. Courtesy of the Ronald Reagan Presidential Foundation and Institute. While researching for a book about Nancy Reagan, Karen Tumulty, columnist for the *Washington Post*, came across this unpublished letter. It first appeared in "Ronald Reagan's Letter to His Dying Father-in-Law," *Washington Post*, September 14, 2018, https://www.washingtonpost.com/news/opinions/wp/2018/09/14/ronald-reagans-letter-to-his-dying-father-in-law-annotated/?utm_term=.e28fc103a5f5. The Nancy Reagan quotation is also in this article.

98: February 22, 1990: Why Did God Spare Me?

1. Gary S. Smith, "George H. W. Bush's Faith Shaped Him and His Presidency," *Morning Call*, June 20, 2017, https://www.mcall.com/opinion/mc-george-h-w-bush-faith-smith-yv-0621-20170620-story.html.

2. George Bush, "Inaugural Address," American Presidency Project, https://www.presidency.ucsb.edu/documents/inaugural-address.

3. 3 C.F.R., *Compilation and Parts 100–102*, 1990, rev. January 1, 1991, International Year of Bible Reading, February 22, 1990: Proclamation

6100 (Washington, DC: Federal Register Division, National Archives and Records Service, General Services Administration, as a Special Edition of the Federal Register, 1991), 21.

4. Smith, "George H. W. Bush's Faith Shaped Him and His Presidency."

5. From multiple media accounts, including Karen Mizoguchi, "James Baker Fights Back Tears During Emotional Eulogy for Best Friend George H. W. Bush in Texas," MSN, December 6, 2018, https://www.msn.com/en-us /news/us/james-baker-fights-back-tears-during-emotional-eulogy-for -best-friend-george-hw-bush-in-texas/ar-BBQARj9?li=AA54ur&index=1.

99: September 11, 2001: The Day We'll Never Forget

1. "United Airlines Flight 93," Wikipedia, updated May 24, 2019, https:// en.wikipedia.org/wiki/United_Airlines_Flight_93.

2. Lisa Beamer, *Let's Roll* (Wheaton, IL: Tyndale House, 2002), 212–14.

3. George Bush, "9/11 Address to the Nation," updated September 11, 2017, American Rhetoric, https://www.americanrhetoric.com/speeches/gwbush 911addresstothenation.htm.

4. Billy Graham, "Billy Graham's 9/11 Message from the Washington National Cathedral, Billy Graham Evangelistic Association, September 9, 2018, https://billygraham.org/story/a-day-to-remember-a-day-of-victory/.

100: February 7, 2019: The National Prayer Breakfast

1. Barack Obama, "Remarks by the President at the National Prayer Breakfast," White House, February 4, 2016, https://obamawhitehouse.archives.gov/the -press-office/2016/02/04/remarks-president-national-prayer-breakfast-0.

2. Donald Trump, "Remarks by President Trump at the 2019 National Prayer Breakfast," White House, February 7, 2019, https://www.whitehouse.gov /briefings-statements/remarks-president-trump-2019-national-prayer -breakfast/.

Conclusion: The Miracle of America

1. Scott S. Greenberger, *The Unexpected President: The Life and Times of Chester A. Arthur* (New York: Da Capo Press, 2017), 163.

2. Greenberger, *Unexpected President*, 168.

3. Harry S. Truman, "Address Before the Attorney General's Conference on Law Enforcement Problems," *Public Papers of the Presidents of the United States: Harry S. Truman*, vol. 6, 1950 (Washington, DC: Office of the

Federal Register, 1965) 157, https://www.trumanlibrary.org/publicpapers
/index.php?pid=657&st=&st1=.

4. George W. Bush, Scholarship Banquet, Union University, Jackson,
TN, October 17, 2017, https://www.uu.edu/news/release.cfm?ID=2518.
Quotations based on my notes.

About the Author

R obert J. Morgan is a writer and speaker who serves as the teaching
pastor at The Donelson Fellowship in Nashville. He is the author
of *The Red Sea Rules*; *Worry Less, Live More*; *The Strength You Need*;
Reclaiming the Lost Art of Biblical Meditation; *Then Sings My Soul*; and
many other titles, with more than 4.5 million copies in circulation. He is
available to speak at conferences and conventions.

Rob was also a homemaker and a caregiver for his late wife of forty-three
years, Katrina, who battled multiple sclerosis and passed away in 2019. He
and Katrina have three daughters and sixteen grandchildren.

Robertjmorgan.com